INDIAN TOURISM

About the Editors

M.R. Biju, (B.1965) is currently Dean, School of Social Sciences and Head of the Department of Public Administration and Policy Studies, Central University of Kerala, Kasaragod, Kerala. He is also working as Member of the Court of the University. He is the Editor of South Asian Journal of Socio-Political Studies (SAJOSPS–UGC Approved) and Editor-in-Chief of International Journal of Political Science (IJOPS) is a prolific writer on socio-political and developmental issues. He has published over twenty-six (26) books, one hundred and forty (145) research papers, seventeen (17) book chapters, and has reviewed over nine hundred books for South Asian Journal of Socio-Political Studies.

His teaching and research experience, spanning more than 24 years, includes several achievements such as completion of three major research projects funded by Ministry of Panchayati Raj, Government of India and University Grants Commission, New Delhi and the post-doctoral fellowship awarded by the UGC in 2004. He has successfully guided doctoral students of the University of Kerala.

He is consistently making professional academic contributions in the capacity of an Associate Board member of Economics and Management, a prestigious journal published by the Technical University of Liberce, Czech Republic; as the Director and Member Secretary of the Asian Institute of Development Research (AIDR); and as a life Member of several Academic and Professional Bodies. He is also serving on the Editorial Board of International Journal of Business and Innovation, Administration. He is a Member of the PG Board of Studies Political Science and Public Administration of the University of Kerala.

Dr. M.R. Biju is one of the widely cited scholars in the field of Social Sciences with 161 citations and H-index of 6 and i10 index of 3. As per UGC Regulations of 2010, 2013 and 2016 Dr. Biju possess a total API Score of 3914 with API Cap of 3739 as on 01.01.2017.

M.R.B. Anantha Padmanabha is working as Deputy Editor of South Asian Journal of Socio-Political Studies [SAJOSPS], has to his credit one book (co-author) a few papers published in International Journals. He has also presented papers in National Seminars. Currently, he is studying International Relations and Politics at Central University of Kerala, Capital Centre, Thiruvananthapuram.

INDIAN TOURISM
Policy Issues and Alternatives

Edited by
M.R. Biju
M.R.B. Anantha Padmanabha

CONCEPT PUBLISHING COMPANY PVT. LTD.
NEW DELHI-110059

ISBN-13: 978-93-86682-54-3

First Published in 2019

Published and Printed by

Concept Since 1974

Concept Publishing Company Pvt. Ltd.
A/15-16, Commercial Block, Mohan Garden,
New Delhi-110059 (INDIA)
T: 91 11 25351460, 91 11 25351794
E: publishing@conceptpub.com; *W*: www.conceptpub.com

Cataloging in Publication Data--Courtesy: D.K. Agencies (P) Ltd. <docinfo@dkagencies.com>

Indian tourism : policy issues and alternatives / edited by M.R. Biju, M.R.B. Anantha Padmanabha.

pages cm
Includes bibliographical references and index.
ISBN 9789386682543

1. Tourism--India. 2. Ecotourism--India. 3. Medical tourism--India. I. Biju, M. R., 1965- editor. II. Anantha Padmanabha, M. R. B., editor.

LCC G155.I4I53 2019 DDC 338.479154 23

Dedicated to

The everloving and everlasting memory of

Jaya Biju

(7th September, 1969 – 31st August, 2012)

Preface and Acknowledgements

Tourism has developed as a major socio, economic and developmental phenomenon of societies cutting across the globe. It is driven by the natural urge of every human being for new experiences and the desire to be both educated and entertained. The motivations for tourism also include religious and business interests, the spread of education has fostered a desire to know and explore more and more about different corners of the world. The information and communication technology electrified the process. The basic human thirst for new experience and knowledge has become stronger as communication barriers are getting overcome by advances in information technology areas. Expenditure on tourism induces a chain of transactions requiring supply of goods and services from the related sectors. The consumption demand, emanating from tourist expenditure also induces more employment and generates a multiplier effect on the economy. The Travel and Tourism Competitiveness Report 2017 ranks India 40th out of 136 countries overall. The report ranks the price competitiveness of India's tourism sector 10th out of 136 countries. It mentions that India has quite good air transport (ranked 32nd), particularly given the country's stage of development, and reasonable ground transport infrastructure (ranked 29th). The country also scores high on natural and cultural resources (ranked 9th). Some other aspects of its tourism infrastructure remain somewhat underdeveloped however. The nation has very few hotel rooms per capita by international comparison and low ATM penetration. The World Tourism Organization reported that India's receipts from tourism during 2012 ranked 16th in the world, and 7th among Asian and Pacific countries.

Tourism in India is economically important and is growing rapidly.

The World Travel & Tourism Council calculated that tourism generated 14.02 lakh crore (US$220 billion) or 9.6 per cent of the nation's GDP in 2016 and supported 40.343 million jobs, 9.3 per cent of its total employment. The sector is predicted to grow at an annual rate of 6.8 per cent to 28.49 lakh crore (US$440 billion) by 2027 (10% of GDP). In October 2015, India's medical tourism sector was estimated to be worth US$3 billion. It is projected to grow to $7-8 billion by 2020. In 2014, 1,84,298 foreign patients travelled to India to seek medical treatment. About 88.90 lakh (8.89 million) foreign tourists arrived in India in 2016 compared to 80.27 lakh (8.027 million) in 2015, recording a growth of 10.7 per cent. Domestic tourist visits to all states and Union Territories numbered 1,036.35 million in 2012, an increase of 16.5 per cent from 2011. In 2014, Tamil Nadu, Maharashtra and Uttar Pradesh were the most popular states for tourists. Delhi, Mumbai, Chennai, Agra and Jaipur have been the five most visited cities of India by foreign tourists during the year 2015. Worldwide, Delhi is ranked at 28 by the number of foreign tourist arrivals, while Mumbai is ranked at 30, Chennai at 43, Agra at 45, Jaipur at 52 and Kolkata at 90.

Keeping this background in view, this volume attempts to address issues pertaining to various accepts of Indian tourism *viz.*, Indian tourism: issues and initiatives, perspectives of tourism, strategies to revamp tourism, initiatives of tourism in Sri Lanka, linkage between human rights, unemployment issues in tourism sector, application of web technology in tourism advancement, aspects of responsible tourism, potentials to stimulate tourism destinations, regional competitiveness and disparity in foreign tourist arrivals, living aspects of eco-tourism communities, segmentations strategy for the promotion of eco-tourism products, rural empowerment through ecotourism, marketing of ecotourism, 'Holsat' approach to destination satisfaction, tea-tourism predictors of behavioural intention of health tourists, dental tourism, connection between tourism and pharma sectors, and management of archaeological sites and promotion of heritage tourism. The research papers and articles are contributed by senior academics, administrators and practitioners of hospitality sector with rich practical and research experience on the core areas of the study. In their submissions they have tried to explore the existing problems faced by the tourism sector in general and hospitality industry in particular. They have also presented solid suggestions to revamp and revitalize tourism sector in India.

These prefatory remarks remain incomplete without expressing our deep sense of gratitude to those who have been kind enough to help us in preparation of this volume. First of all we would like to express our deep sense of gratitude to the esteemed contributors to this anthology of articles. The views and opinions expressed by the contributors are of great value for the researchers, academics and administrators for framing policies and strategies on hospitality sector in India. We are extremely thankful to Sri Ashok Kumar Mittal, Managing Director of Concept Publishing Co. Pvt. Ltd., New Delhi, who brought out the book in an elegant form.

Diwali Day, 2017

M.R. Biju
M.R.B. Anantha Padmanabha
Editors

Contents

Part 3: Dynamics of Health Tourism

List of Contributors

Dr. A.D. Rajeev Kumar, Assistant Professor, Department of Commerce, S.A.R.B.T.M. Government College, Koyilandy, Kerala.

Aishwaryabiju, Sub Editor, South Asian Journal of Socio-Political Studies.

Dr. Ambeeshmon, S., Assistant Professor IMK, University of Kerala, Kerala.

Dr. Amit K. Chakrabarty, Assistant Professor, Department of Commerce, Chakdaha College, Nadia, West Bengal.

Dr. Anitha, R., Assistant Professor in Tourism, Sree Narayana Arts and Science College, Kumarakom, Kottayam, Kerala.

Dr. Anu Chandran, Assistant Professor, Department of Tourism Studies, School of Management, Pondicherry University, Kerala.

Arun Kumar Nambiar, Doctoral Fellow, R & D Centre, Bharathiar University, Coimbatore, (T.N.).

Dr. Balaji, B., Research Supervisor, R & D Centre, Bharathiar University, Coimbatore, (T.N.).

Dr. Bijith, G.A., Research Associate, Centre for the Study of Social Exclusion and Inclusive Policy (CSSEIP), Cochin University of Science and Technology, Kochi-682022, Kerala.

Gaurav Deep Rai, Research Scholar, Department of Commerce, University of North Bengal, West Bengal.

M.R.B. Anantha Padmanabha, Deputy Editor, South Asian Journal of Socio-Political Studies.

Dr. M.A. Joseph, Associate Professor, Department of Commerce & Management Studies, University of Calicut, Kerala.

Dr. M.R. Biju, Dean, School of Social Sciences and Head, Department of Public Administration and Policy Studies, Central University of Kerala, Kasargode, Kerala.

Dr. Manoj, P.K., Assistant Professor, Department of Applied Economics, Cochin University of Science and Technology (CUSAT), Kochi, Kerala.

Dr. Padmasani, Assistant Professor, School of Commerce, Bharathiar University, Coimbatore, Tamil Nadu.

Preji, M.P., Assistant Professor, Indian Institute of Tourism and Travel Management (IITTM), An Organisation of Ministry of Tourism, Government of India, Bhubaneswar, Odisha.

Priyakrushna Mohanty, Doctoral Fellow, Department of Tourism Studies, School of Managemeht, Pondicherry University, Kerala.

Prof. Dr. Rajasenan D., Director, Centre for the Study of Social Exclusion and Inclusive Policy (CSSEIP) Cochin University of Science and Technology, Kochi-682022, Kerala.

Dr. Ravish Mathew, UGC Post Doctoral Fellow, Department of Tourism Studies, School of Management, Pondicherry University, Kerala.

Remya, V., Senior Research Fellow, School of Commerce, Bharathiar University, Coimbatore, Tamil Nadu.

Dr. Renu Malra, Assistant Professor, Department of Tourism, University College, Kurukshetra University, Kurukshetra, Haryana.

Dr. S.V. Sudheer, Professor & Director, UGC Academic Staff College, University of Kerala, Thiruvanathapuram, Kerala.

Dr. Shan Eugene, Assistant Professor, Department of History, Stella Maris College (Autonomous), Chennai, Tamil Nadu.

Shyju P.J., Lecturer in Tourism, Department of History of Art & Tourism Management, Faculty of Arts, BHU, Varanasi, Uttar Pradesh.

Dr. Sujata, Lecturer, Department of AIHC & Archaeology, Faculty of Arts, BHU, Varanasi-221005, Uttar Pradesh.

Dr. Supriya Dam, Assistant Professor, Commerce, Government Degree College, North Tripura, Tripura.

Dr. T.G. Ramaiah, Associate Professor, Centre for Self Employment & Rural Enterprises, NIRD, Rajendranagar, Hyderabad-30, Andhra Pradesh.

Dr. Tejil Thomas, Assistant Professor, Research & PG Department of Commerce, St. Thomas College Pala, Kottayam, Kerala.

Dr. Yashwant Singh, Faculty on ad-hoc basis in P.G. College, under Vir Bahadur Singh Purvanchal University, Jaunpur, Uttar Pradesh.

Introduction

Tourism has developed as a major socio, economic and developmental phenomenon of societies cutting across the globe. It is driven by the natural urge of every human being for new experiences and the desire to be both educated and entertained. The motivations for tourism also include religious and business interests, the spread of education has fostered a desire to know and explore more and more about different corners of the world. The information and communication technology electrified the process. The basic human thirst for new experience and knowledge has become stronger as communication barriers are getting overcome by advances in information technology areas. Expenditure on tourism induces a chain of transactions requiring supply of goods and services from the related sectors. The consumption demand, emanating from tourist expenditure also induces more employment and generates a multiplier effect on the economy. The Travel and Tourism Competitiveness Report 2017 ranks India 40th out of 136 countries overall. The report ranks the price competitiveness of India's tourism sector 10th out of 136 countries. It mentions that India has quite good air transport (ranked 32nd), particularly given the country's stage of development, and reasonable ground transport infrastructure (ranked 29th). The country also scores high on natural and cultural resources (ranked 9th). Some other aspects of its tourism infrastructure remain somewhat underdeveloped however. The nation has very few hotel rooms per capita by international comparison and low ATM penetration. The World Tourism Organization reported that India's receipts from tourism during 2012 ranked 16th in the world, and 7th among Asian and Pacific countries.

Tourism in India is economically important and is growing rapidly. The World Travel & Tourism Council calculated that tourism generated 14.02 lakh crore (US$ 220 billion) or 9.6 per cent of the nation's GDP in 2016 and supported 40.343 million jobs, 9.3 per cent of its total employment. The sector is predicted to grow at an annual rate of 6.8 per cent to 28.49 lakh crore (US$440 billion) by 2027 (10% of GDP). In October 2015, India's medical tourism sector was estimated to be worth US$3 billion. It is projected to grow to $7-8 billion by 2020. In 2014, 1,84,298 foreign patients travelled to India to seek medical treatment. About 88.90 lakh (8.89 million) foreign tourists arrived in India in 2016 compared to 80.27 lakh (8.027 million) in 2015, recording a growth of 10.7 per cent. Domestic tourist visits to all states and Union Territories numbered 1,036.35 million in 2012, an increase of 16.5 per cent from 2011. In 2014, Tamil Nadu, Maharashtra and Uttar Pradesh were the most popular states for tourists. Delhi, Mumbai, Chennai, Agra and Jaipur have been the five most visited cities of India by foreign tourists during the year 2015. Worldwide, Delhi is ranked at 28 by the number of foreign tourist arrivals, while Mumbai is ranked at 30, Chennai at 43, Agra at 45, Jaipur at 52 and Kolkata at 90.

Content of the Volume

The issues, initiatives and challenges of tourism industries in India is the central focus of discussion in the inaugural chapter contributed by the volume editors. To them, tourism in India is economically important and is growing rapidly. The World Travel & Tourism Council calculated that tourism generated 14.02 lakh crore (US$220 billion) or 9.6 per cent of the nation's GDP in 2016 and supported 40.343 million jobs, 9.3 per cent of its total employment. The sector is predicted to grow at an annual rate of 6.8 per cent to 28.49 lakh crore (US$ 440 billion) by 2027 (10% of GDP). In October 2015, India's medical tourism sector was estimated to be worth US$3 billion. It is projected to grow to $7-8 billion by 2020. In 2014, 1,84,298 foreign patients travelled to India to seek medical treatment. About 88.90 lakh (8.89 million) foreign tourists arrived in India in 2016 compared to 80.27 lakh (8.027 million) in 2015, recording a growth of 10.7 per cent. Domestic tourist visits to all states and Union Territories numbered 1,036.35 million in 2012, an increase of 16.5 per cent from 2011. In 2014, Tamil Nadu, Maharashtra and Uttar Pradesh were the most popular states for tourists. Delhi, Mumbai, Chennai, Agra and Jaipur have been the five most visited cities of India by foreign tourists during the year 2015. Worldwide, Delhi is ranked at 28 by the number of foreign tourist arrivals, while Mumbai is ranked at 30, Chennai at 43, Agra at 45, Jaipur at 52 and Kolkata at 90. The hospitality industry of India is economically important and is growing rapidly. The World Travel and Tourism Council calculated that tourism generated INR 6.4 trillion or 6.6 per cent of the nation's GDP in 2012. It supported 39.5 million jobs, 7.7 per cent of its total employment. The sector is predicted to grow at an average annual rate of 7.9 per cent from 2013 to 2023. This gives India the third rank among countries with the fastest growing tourism industries over the next decade. India has a large medical tourism sector which is expected to grow at an estimated rate of 30 per cent annually to reach about 95 billion by 2015. According to provisional statistics 6.29 million foreign tourists arrived in India in 2011, an increase of 8.9 per cent from 5.78 million in 2010. This ranks India as the 38th country in the world in terms of foreign tourist arrivals. Domestic tourist visits to all states and Union Territories numbered 1,036.35 million in 2012, an increase of 16.5 per cent from 2011. The most represented countries are the United States (16%) and the United Kingdom (12.6%). In 2011, Maharashtra, Tamil Nadu and Delhi were the most popular states for foreign tourists. Domestic tourists visited the states Uttar Pradesh, Andhra Pradesh and Tamil Nadu most frequently. Chennai, Delhi, Mumbai and Agra have been the four most visited cities of India by foreign tourists during the year 2011. Worldwide, Chennai is ranked 38 by the number of foreign tourists, while Mumbai is ranked at 50, Delhi at 52 and Agra at 66 and Kolkata at 99.

An attempt has also been made in this first chapter by **M.R.B. Anatha Padmanabha** and **M.R. Biju,** "Hospitality Industry in India: Issues, Initiatives and Challenges", to examine the facets of hospitality sector in an analytical perspective. The chapter has broadly been categorized under two major heads–Part I unfolds the evolution of hospitality sector in a global perspective and Part II critically examines the initiatives undertaken by Government of India for Tourism promotion. After making a deep analytical enquiry the study came to the conclusion that, Indian tourism has vast potential for generating employment and earning large sums of foreign exchange besides giving a fillip to the country's overall economic and social development. Much has been achieved by way of increasing air seat capacity, increasing trains and railway connectivity to important tourist destinations, four-laning of roads connecting important tourist centres and increasing availability of accommodation by adding heritage hotels to the hotel industry and encouraging paying guest accommodation. But much more remains to be done. Since tourism is a multi-dimensional activity, and basically a service industry, it would be necessary that all wings of the Central and State Governments, private sector and voluntary organizations become active partners in the endeavour to attain sustainable growth in tourism if India is to become a world player in the tourist industry.

In Chapter two **Priyakrushna Mohanty, Anu Chandran** and **Ravish Mathew** presented a chapter entitled "Gauging the Pragmatic Perspectives of Tourism in the Ventures of Make in India". The study aims to envisage ways and means by which tourism could play sparkling role in adding value to the campaign. Media reports have been extensively reviewed to make concrete deductions on the prospective role of tourism in strengthening the Make in India ventures. This conceptual work has ample scope given the niche and contemporary vibes associated with the campaign and the far-reaching and pronounced implications of the initiatives.

According to the authors, "Make in India" is an indigenously conceived and developed campaign. Launched on 25th of August, 2014 with lot of fanfare, Make in India, the brainchild of Indian Prime Minister Shri Narendra Modi is a highly sophisticated and well drawn campaign designed to take the Indian economy to the next level by specifically providing thrust to the manufacturing sector. The campaign aims at attracting higher volumes of Foreign Direct Investment (FDI) through simplifying and subsidizing the rules and regulations associated with the establishment of manufacturing units on the Indian soil. Since its launch, the campaign has grown from strength to strength and crossed milestones galore. The campaign outlines 25 major sectors that will be the torchbearers of its triumph. Tourism configures one of those 25 sectors and it would not be an exaggeration if it is counted as one of the most avowed sectors given PM's specific inclination towards tourism sector (which can reinforce with the often repeated mention in his addresses). Amitabh Kant, the Chief Secretary of the campaign, is a highly regarded man for his extraordinary contributions to tourism and being the mastermind behind brand building campaigns like Incredible India and Kerala: God's Own Country. Further, India is blessed with captivating and unspoiled natural and man made assets which are stellar factors for the success of tourism in any country on the globe. The Tourism sector in India has shown exceptional growth in the last two decades and the pattern is a quite sustaining. This work attempts to analyse the stark aspects as regards the intricacies of "Make in India" endeavour.

According to the authors, India is expected to clock 8-10 per cent growth during the next two to three years. The reforms should actually take place and not remain on paper. The good initiatives like Make in India should proliferate with great pace. Make in India is an ambitious campaign which shall roar loudly if the political willpower is good enough. It goes without saying that good governance is central to all the activities related to the campaign. The political acumen would lend a different flavor to the innovative practices that are at the crux of R&D in India. Identification of right talents and opportunities is also part and parcel of it. Tourism can proliferate the campaign as well as act as a goodwill factor as illustrated in this chapter. The noble goals of Indian tourism provides an image makeover for the country abroad and the main implications of that will be reflective in the investment scenario over a period of time. The code of ethics as regards tourism services and ventures become all the more important in this backdrop.

Arun Kumar Nambiar and **Balaji, B.** in their chapter highlight the "Strategies and Mechanisms to Recover Hospitality Industry in India." According to Nambiar and Balaji, the service sector in India and especially the hospitality sector have a huge potential. There seems to be service failures on various fronts in spite of the fact that the country boasts of trained manpower, incredible tourism products, well connected places and enviable heritage. A doctoral-level research was undertaken to ascertain the causes of service failures based on "moments of truth" and in the process hotel managers across star categories were interviewed. The strategies to recover from such failures have been categorized and presented. The changing trends in hospitality industry are also discussed. The study came to the conclusion that the suggested service recovery strategies in Hospitality industry in India are by no means exhaustive. Service sector phenomena change with time and so do expectations and perceptions of consumers. India has a golden treasure and all that the nation needs is creative vision, diligent implementation and sustainable development.

In chapter four the volume editors presented another paper on tourism in the island nation of Sri Lanka. According to them tourism is one of the fastest growing industries globally, including in the developing world. It has grown faster than world gross domestic product since the 1950s with expenditure on tourist goods and services representing some 8 per cent of total world export receipts and 5 per cent of world GDP. Wen and Tisdell rightly observed that this is due to rising global incomes, increasing leisure time, a rising world population, fall in real transport costs, reduced travel time and globalisation. Many developing countries have recognised the possible contribution that this industry can make to economic development and have included it as an integral part of their development strategies. As a result, over the last two decades, an extensive body of literature on issues surrounding this industry in developing countries has been built up. Employment generation, foreign exchange earnings and community welfare are aspects of tourism-induced development considered in most of the relevant literature.

The authors further add that contribution of the tourism industry is heavily influenced by international economic and political stability, as well as by terrorist threats and civil unrest in the tourist destination. There is a widespread view among the tourism analysts that international visitors are very concerned about their personal safety and thus this industry can only thrive under peaceful conditions.

Coming to the core of Asia-Pacific regions, the authors further states that tourism is one of the major foreign exchange earners and main growth sector for many countries especially the small islands which are rich with required natural and cultural resources. The world tourism market has grown at an average of 3.7 per cent over the past five years and is projected to grow by an average of 4.9 cent over the next five years, with Asia and the Pacific regions recording the fastest growth rate. According to World Travel and Tourism Council, Travel and Tourism activity was hit hard by the global slump, Even so, the sector worldwide still provided over 235 million jobs last year. To them, tourism remains the fastest growing service industry in the economies of most of developing countries. Hence, more research has gone into the operations of the sector in order to examine its economic significance and potential. It is known that the industry provides an important impetus to growth in other sectors such as agriculture, transportation, retailing and manufacturing and is therefore seen as a key component of economic development. It plays a major role for the generation of foreign exchange which directly facilitates the improvement of foreign reserves of said economies. Similarly, the sector has shown greater improvements in employment generation both directly and indirectly. Revenue accruing to tourist sites, and increase in number of hotels and similar establishments and other tourism supply establishments.

The authors also adds that, tourism in Sri Lanka is growing rapidly for centuries. Sri Lanka has been a popular place of attraction for foreign travellers. The famous Chinese traveller Fa-Hiuen arrived in Sri Lanka in the late 4th century. In the twelfth century, Italian explorer Marco Polo claimed that Sri Lanka to be the "best island of its size in the world". In view of its fascinating scenic beauty and rich cultural heritage, Sri Lanka is one of the best tourist destinations in the world.

Moreover, Sri Lanka's independence the promotion of tourism was again considered by re-establishing the Ceylon Tourist Board which took over the function of the Tourist Bureau. More formal recognition for the country's tourism sector was given with the enactment of Act No. 10 of 1966. This provided the legislation for the establishment of Ceylon Tourist Board. Since then the Ceylon Tourist Board has functioned as the state agency, responsible for development and promotion of the tourism sector in Sri Lanka. Given its natural advantages, the tourism sector is viewed as one of the most important engines of growth and development in the Sri Lankan economy and as such, is a key focus in the Government's industrial strategy. Tourism main supporting sectors account for more than 8.0 per cent of GDP. In relation to employment, agriculture transport, storage and communication, construction, and distribution are the primary beneficiaries from a dollar spent within the tourism industry. Further, these sectors account for over 7.0 per cent of the employed labour force. However, the descriptive analysis points to the continued low and declining impact of the industry on the overall economy in particular in the context of other countries like Thailand, Malaysia and Kenya. However, the investment share for tourism sector being high, the unstable political situation could be the closest reason for this less performance in the case of comparison. The detailed study came to the conclusion that with the end of civil war, no doubt the expected boom in the industry over the years to come will have a noticeable impact. It has to be kept in mind that there is a strong relationship between the political stability and macro-economic performance in particular with reference to the tourism sector. It is highly recommended to maintain a stable political situation of the country in order for industries like tourism to flourish in the days to come.

In chapter five, **Shan Eugene**, focuses on the interface between tourism and human rights. According to her, human rights are basic principles aimed at ensuring equality and dignity for all. The Universal Declaration of Human Rights embodies the international consensus on human rights and forms the cornerstone of today's human rights law. This law places obligations on states to respect, protect and fulfil the human rights of individual citizens, and these include Civil and Political rights such as the right to association and to participate in civil society, as well as Socio-economic rights such as the right to housing and to health. Although tourism was not widely perceived as an area where the human rights declaration could find application, its ramifications for tourism are far and wide. In fact, a few of the articles of the UDHR are more direct in their application to tourism human rights than to any other sector—for instance, Article 13, and Article 24. Article 13 is very important for tourism as it declares the right to freedom of movement and residence within the borders of each state. No regulations, including unfriendly visa regimes or poor relationships among countries, should be an insurmountable burden upon the one who wants to globetrot. The right to leave a country is juxtaposed with the right to return—which is the spirit of tourism. When Article 13 is read with article 24, a fuller implication upon tourism becomes clear. Article 24 says that everyone has the right to rest and leisure, including reasonable limitation of working hours and periodic holidays with pay. UDHR speaks of the role of Human rights protection in strengthening the development of friendly relations between nations; similarly, one of the goals of tourism is achieving international peace and harmony.

Shan Eugene further adds that a human rights approach to tourism is integral to true sustainability. It is in keeping with emerging international business and human rights norms, standards and practices, especially the United Nations Guiding Principles on Business and Human Rights. Although human rights is an area of inquiry that can potentially address a lot of issues associated with tourism, not more than a handful of studies have been conducted relating the two.

A qualitative study on the unemployment problem is presented by **Amit K. Chakrabarty** in the sixth chapter. It analyses the role of tourism industry in reducing the problem of unemployment in India. Tourism industry is a labour intensive industry. This qualitative study is purely based on the information collected from different sources like websites, articles published in reputed national and international journals, news-papers and reputed reference books related to this field. Unemployment is a curse of developing countries like India but tourism industry has an interesting employment multiplier, i.e. 2.36. So, there is a possibility of employment of large number people in the industry directly or indirectly. The potentiality of this industry in India is very large due to its natural, geographical and historical background. At this time, India stands third in tourism after jam and jewellery and readymade garment. The position of tourism industry, one of the fastest growing industries in world, in respect of globe is just below the oil and automobile industry. So, the author recommends the development of tourism industry in India by improving infrastructure to get rid of unemployment.

Unemployment problem in India according to Amit K. Chakrabarty is a matter of great concern like poverty, illiteracy, malnutrition etc. The nature of the problem is severe in a developing country like India. In India, the number of unemployed persons is increasing consistently.

Organized sectors fail to create sufficient employment opportunity to absorb the unemployed labour force. After independence, Government of India has taken many steps to tackle the problem. But these efforts have failed to solve the alarming problem of unemployment because the main cause behind this problem in India is population-explosion. In this context, tourism industry can play a vital role in Indian economy. Tourism industry is a labour-intensive industry and its employment multiplier is 2.36. A large number of unemployed persons can be employed by this industry. The Government should take necessary steps for development of tourism industry. The Central and State Governments should allocate huge budgetary allocations for tourism industry. And the cooperation and co-ordination on the part of the Central and State Governments, local authorities and local people is needed for the development of the industry. The development of tourism industry mainly depends on adequate hotel accommodation, better transport facilities, medical and communication facilities etc. The Government should take necessary steps to improve these facilities for the growth of tourism industry in India.

The linkage between web and technologies and its scientific application in hospitality sector is the central theme of discussion in chapter seven. According to **Renu Malra**, accessibility of information through web has been increasing in developed countries. Tourism is an area which is getting a lot of attention these days. Tourism means people on move, i.e. mobile and advanced features of mobile ICT suit admirably in the delivering of relevant and timely information that cultural heritage tourists demand. Various mobile ICT techniques like LBS (Location Based Services), Navigation aids have been using by the walkers, cyclists, hikers and others.

This chapter also congregates exploration of the potential of web and Mobile technology in providing the relevant services in the development of tourism. Web and technology according to Renu Malra is shaping the new form of tourism industry, either it is internet booking, social media, mobile technology and apps or gamification, everything is playing a tremendous role in determining the industry. Facebook is the leading social network in the US, but it is experiencing rapid growth throughout Europe. According to comScore Facebook is the most popular social network in 11 out of 17 European countries.

In chapter eight **Anitha R.** and **Ambeeshmon, S.** present a study on the scope of responsible tourism in urban areas. According to Anitha and Ambeeshmon, a responsible tourism initiative at its inception focused only on cultural and environmental aspects and was found to be successful in countries like India, Indonesia, Namibia, Nepal, Philippines, Zambia, Zimbabwe etc. Considering its livelihood aspects we can extend its practices to the urban areas also. Since hospitality sector is the backbone of Tourism industry, the RT practices have a prominent role to uplift the communities by linking RT Practices with the accommodation sector. This practice got momentum after the Cape Town Declaration, in South Africa. Today there are a number of awards and certification schemes for the best responsible tourism practices in the industry. Most of the award programmes highlight the principles of sustainability especially employment quality, biological diversity, local quality of life and social prosperity. The present study analyses the best practices in tourism that can be incorporated with responsible tourism in urban areas which hence can eliminate and reduce poverty of the downtrodden city/urban dwellers. From the study it is observed that the hospitality and tour companies can promote the best practices with the support of both guests and hosts.

Preji, M.P. has presented a chapter entitled "Special Interest Tourism and its Potentials to Stimulate Radical Changes at Destinations: A Study on Event Tourism in Odisha". According to Preji, event tourism traditionally was not a part of mainstream tourism now has got the makeover of a potential segment in special interest tourism (SIT). Many developed nations have carved a niche as far as exploring the prospects of event tourism is concerned. India, being a nation with so many traditional events and ceremonies across the country is yet to explore the chances of attracting potential tourists from this segment. Of late with "Incredible India" campaign which has been launched with the theme "something for everyone", India has reckon the capacity of events in attracting more tourists. Even then, room for improvement is there in the backdrop of planning and coordination are concerned.

Odisha state of India, according to the author has got so many events to its credit which has its roots towards the cultural and societal life of the state. Events can be a better medium in showcasing the cultural and historical richness of a destination and will yield better results if it is promoted in the right direction. The study intends to explore how various cultural and societal events of Odisha can be coined to build destination attributes by duly discovering a pathway for integrated tourism promotion for Odisha which can bring laurels to the tourism industry.

The author also adds that events of Odisha can be instrumental in promoting the state as the most sought after destination globally. Events can be a better medium of cultural appraisals and social understanding of the places that tourists visit during the course of tour. The uniqueness of

Konark and events at such destinations of Odisha can catapult tourism to a different level of augmentation. By building the destination attributes and by enhancing public and private participation, event tourism can be better promoted with forward and backward integration. Inventiveness along with commitment in the segmentation of special interest tourism can bring a paradigm shift in the future development of tourism in Odisha.

Rajeev Kumar, A.D. and **Sudheer, S.V.** presented a study titled "Regional Competitiveness and Disparity in Foreign Tourists Arrivals in Kerala". Kerala according to the authors is the most idyllic state in India, with a unique blend of diverse tourism products, attracts a large number of foreign tourists every year. However, it is evident that the number of foreign tourists arrivals (FTAs) to Kerala is not evenly shared by different regions namely, southern, central and northern. Clearly, the southern and central regions claim the lion share of FTAs to the state leaving the northern region for a meager share of less than 6 per cent. It is observed that, the difference in competitiveness among regions, especially in attractions and facilities acts as a major cause for this disparity in arrivals. In this context, this chapter analyses the regional disparity in foreign tourists arrivals in Kerala in relation to regional competitiveness by examining the preferences of foreign tourists in attractions and facilities. The study used both primary and secondary data. The competitive edge in major factors influencing the tourists preferences like attractions, accommodation and access facilities help the central region for having the highest share of FTAs in most years. Southern region with its competitiveness in above factors managed to receive a comparable share of FTAs in many years and in few years outpaced the central region. Comparing to other regions, northern region, though not lesser in attractions, faces difficulties regarding accommodation and access and hence receives only a meager share of FTAs. The study calls for a balanced regional growth of tourism by bringing the development of northern region in par with those of southern and central regions.

From the above analysis, the authors also state that the international tourism and its impact in northern region is highly insignificant in comparison with southern and central regions. It is clear that central region receives the major share of FTAs to Kerala. The attractions like historic monuments at Fort Kochi and Mattanchery, wildlife at Thekkady, Munnar hill station along with better accommodation and access facilities are the contributing factors for this increased share. As far as southern region is concerned, internationally renowned beaches with various facilities at Kovalam and Varkala, backwaters with houseboat facilities at Alappuzha with a comparable accommodation and access contribute favourably for a good share of foreign tourists. It can be seen that the northern region of the state is completely isolated and poorly benefited from international tourism. Though further improvement is needed, this region is not short of attractions, but in comparison with other regions, it clearly lacks facilities, especially accommodation and access. For instance, in air connectivity, comparing to Calicut airport, both Kochi and Thiruvananthapuram airports are having upper hand in number of flights and their international services. Lack of awareness of the region, absence of long term tourism policy, lack of professional tour operators, highly limited infrastructure and facilities, lack of circuit developments, tough competition from within the state and from neighbouring states etc. are the major reported reasons for this dismal performance of this region (Mammootty and Raveendran, 2008).

According to Rajeev and Sudheer S.V., for the overall development of the state, there should be more evenly distribution of tourists and benefits in all regions. Moreover, to manage the envisaged growth in tourism in a sustainable manner without disturbing the carrying capacity of major transit points and the major destinations of southern and central regions, it is imperative for the state to ensure the judicious dispersal of tourists to other transit points and destinations of the northern districts. This can be made possible through bringing the development of tourism in northern region in par with that of southern and central regions. Development of infrastructure and superstructure facilities, undertaking more promotional programmes, development of tourism circuits connecting various spots in the northern region and with those of other regions, formulating effective tourism marketing strategies, particularly, product positioning strategy etc. can be the recommended actions for the balanced regional growth of international tourism in Kerala. Realising this, government has already initiated some proactive efforts to give a facelift to the major destinations of northern region and the study concludes hoping that this region will improve its performance in international tourism by hosting for a better share of foreign tourists.

Part two of this volume unfolds with a chapter entitled "Socio-Economic Profile and Standard of Living Aspects of the Ecotourism Communities of Kerala". This chapter is contributed by **Bijith, G.A.** and **Rajasenan, D.** The writers are of the firm opinion that, ecotourism development of Kerala and the simultaneous increase in the flow of tourists to these destinations would help in providing livelihood opportunities to the local communities and the betterment of their lives. The theoretical aspect of the study is based on the standard of living index framework, which in a way is connected to their socio-economics. The article uses 600 samples collected from eco-tourism community members from three zones based on active community participation in the area and population proportion. The Standard of Living Index (SLI) with respect to zone, income and education of the eco-tourism communities has been analysed using correspondence analysis. The result obtained from the study shows a well-knit link of income and education of the community members in achieving the standard of living.

Bijith and Rajasenan further say that, there are zone-wise differences with respect to the socio-economic profiles of the community and hence, it reflects in the basic indicators like quality of housing, source of drinking water, use of energy sources and latrine facilities. Standard of living measured in SLI frameworks shows that majority of the respondents have medium SLI values. A zone-wise difference in living standards of community members has also been identified. Majority in the south-zone and the central-zone are in the Medium SLI categories. The result obtained from the study shows that standard of living is mainly depended on income and education of the community members. There exists significant difference between the Standard of Living and income level of the community members as those with impressive living standards are in the high income category. Also, a variation in the SLI value based on the educational qualification attained by the individual can be identified as it shows positive relationship between SLI and the level of educational qualification, which shows that low SLI groups are in the low educational groups.

In chapter twelve **Manoj, P.K.** submitted a presentation on "Segmentation Strategy for Promotion of Ecotourism Products". According to Manoj, P.K., the vast potential of tourism for bringing about economic development and employment generation being widely acknowledged in the literature, promotion of tourism is particularly relevant in developing nations like India. International agencies like the United Nations World Tourism Organization (UN-WTO) have estimated that nations like India and China would become the superpowers in the global tourism map by the year 2020. In spite of the excellent tourism resources in India, the country could not utilize its vast potential because only during the last two decades tourism has been getting due attention in India. While China has already attained a prominent position in global tourism, the progress of India has been slower. India has to traverse a long way to catch up with the top players, including China. Though India is considered unique in its rich bio-diversity and cultural heritage, this rich potential which could be meaningfully utilized for promotion of ecotourism and such other allied tourism segments, is still not being used optimally. In respect of Kerala state in particular—one of the states with the highest tourism resources in India—the situation is more discouraging as Kerala's performance in tourism has not been commensurate with its enviable tourism resources. A few recent studies by the author have revealed the vast prospects of tourism in Kerala for employment creation and economic development. Focusing on Thenmala ecotourism destination, the first planned ecotourism destination in India, this study which is a continuation of the earlier studies of the author analyses as to whether the socio-economic and demographic factors are significantly influencing their decision on tour packages, and suggests the segmentation, targeting and positioning strategies for ecotourism promotion.

The author concludes his study by adding that promotion of ecotourism in Kerala would ensure rich dividend in the days to come, given the huge growth prospects of ecotourism in the state. Careful analysis of the exact tastes and preferences of the customers, considering their socio-economic, demographic and such other factors is very important. The design considerations of various products like Tour Packages and ingredients thereof, should duly take into account the tastes and preferences of various segments. So, a well thought out STP strategy should be used for product design, delivery and re-design on a constant basis.

T.G. Ramaiah in chapter thirteen presented a chapter titled "Rural Empowerment through Ecotourism: A Case Study on Darap Village in Sikkim". In his chapter, the author reiterates that tourism growth potential can be harnessed as a strategy for Rural Development. The development of a strong platform around the concept of Rural tourism is definitely useful for a country like India, where almost 74 per cent of the population resides in its 7 million villages. Across the world, the trends of industrialization and development have had an urban centric approach. Alongside, the stresses of urban lifestyles have led to a "counter-urbanization" syndrome. This has led to growing interest in the rural areas. At the same time this trend of urbanization has led to falling income levels, lesser job opportunities in the rural areas leading to an urbanization syndrome in the rural areas. Rural Tourism is one of the few activities which can provide a solution to these problems. Besides, there are other factors which are shifting the trend towards rural tourism like increasing levels of awareness, growing interest in heritage and culture and improved accessibility, and environmental consciousness. In the developed countries, this has resulted in a new style of tourism of visiting village settings to experience and live a relaxed and healthy lifestyle. This concept has taken the shape of a formal kind of Rural Tourism. Under this Scheme, thrust is to promote village tourism as the primary tourism product to spread tourism and its socio-economic benefits to rural and its new geographic regions. Key geographic regions are identified for development and promotion of Rural Tourism. The implementation is done through a Convergence Committee headed by the District Collector. Activities like improving the environment, hygiene, infrastructure etc. are covered for assistance. Apart from providing financial assistance, the focus is to tap the resources available under different schemes of Department of Rural Development, State Governments and other concerned Departments of the Government of India.

According to author, the Himalayan region is a big boon to promote rural tourism as an economic activity and at the same time promoting rural tourism. The Himalayan range possesses distinct geographical conditions and pattern of culture. The distinct nature of these two resulted in specific economic activities derived through geographical conditions, raw material available, specific skills possessed by the people inhabiting in the vicinity etc. Thus, the Himalayan region has distinct place for promoting "rural tourism." Though, the Himalayan region has been attracting tourism from all-over the world, the region's capacity to attract tourists on the basis of "rural tourism" has not been widely practiced. Only a few such experiments were in vogue. One such experiment which has been considered as one of the successful "rural tourism initiative" is observed in Darap village in Sikkim state.

As referred earlier, the study is based on Darap, a remote village in Sikkim, which has shown the world the immense potential of rural tourism and its role in generating employment and economic development in the region. It has also excelled in how a enterprising and enlightened local people can turn the opportunities into great strength in terms of preservation of culture and at the same time utilizing the same for promoting economic development. The project as well as earned enough attraction from the visiting tourism just by virtue of show-casing the local 'culture' and 'culture products' to the visiting tourists like pattern of agriculture, local artifacts etc. as an attractive elements in promoting rural tourism. The local Eco-tourism committee too displayed enough entrepreneurship skills by dovetailing its efforts with other business organizations. The novel feature of the project is it has been a successful rural tourism venture without disturbing the local culture and geographical terrain. This has been a rare success in the rural tourism sector which was backed by local wisdom, culture, entrepreneurial skills and the local leadership. If these issues are taken care of elsewhere, rural tourism ventures can be promoted in a quicker manner and provide immense employment opportunities to the local youth.

Suprya Dam in her chapter highlights on the marketing of eco-tourism destinations in Tripura. According to the author, nestled in extreme corner of North Eastern Region (NER) of India, Tripura is one of the most industrially backward States in the region. Tranquil atmosphere along with wealth of natural resources and forest reserves makes it an automatic destination for ecotourism. However, ecotourism could not develop as yet as one of the money spinner for the economy. Although, eco-touristic journey had begun in the state nearly twenty years back; but, in spite of possessing abundant ecotourism resources, the State could not capitalize it for want of poor marketing network and initiatives; on the part of stakeholders including the Governments'. Survey reveals that only budget segment of the tourists are venturing into ecotourism sites in Tripura, overlooked by 'high end' visitors. The chapter explores possibilities of forging integrated marketing network to harness plentiful ecotourism products on the one hand and strategies for drawing 'high end' visitors to sustain ecotourism, on the other.

According to Supriya, Tripura tourism has the potential to link it with fishery, agriculture and rubber plantation. Local handicraft industry can also be promoted by showcasing it in international tourism festivals and trade fairs, both in India and abroad. Tourist information centres (TICs) for Tripura tourism has been developed on a limited scale and not covered major airports and trade centres; so, such centres can be opened with the authority to arrange package from there. Tour exchange programme by involving operators from national level and abroad is essential to bring 'high end' visitors from source countries. 'High end' visitors will spent more for realistic "ecotourism experience" by extending overnight stays in the destination; which invariably will bring foreign exchange for the State. Lastly, feedback is regularly sought to take notice of developments and corrective actions whenever needed. The State of Tripura is evenly poised to accept this challenge; however, further research should be carried out to pin-point the linkages and collaborative efforts, which are considered essential to realize such feat.

Tejil Thomas and **Joseph, M.A.** in their chapter titled "The HOLSAT Approach to Destination Satisfaction at Kumarakom Backwaters". This chapter focuses on the assessment of destination satisfaction of domestic tourists by applying the extracts of the HOLSAT model (Tribe & Snaith, 1998). The findings indicate that the tourists have distinct impressions about this holiday destination before and after the travel, which was plotted on a five point scale and was grouped into five dimensions as 'attractions', 'activities', 'accessibility', 'accommodation' and 'amenity'. The level of tourists' experience on these dimensions surpassed the level of expectation. The positive gap scores (experience–expectation) of different destination attributes except public toilet facilities, substantiate the level of tourist satisfaction. Thus, HOLSAT is considered as an apt tool for assessing tourist satisfaction against attributes of a holiday destination.

According to Tejil and Joseph, Kumarakom backwaters offers the tourist one of the most incredible tour destinations for pleasure and holiday enjoyments in Kerala. This backwater destination is made up of interconnected waterways, rivers, lakes and bays. It has a unique ecosystem that perfectly blends scenic beauty, soothing climate, traditional waterways travel on houseboats and delicious spicy foods for both foreign and inland tourists a wonderful experience of an aquatic life. The village of Kumarakom is a cluster of little islands on the Vembanad Lake, and this small water world is part of the tranquil Kuttanad region with lots of coconut trees and shallow waterways. This enchanting backwater destination offers visitors many leisure options like boating, sightseeing and fishing facilities. Holiday packages on the Houseboats, traditional Kettuvallams provide a fabulous experience to tourists. Kumarakom is a beautiful place with a variety of flora and fauna where the natural bird sanctuary is offering a great experience for ornithologists. Many species of birds find shelter in the Bird Sanctuary. Moreover, Kumarakom backwater tourism hub is gaining a strategic place on the tourist map due to its natural charm and aesthetic beauty. The tropical specialities, natural beauty, days at houseboats, spicy foods, Ayurveda and soothing climatic conditions give an unforgettable journey to the tourists. In addition, the backwater destination is a dearest place for domestic tourists for holiday enjoyments and leisure irrespective of seasonable factors. They offer countless support for the tourism industry during the off season too. Therefore, it is advantageous to know about their expectation and experience on various destinations-attributes at Kumarakom to chalk out development strategies and remedial measures to provide them superior facilities and services.

In summary, the authors would like to say that the extracts of HOLSAT model applied in Kumarakom backwaters portray that the destination experience exceeded the level of expectation. Backwater tourism can be considered as a productive strategy for social as well as economic development of Kumarakom region. It is blessed with a number of backwater destinations with high potentials to carve remarkable contributions to the state exchequer. The abstract of findings states that natural beauty, climate conditions, house boat journey and Ayurveda are the main factors influencing domestic tourists to have a trip to Kumarakom Backwaters.

An empirical analysis of tea tourism based on Dargeling is the topic of enquiry in chapter sixteen. This study is carried out by **Gaurav Deep Rai**. To him, the well preserved bungalows of Darjeeling are a few of the last vestiges of the colonial era with lush green tea bushes sprawling wide across, igniting the charm of the British heritage. These tea estates have attracted tourists, researchers and academicians from various disciplines from within the country and abroad, but tourism in these estates have not been given much academic attention. Tea Tourism is a diversification of the tourism and tea industry and is gradually emerging worldwide as a niche market, promoting sustainable cultural and ethnic eco-tourism with enormous potential. The present chapter attempts to unearth the importance of Tea Tourism, the present scenario of the Indian Tea Industry and the perception of tourists regarding the services provided in tea estates adopting tourism activities. A sample size of 86 respondents was selected to comparatively analyse the perception of domestic and foreign tourists to each of the varied services performed by the tea estates. Primary data were analysed through t-tests at .05 level of significance to reveal any variation in the perception levels. Significant variations were perceived with regard to tea plucking sessions, lodging at the heritage buildings, witnessing cultural shows and learning about the history of tea culture. The authorities need to understand the needs of the tea tourists and accordingly design their tourism activities. Apparently, the tea estates lack proper infrastructural facilities and a proper Tea Tourism policy fostering the co-ordination among the government, tea garden managers, trade unions and tourism department is the need of the hour.

Tea tourism according to the author, though relatively new in concept has tremendous potentiality. This chapter attempts to fill a lacuna in the literature of Tea Tourism. This area of tourism has received very little academic attention, but given the proper resources, it will yield additional source of continuous funds. The authorities need to first understand the needs of the tourists (domestic and foreign) and accordingly devise marketing strategies. The participation in the tea tasting sessions, tea plucking, processing in the factories, toy train rides, learning of the history of tea culture and drinking styles have to be given due importance while designing the tourism activities. The purchase of genuine tea produced in the very factory can be an effective measure to curb the blatant imitation of Darjeeling Tea. The enrichment of the lives of the local masses through employment as chauffeurs, waiters, travel guides and entertainers is also a positive contribution towards the local masses and furthermore, there is global transmission of cultures and traditions.

Gaurav Deep Rai also adds that being the second largest producer of tea in the global market, contributing almost 30 per cent of global tea production, still it has not been able to perform effectively in the international arena. With the inherent glitches namely unpredictable weather, high cost of production leading to a high market price, stiff competition faced imitation of tea and high consumption rate of 75 per cent of its own production. The Indian tea is gradually losing its market share in the global arena, which has been reflected through its decline in its exports. Tea Tourism, if properly implemented can be a solution to the glitches and a perfect diversification of its risks. With Tea Tourism, the tea industry, which was in the doldrums, can finally live up to its full potential and can be a major strategy for sustainable economic and regional development.

The concluding part (3) of this volume presents chapter on health and heritage tourism. It starts with a chapter on predictors of behavioural intention of health tourists by **Padmasini** and **Remya, V.** According to them, with the advent of the globalisation and open economy, tourism emerged as one of the world's fastest growing industries and a leading contributor to GDP in many countries. According to a survey by World Tourism Organisation, tourists movement throughout the world can touch 1600 million mark by 2020. This has engrossed considerable attention from the government, practitioners and researchers in many developing nations.

As referred earlier, In India, over the decade, a rapid growth in the tourism industry is witnessed with the tourists arrival of 8.03 million in 2015 compared to 3.92 million in 2005. Tourism, being the biggest foreign exchange earner of India, helps in generating maximum employment opportunity through its interconnection with number of subsidiary industries, brings advancement in the infrastructural development, which in turn, helps in regional and economic development. Thus, acknowledging the great potential of tourism, the Government of India declared tourism as an industry in the year 1980. Though tourism is recognised as an important economic contributor to the nation, it is facing with several challenges. The major challenge faced by the Indian tourism sector is negligible market share in the world tourism market. Thus, it has become crucial for the country to identify its competitive advantage and induce the tourists for greater usage of these services so as to acquire large market share in the world tourism industry.

Padmasani and Remya further states that, developing and fostering behavioural intention as a major source of competitive advantage is an important business strategy in the market economy system and consequently directs the efforts of service managers, academicians and researchers in comprehending the dynamics involved in behavioural intentions. Thus, establishing relationship with customers that shapes behavioural intention has been considered a key factor in obtaining market share and creating a sustainable competitive advantage (Deng *et al.*, 2010). According to Chen & Tsai (2007) by understanding the relationships between future behaviour and its determinants, tourism destination managers would know how to build up an attractive picture and improve their marketing efforts to maximise resource utilisation. Therefore, it is imperative to know the ways to attract the tourists to revisit and to recommend the destination to others for the success of destination tourism development.

This chapter has been organised by presenting the theoretical background and hypotheses of the proposed model, methodology, followed by empirical results and discussions with a conclusion. The study investigated health tourists behaviour by constructing a comprehensive model considering perceived destination image, perceived service quality, satisfaction and behavioural intention. The conceptual model was tested using data obtained from tourists' questionnaire survey at Ayurvedic healthcare centres. The results of the relationship between the constructs suggest important implications for destination marketers. According to the results, the foreign tourists were more influenced by destination image, followed by satisfaction and service quality. Thus, the findings revealed that if the foreign tourists perception towards destination image is favourable, then they may be willing to revisit and recommend the destination in future. Therefore, the destination managers are suggested to capitalise on these dimensions while promoting Kerala as health tourism destination at the international level.

Padmasini and Remya, V. also adds that, increasing the inflow of foreign tourists is extremely important for Kerala Tourism Industry, which is a matured market with very low resource utilisation capacity. Therefore, in addition to retaining existing tourists, more importance should be given to attracting new tourists. A more marketing-oriented approach rather than the traditional supply-oriented approach is thus believed to be more appropriate for Kerala Tourism Industry. From a practical standpoint, the findings offer important implications for the development of destination marketing strategies. In today's competitive climate, creating and managing the right destination image has become vital for effective positioning and differentiation to ensure continuous inflow of foreign tourists into the state.

In chapter eighteen, **Aishwarya Biju**, examines the facets and dynamics of dental tourism, a subset of the sector known as medical tourism. It involves individuals seeking dental care outside of their local healthcare systems. Normally, it may be accompanied by a vacation. Dental tourism is growing worldwide. As the world becomes ever more interdependent and competitive, technique, material, dental tourism enables dental care at significant cost savings when compared with their peers in the developed world. This chapter illustrates and investigates into the facets of dental tourism from hospitality perceptive. The introductory part traces the origin, evolutionary process and significance of hospitality industry in a global perceptive. The second part unfolds, on the rise of dental tourism as a potential element of medical tourism. Part three focuses on the components of dental tourism with special focus on its strategy and concluding part presents the major findings of the study.

According to author, dental Tourism in Kerala, has also been established as a destination for dental tourism for decades. Kerala dental treatments are less susceptible and the patients never ever feel distressed before and after the course. The reasons for the abundance of dental tourists in Kerala are as a result of the excellent dental procedure, quick and easy treatment options and also the specialist's appointments without the need of much waiting. Above all, visitors flock to Kerala owing to its position as the topmost tourism destination round the globe. Dentists are getting appreciated for their degree of professionalism and for their concerned care. Moreover, Dentists in Kerala are highly treasured for their expert dental care. Kerala dental procedures are highly standardised and are done under strict etiquettes of sterilisation and disinfection to keep away from adverse effects of dental treatments.

In chapter nineteen, **Anitha, R.** presents a chapter on "Outbound Business Travel: An Emerging Trend among Pharma Companies". According to Anitha, the Pharmaceutical Industry in India meets around

70 per cent of the country's demands for bulk drugs, drug intermediaries, pharmaceutical formulations, chemicals, tablets, capsules orals and Injectables. There are about 250 large units and about 8000 small scale units which form the core of the Pharmaceutical industry in India (including five central public sector units). These units produce the complete range of pharmaceutical formulation, i.e. chemicals having therapeutic value and used for Production of pharmaceutical formulations. Medical representatives are the major tools of product promotion. Travel cost have emerged as the third largest expense to corporate after salaries and raw materials. The companies offer them outbound business travel for motivating their field force and achieving sales target. Normally a field executive who achieves 110-120 per cent sales target gets the advantage of outbound business travel. The studies show that most of them are visiting a foreign destination for the first time. All the companies seek the assistance of corporate travel agents. Duration of the visit is usually 3 to 4 days. Pharmaceutical companies offer incentive travel for attending international conferences, for updating scientific and academic knowledge, sharing of their experiences, familiarization of the application of modern technologies etc. Other than the above reasons some sort of entertainment mixed with leisure is common. They are cultural performances at the venue, discount for shopping in malls, duty free outlets etc. Preferred destinations of demand are Malaysia, Singapore, Hongkong, Thailand. The trend among16 major companies during 2006, 2007, 2008 were studied in detail.

Anitha concludes her investigation by stating that outbound business travel is a new trend among pharma companies. Even though companies are following the cost cutting norm the trend still exists. Those who achieve the sales target are only eligible for incentive travel. So every person is striving for achieving sales target and they get monitory benefit as well as out bound incentive travel. It is also considered as a prestigious one for marketing executives. A recent study by the National Business Association (NBA) has shown that Companies are recognizing the value of face to face meeting with customers, prospects, partners and colleagues, to build relationships and set the stage for topline growth. For this outbound business travel for conference, conventions, meetings, award presentations etc. will always be one of the best ways to reward and retain top talent. Even in the background of global economic recession the trend is still existing.

In the concluding chapter **Sujatha, Yashwant Singh** and **Shyju, P.J.** present a chapter titled "Management of Archaeological Sites and

Promotion of Heritage Tourism: Study of Nalanda". To them, archaeological sites represent the identity of a nation, and excavated item, the remains of historical monuments are part of the rich heritage of the people of that country. Archaeological Survey of India, had declared many sites in India as protected monuments, but the management of many sites raise several questions when tourism activity is promoted in a big scale. The real intention of protection redirects to earning. Researches show that tourist perception changes according to the nature of destinations. Dissatisfaction of tourists is an indication of poor site management; several questions arise here on priorities. This chapter focuses the key aspects of management of archaeological sites and how heritage tourism can be linked with ancient sites.

The debate of impacts of heritage tourism according to the authors, in preserving our cultural heritage opens new areas of research. The process of convergence between heritage management and tourism activity certainly help to protect the site, and at the same time make the project sustainable. In order to maintain the site as a destination, a detailed study of individual preference pattern, motivating forces etc., should be carried out at a site. The result of this study will help the administrators to change the approach towards an archaeological site and how efficiently they can incorporate with heritage tourism. Tourism acts as a tool for sustainability here. However, promotion of tourism activity should not disturb the existing conditions of a site. Tourism highlights the importance of a site, at the same time modifications are required from the side of the archaeological department authorities regarding the management of information, site interpretation, behaviour of the staff, amenities for visitors etc.

Keeping this background in view, this volume attempts to address issues pertaining to various aspects of Indian tourism *viz.*, Indian tourism: issues and initiatives, perspectives of tourism, strategies to revamp tourism, initiatives of tourism in Sri Lanka, linkage between human rights, unemployment issues in tourism sector, application of web technology in tourism advancement, aspects of responsible tourism, potentials to stimulate tourism destinations' regional competitiveness and disparity in foreign tourist arrivals, living aspects of ecotourism communities, segmentations strategy for the promotion of ecotourism products, rural empowerment through ecotourism, marketing of ecotourism, HOLSAT approach to destination satisfaction, tea-tourism predictors of behavioural intention of health tourists, dental tourism, connection between tourism and pharma sectors, and management of archaeological sites and promotion of heritage tourism. The research papers and articles are contributed by senior academics, administrators and practitioners of hospitality sector with rich practical and research experience on the core areas of the study. In their submissions they have tried to explore the existing problems faced by the tourism sector in general and hospitality industry in particular. They have also presented solid suggestions to revamp and revitalize tourism sector in India.

Diwali Day, 2017

M.R. Biju
M.R.B. Anantha Padmanabha
Editors

Part 1: Dynamics of Tourism

1

Hospitality Industry in India
Issues, Initiatives and Challenges

M.R.B. Anantha Padmanabha and *M.R. Biju*

The hospitality industry of India is economically important and is growing rapidly. The World Travel and Tourism Council calculated that tourism generated INR 6.4 trillion or 6.6 per cent of the nation's GDP in 2012. It supported 39.5 million jobs, 7.7 per cent of its total employment. The sector is predicted to grow at an average annual rate of 7.9 per cent from 2013 to 2023. This gives India the third rank among countries with the fastest growing tourism industries over the next decade. India has a large medical tourism sector which is expected to grow at an estimated rate of 30 per cent annually to reach about 95 billion by 2015. According to provisional statistics 6.29 million foreign tourists arrived in India in 2011, an increase of 8.9 per cent from 5.78 million in 2010. This ranks India as the 38th country in the world in terms of foreign tourist arrivals. Domestic tourist visits to all states and Union Territories numbered 1,036.35 million in 2012, an increase of 16.5 per cent from 2011. The most represented countries are the United States (16%) and the United Kingdom (12.6%). In 2011, Maharashtra, Tamil Nadu and Delhi were the most popular states for foreign tourists. Domestic tourists visited the states Uttar Pradesh, Andhra Pradesh and Tamil Nadu most frequently. Chennai, Delhi, Mumbai and Agra have been the four most visited cities of India by foreign tourists during the year 2011. Worldwide, Chennai is ranked 38 by the number of foreign tourists, while Mumbai is ranked at 50, Delhi at 52 and Agra at 66 and Kolkata at 99.

The Travel and Tourism Competitiveness Report 2013 ranks India 65th out of 144 countries overall. The report ranks the price competitiveness of India's tourism sector 20th out of 144 countries. It mentions that India has quite good air transport (ranked 39th), particularly given the country's stage of development, and reasonable ground transport infrastructure (ranked 42nd). Some other aspects of its tourism infrastructure remain somewhat underdeveloped However,. The nation has very few hotel rooms per capita by international comparison and low ATM penetration. The World Tourism Organisation reported that India's receipts from tourism during 2012 ranked 16th in the world, and 7th among Asian and Pacific countries. The Ministry of Tourism designs national policies for the development and promotion of tourism. In the process, the Ministry consults and collabourates with other stakeholders in the sector including various Central Ministries/agencies, State Governments, Union Territories and the representatives of the private sector. Concerted efforts are being made to promote new forms of tourism such as rural, cruise, medical and Ecotourism. The Ministry also maintains the Incredible India campaign. India's rich history and its cultural and geographical diversity make its international tourism appeal large and diverse. It presents heritage and cultural tourism along with medical, business, educational and sports tourism.

Against this backdrop, an attempt has been made in this chapter to examine the facets of hospitality sector in an analytical perspective. The chapter has broadly been categorized under two major heads–Part I unfolds the evolution of hospitality sector in a global perspective and Part II critically examines the initiatives undertaken by Government of India for Tourism promotion.

PART I : EVOLUTIONARY PROCESS

World tourism is considered as a significant factor in the economy of many nations. Today tourism related infrastructure in various parts of the country has improved the quality of life of the local people and helped to promote local arts and crafts. Tourism has contributed to increase awareness about conservation of the environment and the cultural heritage. Tourism is the fastest growing industry in modern world. People have always travelled to distant parts of the world to see monuments, arts and culture, taste new cuisine etc. The term tourist was firstly used as official term in 1937 by the League of Nations. Tourism was defined as people travelling abroad for period of over 24 hours.

The word tour gained acceptance in the 18th century, when the Grand Tour of Europe became part of the upbringing of the educated and wealthy

British noblemen. Tourism is a service industry, consisting of transportation, accommodation and hospitality. The term "tourism and travel" are often used interchangeably though literally there is a difference. A person who indulges in tourism is known as tourist. Tourism is multi-faceted phenomenon which involves movement to and stay in destination outside the normal place of residence. Tourism is composed of three basic elements:

(a) A dynamic element which involves travel to a selected destination or destinations.
(b) A static element which involves the stay in the destination.
(c) A consequential element resulting from the two preceding elements, which is concerned with effect on the economic, physical and social subsystems with which the tourist is directly or indirectly in contact.

Therefore, it has been rightly said that the core concept of tourism revolves around for 4 A's (a) Attraction, (b) Accessibility, (c) Amenities, and (d) Ancillary services.

Important Highlights of Indian Tourism

(1) The number of Foreign Tourist Arrivals (FTAs) in India during 2010 increased to 5.78 million as compared to 5.17 million in 2009. The growth rate in FTAs during 2010 over 2009 was 11.8 per cent as compared to (–) 2.2 per cent during 2009 over 2008. The growth rate of 11.8 per cent in 2010 for India was better than UNWTO's projected growth rate of 5 per cent to 6 per cent for the world in 2010.

(2) The share of India in international tourist arrivals in 2010 was 0.61 per cent, which is 0.02 per cent improvement over 2009. However, India's rank improved to 40th in 2010, from 41st in 2009. India accounted for 2.83 per cent of tourist arrivals in Asia Pacific Region in 2010, with the rank of 11.

(3) Tourism continues to play an important role as a foreign exchange earner for the country. In 2010, foreign exchange earnings (FEE) from tourism were Rs. 64,889 crore as compared to Rs. 54,960 in 2009, registering a growth of 18.1 per cent.

(4) Number of domestic tourist visits in India during 2010 was 740.21 million as compared to 668.80 million in 2009, with a growth rate of 18.8 per cent.

Foreign Tourists Arrivals in India (FTAs)

Tourism is an important sector of the economy and contributes significantly in the country's GDP as well as Foreign Exchange Earnings (FEE). With its backward and forward linkages with other sectors of the economy like transport, constriction, handicrafts, manufacturing, Swiss Professor Walter Hunzikar and Kurt Krapf (1994), describe the concept of tourism "Tourism is the sum of phenomena and relationship arising from the travel and stay of non-residents, in so far as they do not lead to permanent residence and are not connected with any earning activity".

As per the International Union of Official Travel Organisation (IUOTO), now called as World Tourism Organisation (WTO), has defined tourist as a temporary visitor staying for at least 24 hours in a country visited when the purpose of the journey can be classified under one of the following headings:

(a) *Leisure*: recreation, holiday, health, study of religion and sports or
(b) Business, family, mission meetings.

As per the IASET and Tourism Society of Cardiff in 1981, "Tourism may be defined in terms of particular activities selected by choice and undertaken outside the home environment. Tourism may or may not involve overnight stay away from home."

Herman Von Schullard, An American Economist, defined it as, "The sum of the total operations, mainly of an economic nature which directly relates to the entry, stay and movement of foreigners inside and outside a certain country, city or region."

According to Tourism Society in Britain, "Tourism is the temporary short-term movement of people to destination outside the place where they normally live and work and their activities during the stay at their destinations, includes movement for all purposes, as well as day visit or excursions".

In 1981, the International Conference on Leisure-Recreation-Tourism, held by Tourism Society in England, defined it as, "Tourism may be defined in terms of particular activities selected by choice and undertaken outside the home environment. Tourism may or may not involve overnight stay away from home". This definition was subsequently accepted by the IASET (Burkart & Medlik, 1974).

All the above definitions bring out the following distinct features of tourism:

(a) Involvement of a mobile population of travellers who are stranger to the place they visit.
(b) Their stay is of a temporary nature in the area visited.
(c) It is essentially a pleasure and recreational activity.
(d) Their stay is not connected with any remunerated activity or an activity involving earnings.

WTO has taken the concept of 'tourism' beyond a stereotype image of 'holiday making'. The official accepted definition in the report is: "Tourism comprises the activities of persons travelling to and staying in places outside their usual environment not for leisure, business and other purposes".

WTO has classified three types of tourism:

(a) **Domestic Tourism:** It consists of residents visiting within their own country. No formalities are required in this kind of travel.
(b) **Inbound Tourism:** Comprises non-residents travelling into a country of their choice.
(c) **Outbound Tourism:** Comprises residents of a nation travelling out to foreign country.

These three basic forms of tourism can be in turn being combined to derive three categories of tourism.

(a) **Internal Tourism:** This comprises domestic and inbound tourism.
(b) **National Tourism:** Domestic and outbound tourism.
(c) **International Tourism:** Inbound and outbound tourism.

Geographers study the spatial expression of tourism as a human activity, focusing on tourist generating and tourist receiving areas. The study can incorporate a variety of scales, climate, tourist recourses to local landscape, resorts etc. From the geographical point of view, tourism has three main components:

(1) The tourist from one country to another country is known as generating areas.

(2) The destination area of tourist receiving countries or region or local areas.

(3) The route travelled between respective destinations.

Tourism Flow

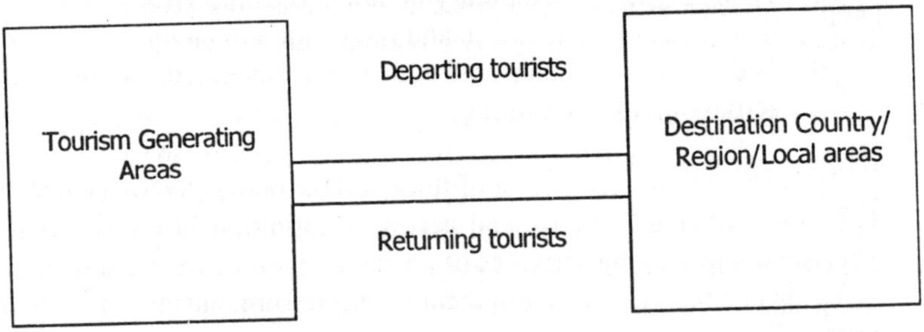

Tourism flow depends on pull and push factors. Push factors depend on the stage of economic development in generating market, number of holidays available and income. Also pull factor influence on tourist flow, it includes accessibility and the relative cost. Due to growing economic significance of tourism, it has a spectacular increase in tourism worldwide and increase in tourist earning. That money is absorbed by the local economies of the nation, and helps to increasing jobs as well as opportunities. Tourism mostly depends on the range and types of accommodation available at the destination. Accommodation is a core of the tourist industry, and plays a distinctive role in the development of this ever-expanding industry. Tourism also tends to give support to local handicrafts and cultural activities; both in urban and rural areas. Expenditure by tourists has a multiplier effect and also generates considerable tax revenue for local economy.

Tourism has become a major and an integral part of economic, social and physical development. It comprises complete system of nature, the universe, the space and the galaxy which includes the man and his activities, wildlife, mountain and valleys, rivers and waters, forest and trees, social and cultural system, flora and fauna, weather and climate, sun and the sea. The whole system requires an environmental and ecological preservation, which can be expressed in terms of following equation:

$$\text{Tourism} = (N + W + M)^{EE}$$

Whereas,

N = Nature, W = Wildlife, M = Man and his activities, EE = Environment and Ecology.

The environment and ecological aspect on all the components as regard to the development of tourism. The equation can further simplified in nature-Tourism = $(\text{Wildlife} + \text{Man})^{EE}$.

Without planning and controlling mechanism the development of tourism may end by having social, cultural and economic distortions, which will be reflected in the relationship between tourists and local people. As soon as tourism grows and expands, it brings the social and economic changes in the respective region. This can be positive as well as negative.

Tourism 2020 vision is the World Tourism Organisation long-term forecast and assessment of the development of tourism up to the first 20 years of the new millennium. An essential outcome of the Tourism 2020 vision is quantitative forecasts covering a 25 years period, with 1995 as base year and forecasts for 2000 and 2020. Tourism 2020 vision calls these motivating factors the three E's–Entertainment, Excitement and Education.

Attraction, accommodation, supporting facilities, and infrastructure are the basic elements of tourism. For the better development of tourism, these facilities should be developed in respective areas and for this public as well as private sector should take a lead. The flow of domestic tourists will depend on the location of tourist spot and population density of an area. Accessibility is an essential factor for better development of tourism.

Tourism in India

India's glorious traditions and rich cultural heritage are closely related with the development of tourism. Its magnificent monuments attract a large number of tourists from all-over the world. The natural surroundings, the architectural masterpieces, the music, dance, paintings, customs and languages all these go to make India as tourist paradise. In ancient India, there were no travel formalities for travelling in the period of Chandragupta-II, and that time the famous Chinese pilgrim Fa-Hiuen travelled between A.D. 401 and 410 without a passport. But in the 3rd century B.C., a passport or *mudra* was essential, according to Kautilya's *Arthashastra,* for all travellers. During the Vedic period, the tourists were accommodated at *'dhams'* or holy place of the country.

There was a remarkable increase in the number of traveller coming to India, as a result of the discovery of the new sea route by Vasco-da-Gama. When Alexander the Great reached in India, he found well maintained roads lined with trees and wells, and rest houses. Along with the royal highway which is 1920 km long and 19 meters wide, men travelled in Chariots, palanquins, bullock-carts, on donkeys, horses, camels and elephants. During the British period, tourism in India becomes more organised. They built Dak Bungalows on the road side for the convenience of dak traveller. The finest of India's cuisines is as rich and diverse as its civilisation. In Sanskrit literature the three famous words *"Atithi Devo Bhavah"* means "the guest is truly god" are a dictum of hospitality in India. India is a storehouse of art, paintings; crafts appeared on pots found in the Indus valley civilisation as early as the 3rd century B.C. The cave paintings of Ajanta and Ellora date back to the 1st to 5th century A.D. The British set up the Archaeological Survey of India in the 19th century to document the wealth of material available in the country viewing Indian art and culture as an integral part of the century's heritage.

India is a land of geographical diversity, blessed with a long history of rich civilisation and culture. It is a potential tourism paradise with a wide variety of attractions ranging from beautiful beaches, hill stations, scenery, forts, monuments, fairs, festivals, art, crafts, culture, forest, wildlife, and religious centres etc. India has one of the world's richest natural heritage: 65,000 species of fauna including 350 of mammals (7.6% of the world's total), 408 of reptiles (6.2%), 197 of amphibians (4.4%), 1244 of birds (12.6%), 2546 of fishes (11.7%) and as well as 15,000 species of flora (6%) attract the tourists for the development of tourism. India's forest, rivers, streams are bursting with rich wildlife. In India, there are 80 national parks and 441 sanctuaries. The largest wildlife sanctuaries in Asia *viz.* Kanha National Park–Madhya Pradesh (Tiger project), Jim Corbett National Park (Utter Pradesh), Gir (Gujarat) (Lion), Ranthambor (Rajasthan) (Peacock), Kaziranga (Assam) (Rhinoceros), Bandipore (Karnataka) etc.

The temples trails in India like *Gurudwara* in Amritsar, Tirupati Balaji, Mathura, Ayodhya, Badrinath, Haridwar and Rishikesh. The hill stations like Simla, Kullu, Manali, and Mussoorie in the north, Shilling and Darjeeling in the east, Ooty, Kodaikanal, and Munnar in the south and Mahabaleshwar, Matheran, Chikaldara, and Amboli in the central. All these tourist places are most popular, which attract large number of tourists. The tourist organisation of India had its beginning from the year 1945. A committee was appointed in 1945 under the Chairmanship of Sir John Sargent, Educational Advisor, by Government of India. The Sargent Committee submitted their interim report in October 1946, but implication of the suggestions given by this committee was implemented after Independence. As per the report of Sargent Committee, Tourist Traffic Committee was appointed in 1948. On the recommendation a Tourist Traffic Branch was set-up in 1949 with regional offices at Kolkata and Chennai. The tourist traffic branch was further expanded in 1955-56 from one branch to four branches and hand over a function to them *viz.* (1) Tourist Traffic, (2) Tourist Administration, (3) Tourist Advertisements, (4) Distribution Section. On March 1, 1958, a separate Department of Tourism was created in place of a Tourist Traffic Branch under the Ministry of Transport and Communication, which provides services such as accommodation, food facility, hospitality etc.

One committee was appointed in March, 1963 under the Chairmanship of L.K. Jha. This Committee made several recommendations to improve tourist flow in India, especially in regards to facilitation; three new corporations were setup in 1965, *viz.* Hotel Corporation, Indian Tourism and India Tourist Traffic Corporation, but they did not work well and therefore merged to make a single unit as India Tourism Development Corporation (ITDC) on October, 1966. ITDC is the main agency of the Ministry of Tourism and Civil Aviation, which promoted tourism in India.

Regional offices are located in all capital cities in India. Besides, there are several other offices at focal point of international tourist interest. Tourist destination in the country are improved and provided more facilities to attract the foreign tourists. India is a land of great variety and contrast. Its unique cultural mystique, exotic heritage, aesthetic environment and outstanding natural resources have attracted international tourists. Tourism has emerged as one of India's important industry. Today tourism is a major source of foreign exchange earnings and employment. India is a huge market for tourism for outbound and inbound tourists.

The main elements of culture which attract tourist to a particular destination fall under following categories: (1) Pleasure climate, (2) Scenic attraction, (3) Historical and cultural attraction, (4) Accessibility, (5) Shopping, (6) Adventure, (7) Variety of cuisines, (8) Accommodation, (9) Relaxation and horticulture, agriculture etc., tourism has the potential to not only be the economy driver, but also become an effective tool for poverty alleviation and ensuring growth with equity. Table 1.1 shows the number of foreign tourists' arrivals in India during 2000-2011:

Table 1.1: India Foreign Tourists Arrivals (FTAs) 2000-2011

Years	*FTAs (in millions)*	*Annual Growth (%)*
2000	2.65	6.7
2001	2.54	-4.2
2002	3.38	-6.0
2003	2.73	14.3
2004	3.46	26.8
2005	3.92	13.3
2006	4.45	13.5
2007	5.08	14.3
2008	5.28	4.0
2009	5.17	-2.2
2010	5.58	8.1
2011 (Jan.-June P)	2.92	10.9 @

P-Provisional @ Growth rate over Jan-June 2010.
Source: Annual Report of Tourism Department, 2010.

It is understood from Table 1.1 that, the foreign tourists arrivals in India continued to grow from 2.65 million in 2000, 2.73 million in 2003, 4.45 million in 2006, 5.17 million in 2009 and reaching 5.58 millions in 2010. The compound annual growth rate in FTAs in India during 2000-2010 was 13.5 per cent. Figure 1.1 shows the FTAs in India during the period of 2000-2011:

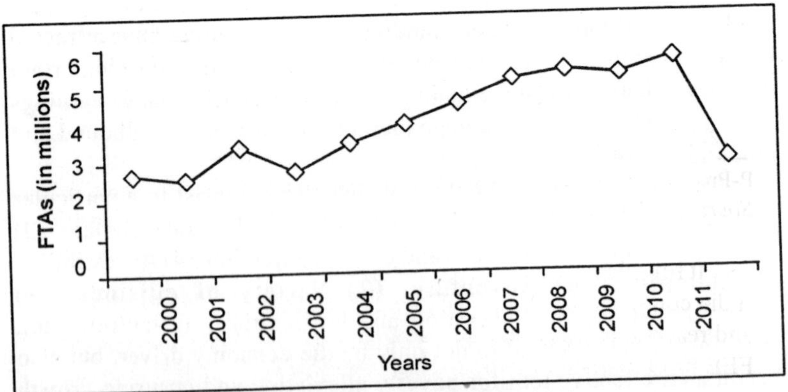

Fig. 1.1: Arrivals of Foreign Tourists in India, 2000-2011.
Source: Annual Report Tourism Department, 2010.

As shown in Fig. 1.1 during the year 2009, India witnessed a negative growth rate of 2.2 per cent over 2008. Because of global financial meltdown, terrorist activities, H_1N_1 influenza pandemic etc. However, growth rate for India was better than that the negative growth of 4.2 per cent registered for the world during 2009. In the year 2010, the tourism sector witnessed substantial growth as compared to 2009. The Foreign Tourists Arrivals (FTAs) in India during 2010 of 5.58 million as compared to the FTAs of 5.17 million in 2009, shows a growth of 8.1 per cent.

Foreign Exchange Earning (FEE) from Tourism in India

The revenue through foreign exchange is analysed in respect of growth of exchange earnings from tourism over a period of time and percentage of exchange earnings from tourism. Tourism is one of the important sectors in India for Foreign Exchange Earning. Table 1.2 depicts the Foreign Exchange Earning from tourism in India, from 2000 to 2011:

Table 1.2: India Foreign Exchange Earning (FEE), 2000 to 2011

Years	*FEE (in Rs. Crore)*	*Annual Growth (%)*
2000	15626	20.5
2001	15083	-3.5
2002	15064	-0.1
2003	20729	37.6
2004	27944	34.8
2005	33123	18.5
2006	39025	17.8
2007	44360	13.7
2008	51294	15.6
2009	54960	8.3
2010	64889	18.1
2011# (Jan.-June)	35163	12.1@

P-Provisional, # Advance Estimate, @ Growth rate over Jan-June 2010.
Source: Annual Report of Ministry of Tourism, 2009.

It reveals that, the foreign exchange earnings (FEE) from tourism in India continued from Rs. 15626 crore in 2000, Rs. 54960 crore in 2009 and reached up to Rs. 64889 in 2010. Figure 1.2 shows clear picture of FEE from tourism in India during 2000-2011:

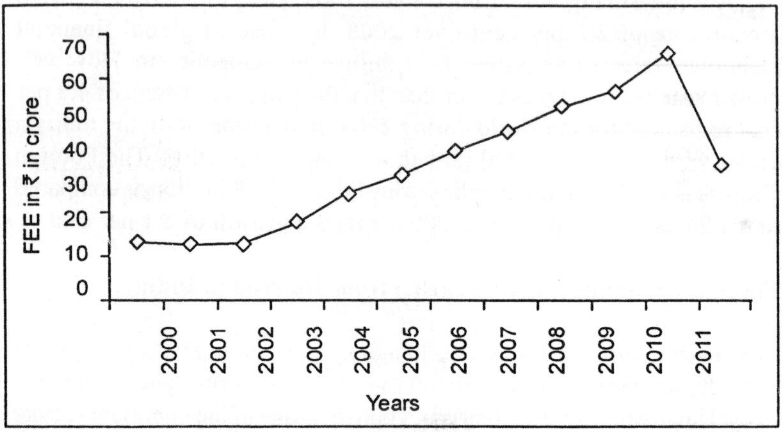

Fig. 1.5: Foreign Exchange Earning (FEE) 2000-2011.

Source: Annual Report Tourism Department, 2010.

As shown in Fig. 1.2, FEE from tourism during 2010 were Rs. 64889 crore as compared to Rs. 54960 crore during 2009, registering a growth rate 18.1 per cent. The growth rate in FEE from tourism during 2009 over 2008 was 8.3 per cent. The decline in growth rate in FEE in 2009 over 2008 was due to global financial crisis, terrorist activities H_1N_1 epidemic etc.

Growth of Domestic Tourism

The buoyancy in the Indian tourism industry can be attributed to several factors. Firstly, the tremendous growth of Indian economy has resulted in more disposable income in the hands of middle class, thereby promoting increasingly large number of people to spend money on vacations abroad or at home. Secondly, India is a booming Information Technology hub and more and more people are coming to India on business trips. Thirdly, aggressive advertising campaign "Incredible India" by Tourism Ministry has played a significant role in changing the image of India from that of the land of snake charmers to a hot and happening place and has sparked renewed interest among foreign travellers. Table 1.3 shows the number of domestic tourist visits to all states and Union Territories in India during the year 2000 to 2010:

Table 1.3: Number of Domestic Tourist Visits to All States and Union Territories 2000-10

Year	*No. of Domestic Tourist Visits (in millions)*	*Annual Growth (%)*
2000	220.11	15.4
2001	236.47	7.4
2002	269.60	14.0
2003	309.04	14.6
2004	366.27	18.5
2005	391.95	7.0
2006	462.31	18.0
2007	526.56	13.9
2008	563.03	7.0
2009	668.80	18.8
2010(P)	740.21	10.7

P: Provisional data

Source: Annual Report of Ministry of Tourism, 2010.

Table 1.3 presents the statistics on domestic and foreign tourist visits to various States and Union Territories during the years 2000 to 2010. There has been a continuous increase in domestic tourist visits from 2000-2010, with the Compound Annual Growth Rate (CAGR) of domestic tourist visits to all States and Union Territories from 2000 to 2010 being 13.2 per cent. Fig. 1.3 shows the number of Domestic Tourist Visits to all states and Union Territories, 2000-10.

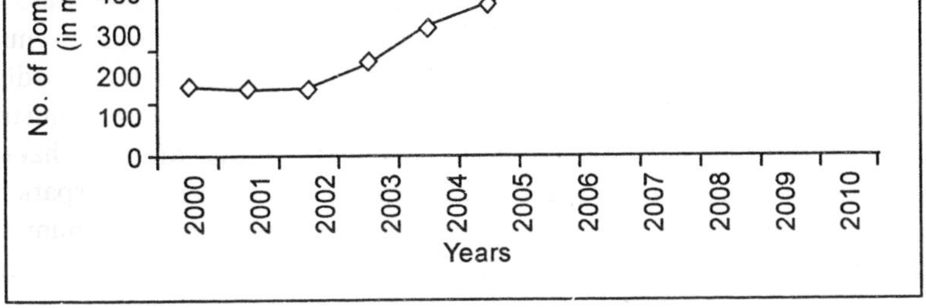

Fig. 1.3: Number of Domestic Tourist Visits to all States and Union Territories in India, 2000-2010.

Source: Annual Report Tourism Department, 2010.

As shown in Fig. 1.3, the year 2010 witnessed a growth of 10.7 per cent in domestic tourist visits over the year 2009, which is lower than the growth of 18.8 per cent in the year 2009 over 2008. It is apparent that number of domestic tourist visits to states and union territories during last 10 years have been consistently registering an increasing trend.

PART II
INITIATIVES BY THE GOVERNMENT FOR TOURISM PROMOTION

'Hunar se Rozgar' Programme

A special initiative was launched in 2009-10 for the creation of employable skills among youth belonging to economically weaker sections of the society in the age group of 18-25 years (upper age limit raised to 28 years in November, 2010) with the basic objective to reduce the skill gap affecting the hospitality and tourism sector and to ensure the spread of economic benefit of tourism to the poor. The programme offers short duration courses of 6 to 8 weeks which are fully funded by the Ministry of Tourism. Initially covering two courses *viz.* (i) food and beverage service; and (ii) food production, courses in Housekeeping, Utility, Bakery and Patisserie were added subsequently. With the growing acceptability of the initiative more trades/training areas were added like—to bring up drivers, golf caddies, stone mason, security guards and tourist facilitators etc. For the year 2012-13, 21,175 persons have been trained under the initiative up to 31 January, 2013.

Visa on Arrival (VoA)

Considering the importance of Visa facilities in enhancing tourist inflow, the facility of "Long Term Tourist Visas" of five years duration with multiple entry, carrying a stipulation of 90 days for each visit, has been introduced on a pilot basis for the nationals of the 18 selected countries. The findings of an evaluation study conducted by this Ministry have reinforced the belief that the presence of the facility of "Visa on Arrival" (VoA) significantly influences the tourists' travel plans to any country. During 2012, a total number of 16,084 VoAs (Visa on Arrival) were issued as compared to 12,761 VoAs during the corresponding period of 2011, thereby showing a growth of 26 per cent. Efforts are on to extend the VoA facility for the nationals of more countries.

Publicity and Marketing Strategy

As part of its domestic and global publicity and marketing strategy to promote tourism and create social awareness through the print and electronic media, the Ministry of Tourism launched campaigns on Clean India, "Atithi Devo Bhava and Hunar Se Rozgaar" through radio channels. Campaigns highlighting the tourism potential of North-East and J&K were also carried out through Doordarshan. Campaigns were also taken up for "Incredible India" branding on TV during 2nd Formula Grand Prix and London Olympics, 2012, during the International Film Festival of India (IFFI) held in Goa, and during the International Indian Film Academy (IIFA) Awards 2012 in Singapore.

The Ministry had participated in major international Travel Fairs and Exhibitions in important tourist generating markets the world over, as well as in emerging and potential markets, to showcase and promote the tourism products of the country. These included Arabian Travel Market (ATM) in Dubai, International Trade Business (ITB-Asia) in Singapore, World Travel Market (WTM) in London, International Meetings Exhibitions (IMEX) in Frankfurt, International Tourism Trade Fair (FITUR) in Madrid etc.

To showcase and project the Buddhist Heritage of India, an International Buddhist Conclave was organised by the Ministry of Tourism in Varanasi in September 2012 and attended by 132 international delegates from around 30 countries. The delegates were taken for a visit to Sarnath and Bodh Gaya. For the first time, an International Tourism Mart was held at Guwahati in January 2013 to showcase the largely untapped tourism potential of the North-Eastern Region in the domestic and international markets.79 International Buyers and media delegates from 23 countries and hundreds of tour operators from different parts of India participated in the Mart and engaged in one-to-one meetings with sellers from the North-East Region and West Bengal. The international delegates were taken on Familiarisation Tours of the North-Eastern Region.

Niche Tourism Products

The Ministry of Tourism has also taken the initiative of identifying, diversifying, developing and promoting the nascent/upcoming niche products of the tourism industry. This is done in order to overcome the aspect of 'seasonality' to promote India as a 365 days destination, attract tourists with specific interests and to ensure repeat visits for the products in which India has comparative advantage. Accordingly, the following Niche Products have been identified by the Ministry of Tourism for development and Promotion:

(i) Cruise
(ii) Adventure
(iii) Medical
(iv) Wellness
(v) Golf
(vi) Polo
(vii) Meetings Incentives Conferences and Exhibitions (MICE)
(viii) Ecotourism
(ix) Film Tourism

Cruise Tourism

'Cruise Shipping' is one of the most dynamic and fastest growing components of the leisure industry worldwide. India with its vast and beautiful coastline, virgin forests and undisturbed idyllic islands, rich historical and cultural heritage, can emerge as an attractive tourist destination for cruise tourists. Central financial assistance for Cruise Tourism project of Rs. 1450.00 lakh was sanctioned by the Ministry of Tourism for development of Tourism Infrastructure in Willing Island, Cochin Port, during the year 2008-09. An amount of Rs. 491.53 lakh had been sanctioned and Rs. 245.77 lakh released during 2011-12 to Cochin Port Trust for the development of Cruise Passenger facilitation centre at Cochin Port.

Adventure Tourism

Adventure tourism involves travel to remote, exotic areas, for exploration as for undertaking activities which test the endurance of both a person and his equipment. Adventure tourism is rapidly growing in popularity as tourists seek different kinds of vacations. Central Financial Assistance is being extended to State Governments/Union Territory Administrations for development of tourism infrastructure in destinations including adventure tourism destinations. These include facilities for trekking, rock climbing, mountaineering, aero-sports, winter/water related sports, trekker huts, wildlife viewing facilities etc. Financial assistance to State Governments is also provided for the purchase of water sports equipments consisting of kayaks, canoes, paddle boats, fibre glass boats, hovercrafts, water scooters, etc. This year, the Ministry of Tourism has sanctioned an amount of Rs. 220.76 lakh to the Indian Institute of Sking and Mountaineering, Gulmarg (IISM) for conduct of adventure courses as follows:

Sl. No.	*Courses*	*No. of Courses*	*No. of Trainees*	*Total Expenditure (Rs. in Lakh)*
1.	Snow Skiing	6	480	40.30
2.	Water Skiing	10	300	84.80
3.	Trekking	10	200	33.95
4.	Parasailing	10	200	24.41
5.	Hot Air Balloon	5	100	37.30
	Total		**1280**	**220.76**

Source: Ministry of Tourism, *Annual Report 2012-13.*

Medical Tourism

Medical tourism (also called medical travel, health tourism or global healthcare) is a term used to describe the rapidly-growing practice of travelling across international borders to obtain healthcare. Services typically sought by travellers include elective procedures as well as complex specialised surgeries such as joint replacement (knee/hip), cardiac surgery, dental surgery, and cosmetic surgeries. Besides India, there are several Asian destinations like Singapore, Malaysia and Thailand that are offering Medical care facilities and promoting medical tourism. India excels among them for the following reasons:

- State of the Art Medical facilities
- Reputed healthcare professionals
- Quality nursing facilities
- No waiting time for availing the medical services

India's traditional healthcare therapies like Ayurveda and Yoga combined with allopathic treatment provide holistic wellness. Financial support as per guidelines and availability of funds under the Market Development Assistance Scheme (MDA) is provided to following approved Medical Tourism Service Providers:

- Representatives of Hospitals accredited by Joint Commission International (JCI) and the National Accreditation Board of Hospitals and Healthcare Services (NABH).
- Medical Tourism facilitators (travel agents/tour operators) approved by Ministry of Tourism, Government of India.

Wellness Tourism

Wellness Tourism is about travelling for the primary purpose of achieving, promoting or maintaining maximum health and a sense of well-being. Health Tourism holds immense potential for India. The Indian systems of medicine, that is Ayurveda, *Yoga*, *Panchakarma*, Rejuvenation Therapy etc., are among the most ancient systems of medical treatment, in the world. India can provide medical and healthcare of international standard at comparatively low cost. Most of the hotels/resorts are coming up with Ayurveda Centres. The leading tour operators have included Ayurveda in their brochures. The Ministry of Tourism also provides financial assistance under the Market Development Assistance Scheme (MDA) to approved wellness centres, i.e. representatives of wellness centres accredited by NABH or the State Governments. The MDA assistance is for participation in medical/ tourism fairs, medical conferences, wellness conferences, wellness fairs, and allied road shows. Yoga/Ayurveda/Wellness has been promoted in the past years in the print, electronic, internet and outdoor media under the Ministry of Tourism's "Incredible India Campaign".

Golf Tourism

Sports Tourism in India is gaining interest. One of the latest trends in golf tourism is the fact that there has been a recent surge in the interest levels amongst youth the world over. India has several golf courses of international standards. Further, golf events held in India also attract domestic and international tourists. Recognising this potential to develop Golf as a niche tourism product for attracting both international and domestic tourists, the Ministry of Tourism had organised a one day Workshop on "Promotion of Golf Tourism" on 21 January, 2011. The objective of this workshop was to evolve a road map for formulating strategies for development and promotion of golf tourism in India.

Polo Tourism

India has rich historical ties with many of the sporting traditions including

Polo. The game of Polo originated in India and India is one of the few countries in the world where this game is still preserved and practiced. The Kolkata Polo Club is the oldest Polo club in the world and is 150 years old. Therefore, Polo can rightly be termed as "Heritage Sports" of India. The Ministry of Tourism had sanctioned an amount of Rs. 5 Lakh to the Government of Manipur for organising the 6th International Polo Festival 2012, held at Imphal from 22-29 November, 2012, coinciding with the Sangai festival.

Meetings Incentives Conferences and Exhibitions (MICE)

In order to promote India more effectively as a convention destination, the travel industry had, under the patronage of the Ministry of Tourism, set up the India Convention Promotion Bureau (ICPB) in 1988, a non-profit organisation, with members comprising of national airlines, hotels, travel agents, tour operators, tourist transport operators, conference organisers, etc. The important objectives of ICPB are as under:

- To promote India as a venue for International Congresses and Conventions.
- To undertake a continuing programme of creating awareness of the role and benefits of Congress and Conventions in the context of national objectives.
- To undertake research on the international conference market for development of India's conference industry.
- To diffuse knowledge to conference industry personnel through educational programmes, seminars, group discussions, courses of study and exchange of visits with India Associations/ Organisations.

Ecotourism

Ecotourism means making as little environmental impact as possible and helping to sustain the indigenous populace, thereby encouraging the preservation of wildlife and habitats when visiting a place. This is responsible form of tourism and tourism development, which encourages going back to natural products in every aspect of life. It is also the key to sustainable ecological development. Ecotourism focuses on local cultures, wilderness adventures, volunteering, personal growth and learning new ways to live on our vulnerable planet. It is considered the fastest growing market in the tourism industry, according to the World Tourism Organisation with an annual growth rate of 5 per cent worldwide and representing 6 per cent of the world Gross Domestic Product, 11.4 per cent of all consumer spending. Ecotourism in India is still at a very nascent stage, but there are conscious efforts to save the fragile Himalayan Eco system and culture and heritage of the indigenous people, which is probably the largest concentration in the world.

The details of year-wise financial achievement under Scheme "Ecotourism" are:

Plan Period	*Years*	*Expenditure (Rs. in lakhs)*
Tenth Plan (2002-07)	2002-03	7.41
	2003-04	14.36
	2004-05	15.12
	2005-06	35.43
	2006-07	31.68
Total		**104.00**
Eleventh Plan (2007-12)	2007-08	47.79
	2008-09	49.79
	2009-10	62.54
	2010-11	12.97
Total		**173.00**

Source: Answer to Lok Sabha Unstarred Question no. 4653 dated 8.12.2010.

Film Tourism

The Ministry of Tourism has recognised films as powerful tool for the development and promotion of destinations under Niche Tourism Product. The Ministry of Tourism has taken following steps to promote Film Tourism in the country:

- Signing of a Memorandum of Understanding with the Ministry of Information and Broadcasting in 2012;
- Joint participation with the Ministry of Information and Broadcasting in the Cannes Film Festival and Market, International Film Festival of India (IFFI, Goa), and European Film Market, Berlin;
- Institution of a National Tourism Award in 2012 in the category "Most Film Promotion Friendly State/UT" to encourage the State Governments and Union Territories to facilitate filming in their region; and

- The Ministry of Tourism has formulated guidelines for extending financial support to State Governments/Union Territory Administrations for promotion of Film Tourism. As per these guidelines, Central Financial Assistance of Rs. 2 lakh per film will be given to each of the State Governments/UT Administrations during each financial year.

Tiger Tourism

As per the Supreme Court directions, the Ministry of Environment and Forests has issued guidelines for tourism activities in tiger reserves in the country. As per this guideline, no tourism activity is permitted in the core areas of Tiger Reserves. The Ministry of Tourism is in favour of regulated tourism in Protected Areas of the country. Tourism should be based on scientific carrying capacity and sustainability principles. The Ministry of Tourism does not favour a total ban in protected areas including Tiger Reserves. International Practices/best National practices should be taken into consideration by the Ministry of Environment and Forests in finalising Ecotourism guidelines for Protected Areas. The Ministry of Tourism extends Central Financial Assistance (CFA) to the State Governments/ Union Territory Administrations for development of Tourism Products under the scheme of Product/Infrastructure Development for Destinations and Circuits, based on the proposals identified in consultations with them, subject to availability of funds and *interse* priority and adherence to scheme guidelines.

Rural Tourism

Rural Tourism is essentially an activity which takes place in the countryside. It is multifaceted and may entail farm/agricultural tourism, cultural tourism, nature tourism, adventure tourism, and ecotourism. As against conventional tourism, rural tourism has certain typical characteristics: It is experience-oriented; the locations are less populated, it is predominantly in natural environments and it is based on the preservation of culture, heritage and traditions.

The scheme of Rural Tourism was started by the Ministry of Tourism in 2002-03 with the objective of highlighting rural life, art, culture and heritage at rural locations and in villages which have core competence in art, craft, handloom, textiles and natural environment. The intention was to benefit the local community economically and socially as well as to enable interaction between tourists and local population for a mutually enriching experience. The promotion of village tourism was also aimed towards generating revenue for rural communities through tourist visits, which may stop exodus from rural to urban areas.

Infrastructural Development for Rural Tourism

Rural Tourism can be harnessed as a strategy for rural development. The development of a strong platform around the concept of Rural Tourism is definitely useful for a country like India where almost 74 per cent of the population resides in its 7 million villages. On the other hand, the growing trend of urbanisation has led to falling of income levels, lesser job opportunities leading to desertion of villages. Rural Tourism could be a solution to this.

Challenges in Rural Tourism

The major challenges of Rural Tourism are *viz.* need to preserve the environment and natural resources, the need for education, proper understanding for both tourists and local people, and the need to generate a democratic movement which helps people at all levels to participate in tourism development. Also they need to focus on occupation training, handicraft promotion, and improvement of both the landscape and the basic infrastructure, to increase the quality of life of villagers by creating a healthy environment. The cooperative system in Rural Tourism can be an effective approach in bringing positive impact in rural areas. Local people can monitor and control the negative impacts of tourism on their own society, if they have an equal stake and authority in management and development. Rural Tourism projects at 186 villages in 29 States/ Union Territories have been sanctioned by the Ministry of Tourism since the inception of the scheme. 56 of these sites are located in the North-Eastern Region. A total amount of Rs.55.40 crores was sanctioned for Rural Tourism projects during the Eleventh Five Year Plan. Projects at 90 sites have been completed by December 2012. During the Twelfth Five Year Plan, the scheme of Rural Tourism is being replaced with the scheme of Rural Tourism Cluster. The Modified scheme aims at developing a cluster of villages a Tourism Product.

Agri-Tourism

Agri-tourism is considered as the fastest growing sector in the tourism industry. The concept has been successfully implemented in states like Maharashtra, Kerala, Rajasthan, Jharkhand, Gujarat and Himachal Pradesh. It has become a new avenue for earning the income for the rural farmers. In Maharashtra, rural areas have formed an organisation named Maharashtra State Agri and Rural Tourism (MART). There are about 150 Agri-tourism centres in the state working without financial assistance of the Government schemes. In Kerala, the Government has played a key role in boosting up the Rural and Health Tourism. Rajasthan is one of the preferred ventures to attract the foreign visitors. In Himachal Pradesh, the State Government is motivating the rural people to create required facilities in rural areas for tourism purpose.

Tourism in the North-Eastern Region

The North-East has a wide array of products in the form of its pristine natural beauty, forests and wildlife, rivers and mountains, and a unique multi-ethnic cultural heritage to offer to the tourist. The region is endowed with diverse tourist attractions and each state has its own distinct features. For the development and promotion of North-East Region. Ten per cent of the plan allocation of the Ministry has been earmarked. An amount of Rs. 100.00 crore has been earmarked in Budget Estimate 2012-13 for the region. In order to develop and promote tourism in the region, Ministry of Tourism has organised the International Tourism Mart with the objective of showcasing the largely untapped tourism potential of the North-East region in the domestic and international markets from 18-20 January, 2013 in Guwahati.

International Cooperation

In the arena of international cooperation, India participated in the 4th Meeting of Association of South-east Asian Nations (ASEAN)–India Tourism Ministers meeting held in Vientiane, Lao PDR, in January 2013; 93rd Session of UNWTO Executive Council in Madrid, Spain in June, 2012 and the 94th Session of UNWTO Executive Council in Campeche, Mexico in October, 2012. A meeting of the Joint Working Group on Tourism Cooperation between India and Israel was held in Jerusalem, Israel in June, 2012 for enhancing further development of tourism in both the countries. A similar meeting of India and Philippines was held in Delhi in September, 2012. A special mention must be made of the 4th T-20 Tourism.

Ministers meeting held in Mexico in May 2012 which unanimously emphasised the role of tourism as a major engine for job creation particularly for youth and women. This led to the G-20 Leaders of Nations Summit held in Mexico in June 2012 acknowledging tourism as a major sector for employment generation, poverty reduction and economic growth. India participated in events to coincide with the visit of INS Sudharshini, the 40th Anniversary Celebrations of Diplomatic Relations between India and Vietnam and the 20th Anniversary of India-ASEAN Partnership in Danang, Vietnam in January, 2013.

Concluding Observations

To sum up, Indian tourism has vast potential for generating employment and earning large sums of foreign exchange besides giving a fillip to the country's overall economic and social development. Much has been achieved by way of increasing air seat capacity, increasing trains and railway connectivity to important tourist destinations, four-laning of roads connecting important tourist centres and increasing availability of accommodation by adding heritage hotels to the hotel industry and encouraging paying guest accommodation. But much more remains to be done. Since tourism is a multidimensional activity, and basically a service industry, it would be necessary that all wings of the Central and State Governments, private sector and voluntary organisations become active partners in the endeavour to attain sustainable growth in tourism if India is to become a world player in the tourist industry.

REFERENCES

Adhikari, P.S. (1990), Tourism and its impact on Himalaya Environment, *Himalaya, Man and Nature*, Vol. 14, No.1, Himalaya Seva Sangh, New Delhi.

Bansal, S.P. (2002), *Tourism in the New Millennium*, Abhishek Publications, Delhi.

Bedi, R. (1985), *Corbett National Park*, Clarion Books, Delhi.

Chakraborty, P. (1996), Adventure Tourism in the Himalaya, *Yojana*, Vol. 40, No. 8.

Dixit, Manoj, (2001), *Dimensions of Indian Tourism*, BBC, Lucknow.

Gopal, Rajesh, (1993), *Fundamentals of Wildlife Management*, Justice Home, Allahabad.

Iyer, H.R.S. (1997), Towards an eco-environment friendly society, *Kurukshetra*, Vol. XLV, No. 55.

Kohli, M.S. (1989), *Mountaineering in India*, Vikas Publishing House, New Delhi.

Negi, S.S. (1995), *Handbook of National Park*, Indus Publications, New Delhi.

Sharma, M.M. (1985), *The Value of Flowers*, Vision Books, New Delhi.

Williams, P. (1990), Tourism Technology and Environment, *Journal of Travel Research*, Vol. 29, No. 2.

Yale, P. (1995), *The Business of Tour Operations*, Longman.

http://en.wikipedia.org/wiki/Tourism_in_India

http://shodhganga.inflibnet.ac.in/bitstream/10603/6703/6/06_chapter%201.

http://164.100.47.134/intranet/TourismSectrinIndia.pdf.

2

Gauging the Pragmatic Perspectives of Tourism in the Ventures of Make in India

Priyakrushna Mohanty, Anu Chandran and *Ravish Mathew*

In the recent past, India has witnessed an array of sector specific campaigns like Swachh Bharat, Digital India, Smart Cities, NITI Aayog, Pradhan Mantri Jan Dhan Yojana, AMRUT-Atal Mission for Rejuvenation Programme and Urban Transformations, Beti Bachao, Beti Padhao: Caring for the Girl Child, DD KAUSHAL Kendra, HRIDAY-Heritage City Development and Augmentation, Pradhan Mantri Ujjawala Yojana and Start up India etc. One such path breaking campaign, "Make in India" is a move towards promoting India as a manufacturing hub. The campaign spelt out 25 sectors that will provide the platforms for the manufacturing sectors to prosper. Tourism is one of those 25 sectors and a very potent one given its labour intensive and rapid growing capacity.

Tourism industry has earned the reputation of being an economic driver (Rogerson & Lemon, 2002) and poverty alleviator (Muganda, Sahil & Smith, 2010). It is recognised as an industry that not only provides economic benefit, but also acts both directly and indirectly towards building a favourable image in the minds of the tourists about the country. Subsequently, those tourists act as the live agents for word-of-mouth promotion. This holistically helps in brand building of the nation. To attract any kind of investment, the destinations have to be portrayed in a nice manner; that it is devoid of problems and possess a conducive environment which is utmost favourable for the sectors to thrive. Such an image does not come effortlessly. It is indeed a tedious affair and any move can make or mark the process, which means it is so volatile. Tourism has a superlative capacity in triggering scores of sectors and stimulates investment. Furniture, IT, Food and Beverages, Handicrafts, Cottage Industries, Transport, Leather, Cruise and Entertainment are a few to mention. Thus, tourism can in every sense provide fillip to the entire Make in India ventures.

Make in India is a campaign to urge the potential investors to manufacture in India. But then, India is not considered very high in the eyes of other developed countries in terms of investment climate. Indian markets are characterised by restrictive trade policies, high taxation, stringent rules and corruption. If Make in India is to make progress in prospect, it has to take corrective actions and change these stereotypes existing in the minds of the major investors. Tourism industry can come handy here. This industry as noted earlier, can act towards national brand building and at the same time provide economic development (Gnoth, 2002).

It has been roughly two years since the campaign was launched and a sizable amount of progress has also been reported since then. However, there remains a scarcity of academic works based on this topic. This shows the contemporary nature of the topic and also the gap existing in the academic discourse. Moreover, there is almost no study linking tourism and Make in India. However, the campaign and its impacts have been frequently reported in newspapers and press releases of the Government. This has served as the inspiration to come up with the chapter. This has prompted the researchers to garner the reports and dossiers connected with the role of tourism in the Make in India campaign and prepare an analytical study.

Thus, this chapter is an attempt to project the importance of Tourism industry for the success of Make in India and for the betterment of the dynamics of Indian destinations. The chapter commences by providing a brief overview of the campaign and then shifts the attention to the issues and challenges faced by the campaign in general. Further, the spotlight is turned on the lead question: "How can multifaceted service sector like Tourism can impact the Make in India campaign?" Relying on the qualitative and statistical projections featured on the campaign, this study deliberates on the prospective implications and attempts to draw inferences.

Make in India—A Kaleidoscope

Launched on 25th of September, 2014, Make in India, the novel initiative of the NDA Government is an attempt to persuade the companies may it be multinational or domestic to produce in India (Choudhury, 2014). The campaign works with a major aim to make a boom in the manufacturing sector of India. The premier global companies were urged to consider India as a place of opportunities and not as a mere market. The importance of Foreign Direct Investment (FDI) as a premium catalyst in holistically developing various sectors was stressed. The crux of the campaign centres around the idea that as the investors create more employment opportunities, more number of poverty-stricken people will be exposed to the opportunities for improving their standard of living whereby a "Handsome Buyer Base" will be created. India is avidly showcased as a favourable investment destination with optimum avenues for manufacturing (www.narendramodi.in, 2016). It is forecasted that the policies associated with the Make in India campaign would be able to nurture 100 million jobs and an escalation is expected to the contribution to the national output from the current rate of 17 per cent to 25 per cent (Chitravanshi, 2016).

The official website of Make in India, i.e. www.makeinindia.com defines the campaign as "a major new national programme designed to facilitate investment, foster innovation, enhance skill-development, protect intellectual property and build best-in-class manufacturing infrastructure." The campaign is a major aid to the manufacturing sector and it was estimated that this campaign will increase the manufacturing rate from the current 15 per cent to 25 per cent by the end of 2022. The campaign is headed by an eight member expert panel that was jointly constituted by Department of Industrial Policy and Promotion (DIPP) and Federation of Indian Chambers of Commerce and Industry (FICCI). The *modus operandi* of the campaign has four basic objectives (Mehra, 2014) which are enlisted as follows:

(a) Developing an interface with the global investors;
(b) Grievance redressal and establishing a help desk;
(c) Providing Suggestions to both the centre and the state to de-bureaucratise and deregulate; and
(d) Resolve policy issues and simplify business procedures.

The campaign outlined 25 major sectors that have optimum potential for generating jobs and enhancement of skills. The list of sectors has been noted below:

Automobiles	*Ports*	*Railways*	*Bio-Technology*	*Thermal Power*
Chemicals	Aviation	Auto Components	Pharmaceuticals	Media and Entertainment
IT and BPM	Leather	Design Manufacturing	Electronics	Oil and Gas
Pharmaceuticals	Tourism & Hospitality	Renewable Energy	Construction	Electrical Machinery
Textiles	Wellness	Mining	Defense Manufacturing	Roads and Highways

Source: Official website of Make in India, http://www.makeinIndia.com/sectors.

Since its launch, the campaign has grown from strength to strength to be more effective in channelising a huge amount of FDI into the Indian markets and also simplifying the processes associated with the starting up a business. The campaign has showed multifaceted growth and developments in terms of business propositions in India. For example, India's rank in terms of Ease of Doing Business aspect (An assessment by World Bank) has moved 12 spots up since the launch of the campaign and India now ranks at 130 in a list of 189 countries. The Chief Economist of World Bank, Mr. Kaushik Basu iterated the improvement as "Remarkable Achievement" (*NDTV Profit*, 2015). India has been ranked as the top notch investment destination by a large number of organisations including the International Monetary Fund (IMF), Ernst & Young (EY), Frost and Sullivan Foreign Policy Magazine, Financial Times etc. (Mehra, 2015).

The FDI inflow showed a growth of 48 per cent within seven months since the launch of Make in India in September. And this progress has happened in a time when global FDI inflow slipped down by 16 per cent (*Business Standard*, 2016). Further, Wharton School of the University of Pennsylvania terms the current decade as the best time to do business in India (Suri, 2014).

In order to achieve the growth in manufacturing sectors, FDI investment limits have been raised substantially. In some sectors like Telecom, Tourism and Hospitality, Automobiles etc. the FDI limits have been raised to 100 per cent. Along with this, promise has been provided to make necessary corrections in the current tax structure and wipe out any retrospective taxes (Web Team, 2016). In addition to this, creative initiatives like Digital India, Waste to Wealth, Smart Cities and MUDRA Micro Units Development and Refinance Agency Bank (for development of MSMEs) will act as supporting bases for the campaign to flourish and be productive.

Issues and Challenges to Make in India Initiatives

In spite of all these achievements, Make in India has some barriers and challenges to overcome. The major criticism Make in India has been facing is that India's economy is majorly based on Agriculture and a sudden shift of the focal points economy may give rise to uncertain and unforeseen developments. Furthermore, the key policies like labour and policy reforms which are important for the successful implementation of the campaign has not been implemented fully. Indian markets face a serious challenge of having a "tough business environment" reputation (Barhat, 2015). India's business environment is full of stringent laws and is highly regulated. It is yet to be seen how this campaign will revitalize the environment in favour of investors (Maps of India.com, 2015). Moreover, Make in India is accused of showing developments only in few sectors like tourism and hospitality, electronics, IT and BPM and aviation while it is shifting the focus from primary sectors, i.e. agriculture, construction, energy etc.

Dr. Raghuram Rajan, the then Governor of Reserve Bank of India (RBI) has cautioned the sectors not to ape China's growth trajectories as Indian economy is very different from the dragon economy. The economic meltdown and slow pace of the global economic growth pose several impediments to the Make in India programme as the principles of the campaign revolve around export based growth (Mehra, 2016). Another criticism is that Make in India is a call to investors to "Come to India" and "Stay in India" which is quite paradoxical since in the last few decades the opposite has happened, i.e. many talented skilled people have left India for better job opportunities (Jagannathan, 2014). When it comes to manufacturing, China has the supremacy in the world economy. Team Make in India has to consistently develop and create strategies to outpace China in the days to come (*Zee News*, 2014).

Adding to the woes is the issue of lack of concrete infrastructure. To woo the investors, the country needs good transportation facilities, uninterrupted power supply, skilled labourforce and equipped machineries. India has not been regarded very high when it comes to some of these aspects. Hindrances in availing timely credit, restrictive labour regulations and rising taxations have made the prospective investors think twice before they establish manufacturing units in India. Seventy per cent of our workforce have an education base either up to primary or lower than that. Eighty per cent of new entrants to workforce, have no opportunity for skills' development training. Against 12.8 million per annum new entrants to the workforce the existing training capacity is 3.1 million per annum. About 2 per cent of existing workforce has skill training against 96 per cent in Korea, 75 per cent in Germany, 80 per cent in Japan, and 68 per cent in the United Kingdom (Planning Commission of India, n.d.).

The Configuration of Tourism in the Spectrum of Make in India

Among the 25 sectors that the Make in India campaign identified for progression of the economy, Tourism is considered to be one of the most prime and crucial factors. This is owing to the fact that, tourism is emerging as a primary growth engine of the economies of the third world and developing countries (Lee & Chang, 2008). The Honourable President of India Shri Pranab Mukherjee himself has endorsed the fact stating that tourism is a development agent, economic growth engine, and the biggest employer in India (*Business Standard*, 2015). Tourism in India is riding the waves of growth showing a steady progress in terms of the number of foreign tourist arrivals and spending. India received 8.016 million foreign tourists with an aggregate foreign exchange earnings of Rs.1,26,211 crore during January–December 2015 (Ministry of Tourism, GoI, 2016a). India ranks 15th and 41st in the world in terms of the International Tourism Receipts and International Tourism Arrivals respectively (Ministry of Tourism, GoI, 2016b).

The total contribution of travel and tourism sector to the Indian GDP is estimated to be Rs. 642.5bn which is about 6.7 per cent of the total GDP; in terms of the contribution to GDP, tourism stands as the 12th biggest sector in India. Furthermore, Travel and Tourism *in toto* comprises 8.7 per cent (3,66,95,500 jobs) of the total employment in the country (WTTC, 2015). In India, for every USD 1 million spent on tourism creates 78 jobs whereas an equal amount spent in manufacturing sector generates only about 45 jobs (Narendra, 2014).

After Gems, Jewellery and Readymade garments, Tourism is the third biggest earner of foreign exchange and the largest in service sectors (Mukhopadhyay, 2010). In terms of the Tourism and Travel Competitive Index (TCI), published by World Economic Forum, India dotted 52nd position in the world in 2015 (Ministry of Tourism, GoI, 2015). A survey by Google estimated that bookings of hotel rooms through on-line resources are expected to double by the end of 2016 (*Business Line*, 2016).

The Electronic Travel Authorisation (ETA) which was rechristened as e-Tourist Visa (e-TV) on 15 April, 2015 (*NDTV*, 2015) has extended the Visa-on-Arrival (VOA) status to 113 countries from 15th August, 2015. This has turned out to be one of the biggest positive and strategic moves from the Government as a result of which a growth of 252.3 per cent has been reported in arrivals on e-Tourist Visa in January 2016 over the same Period in 2015 (Ministry of Tourism, GoI, 2016c). Similarly, compared to the total 20,294 Visa-on-Arrival cases in 2013, India registered a growth of 92.4 per cent growth in 2014, taking the figures on to 39,046 (Bhalla, 2015). The Ministry is expected to extend Visa-on-Arrival status to 150 countries in March, 2016 (*The Hindu*, 2015).

The statistical reportage brings forth the booming nature of tourism industry and, therefore, demands for much closer attention in the Indian context. When more attention is accorded to tourism industry in the country by providing more benefits and incentives, the ramifications will be sprucing up the brand image of India as a conducive investment destination. India has a very bad reputation in the realm of investments in various spheres due to the stringent procedures and highly regulated business environs. Studies conducted by Gnoth (2002) points out that a destination or nation which provides exceptional services facilitating mind blowing tourism experiences are expected to generate a favourable brand image for the country as a whole. Viewing from such lens, it could be justified lucidly that tourism is a thrust factor that revitalizes the 360 degree brand image of the country.

Apart from the above mentioned reasons, the natural and cultural assets with which India is blessed provide it with great advantages over the other countries in the world. The country is home to 32 World Heritage Sites, 25 Bio-Geographical Zones and 18 Biosphere Reserves (from which 9 are included in the World Network of Biosphere Reserves). The Indian culture has a niche place given the fact that it is the world's largest, oldest and living civilisation and the largest democracy in the world. It was administered by both Mughals and British and the traces of their architecture and expressions have only been able to provide further diversity to the land. India is the birthplace of so many languages, religions, cultures and traditions. This incredible land is considered to be wooing tourists with its acclaimed multiple USPs (Unique Selling Propositions).

Apart from being a cultural, religious and architectural destination, India in the recent past has shown a lot of diversity by taking exemplary strides in Medical Tourism and Wellness Tourism. Equipped with state-of-the-art infrastructure, cutting edge technology and finest doctors India provides better quality and cost-effective treatment to patients with zero waiting time (www.indiahealthcaretourism.com, n.d.). A heart bypass (without insurance) costs US$ 7000 in India as compared to a hefty US$ 1,40,000 in the US. Similarly, medical procedures such as knee and hip replacement, gastric, bypass, face lift and heart valve replacement is very cost-effective in India (Jayaraman, 2014). The positive slanted demand for herbal products and AYUSH, i.e. Ayurveda, Yoga, Naturopathy, Unani,

Siddha and Homoeopathy is at all time peak and a Study by SRI international estimated that India will be the No. 1 tourism destination for wellness tourism by 2019 (*Economic Times*, 2014). Plans have also been devised to promote India as Honeymoon, Adventure, MICE, Rural and Film Tourism Destination. A whooping amount of INR 200 crore has been assigned to develop tourism projects. The Public Private Partnership (PPP) for developing the sustainable attributes and components of the projects, are strengthened by initiatives like *Swadesh Darshan*, PRASAD, MDA Market Development Assistance. Brand building campaigns like *Atithi Devo Bhavah* and Incredible India are changing the face of Indian Tourism like never before.

Inferences and Discussions

The salient features of Tourism *vis-à-vis* the progression of Make in India campaign are:

- There is heavy demand among tourists for the souvenir articles and indigenous artifacts made in the country and which are authentic. Expertise of foreign investors and Indian conglomerates may be sought to add teeth to the initiatives of souvenir manufacturing country. Artifacts such as Kondapalli Toys, Kancheepuram Sarees, Mahabalipuram Black Granite idols, Aranmula Metal Mirrors, Kashmiri Shawls, Rajasthan Mirror objects, Appliqués from Pipili, Silver Filigree Work from Cuttack, Cane and Bamboo Handicrafts known as Tlieng from Meghalaya, Indian Puppets from Rajasthan, Madhubani or Mithila paintings from Bihar, Kolhapuri chappals from Maharashtra, Mekhela *sarees* from Assam, Banjara embroidery in Telangana and a host of such materials sought after by tourists can be creatively made with the involvement of proficient companies. Workshops for the artisans with collaborative ventures will leverage their talent and quality of making the artifacts.
- Tourist visitation would strengthen the bilateral relationships of India with other countries. The industry representatives from the tourist generating markets to India who arrive as tourists eventually may develop interests in investing the projects gaining traction in the country. Similarly, outbound tourists many a time get ample exposure to witness and learn about the best industry

practices in premier foreign destinations. Those advanced practices and propositions could be effectively implemented in India.

- Tourism is a multifaceted industry nurtured and nourished by several players from diverse sectors such as Transportation, Information Technology, and Accommodation etc. To cater to the requirements of tourists hordes of gadgets and equipments are required. At present lot of such things like amusement park equipments, recreation vehicles etc. are imported; Make in India campaign has an opportunity in manufacturing the machinery and apparatus sought by tourism industry. Likewise, the paradigm shift that took place in the realm of tourism resulted in the emergence of many off beat forms such as Fashion Tourism, Medical Tourism, Accessible Tourism etc. The tangible objects and manifests that enhances tourist experience at the destination namely ethnic wears, state-of-the-art medical equipments and facilities, accessible tourism infrastructures could be made in the country opening-up the investment avenues.
- Tourism infrastructure and superstructure amenities would also be ingrained as part of the Make in India campaign.
- Eco-friendly tourism has become the buzz word in the present day. The machines and gadgets for conservation of resources like water and power may be produced in the country.
- Advanced equipments are needed for the refurbishment of monuments and sites which are unique tourism products; beautification and landscaping; beach cleaning and other activities. Make in India campaign could also address the current lacunas in the shortage of such equipments.
- Volunteerism is steadily attaining traction in India. The volunteerism initiatives which are in focus could be intertwined with Make in India campaign. The skills and versatility of foreign visitors who arrive as volunteer tourist can be tapped by the manufacturing sectors.

Epilogue

India is expected to clock 8-10 per cent growth during the next two to three years. The reforms should actually take place and not remain on chapter. The good initiatives like Make in India should proliferate with great pace. Make in India is an ambitious campaign which shall roar loudly if the political will-power is good enough. It goes without saying that good governance is central to all the activities related to the campaign. The political acumen would lend a different flavour to the innovative practices that are at the crux of R & D in India. Identification of right talents and opportunities is also part and parcel of it. Tourism can proliferate the campaign as well as act as a goodwill factor as illustrated in this chapter. The noble goals of Indian tourism provides an image makeover for the country abroad and the main implications of that will be reflective in the investment scenario over a period of time. The code of ethics as regards tourism services and ventures become all the more important in this backdrop.

REFERENCES

Barhat, V. (2015). Shedding Light on Business in India. *BBC Capital*. Retrieved from http://www.bbc.com/capital/story/20151109-driving-success-in-india

Bhalla, A. (2015). PM Pushes for Chinese Tourists to get 'visa on arrival'. *Mail Online India*. Retrieved from http://www.dailymail.co.uk/indiahome/indianews/article-3010151/PM-pushes-Chinese-tourists-visa-arrival.html

Business Line (2016). Online Booking of Hotel Rooms Set to More than Double by 2016: Google Survey. Retrieved from http://www.thehindubusinessline.com/news/online-hotel-booking-industry-to-touch-18-bn-by-2016-google/article7105172.ece

Business Standard (2015). Tourism "An Engine for Economic Growth, Employment Generation": Prez. Retrieved from http://www.business-standard.com/article/news-ani/tourism-an-engine-for-economic-growth-employment-generation-prez-115091800842_1.html

Business Standard (2016). FDI India Growing 48 per cent, Falling Elsewhere: Sitharaman. Retrieved from http://www.business-standard.com/article/news-ians/fdi-india-growing-48-per cent-falling-elsewhere-sitharaman-116020800618_1.html

Chitravanshi, R. (2016). Make in India: Government Looking to woo Global Investors; PM Modi Expects Policies to Boost Manufacturing. *The Economic Times*. Retrieved from http://economictimes.indiatimes.com/news/economy/policy/make-in-india-government-looking-to-woo-global-investors-pm-modi-expects-policies-to-boost manufacturing/articleshow/51002115.cms

Choudhury, G (2014). Look East, Link West, says PM Modi at Make in India launch. *Hindustan Times*. Retrieved from http://www.hindustantimes.com/business/look-east-link-west-says-pm-modi-at-make-in-india-launch/story-mGj6f6mlUmos0BAi27Rl1O.html

Economic Times (2014). India to be Number one for Growth in Wellness Tourism by 2019: Study. Retrieved from http://articles.economictimes.indiatimes.com/2014-06 13/news/50564535_1_indian-business-tourism-spending-tourism-industry

Gnoth, Juergen. "Leveraging Export Brands through a Tourism Destination Brand." *The Journal of Brand Management*, 9.4 (2002), pp. 262-280.

The Hindu (2015). Visa on Arrival to be Extended to 150 countries. Retrieved from http://www.thehindu.com/news/national/visa-on-arrival-to-be-extended-to-150-countries/article6946563.ece

Jagannathan, K. (2014). Hurdles to 'Make in India'. *The Hindu*. Retrieved from http://www.thehindu.com/business/Industry/hurdles-to-make-in-india/article6324344.ece

Jayaraman, V. (2014). 4 things to know about India's next crown jewel, Medical Tourism Read more: http://forbesindia.com/blog/health/4-things-to-know-about-indias-next-crown-jewel-medical-tourism/#ixzz40yVIvbjW. *Forbes India*. Retrieved from: http://forbesindia.com/blog/health/4-things-to-know-about-indias-next-crown-jewel-medical-tourism/

Lee, C.C., and Chang, C.P. (2008). Tourism Development and Economic Growth: A Closer look at Panels. *Tourism Management*, *29*(1): 180-192.

Make in India.com,. (2016). *Sectors—Make in India*. Retrieved 18 February, 2016, from http://www.makeinindia.com/sectors

Maps of India.com. (2015). *Make in India—Vision, Criticism, Sectors, Benefits, and Disadvantages*. Retrieved 18 February, 2016, from http://www.mapsofindia.com/government-of-india/make-in-india.html

Mehra, P. (2014). "Make in India" pitch from Sept. 25. *The Hindu*. Retrieved from http://www.thehindu.com/business/Economy/modi-to-launch-make-in-india-campaign-on-sep-25/article6422804.ece

Mehra, P. (2015). India ranked best for investment. *The Hindu*. Retrieved from http://www.thehindu.com/business/Economy/india-ranked-best-for investment/article7359257.ece

Mehra, P. (2016). Better to "Make for India": Rajan. *The Hindu*. Retrieved from http://www.thehindu.com/todays-chapter/better-tomake-for-india-rajan/article6687945.ece

Ministry of Tourism, GoI (2016a). *3.2 per cent Growth in Foreign Tourist Arrivals in December 2015 over the same Period in 2014*. Retrieved 22 February, 2016, from http://pib.nic.in/newsite/PrintRelease.aspx?relid=134298

Ministry of Tourism, GoI (2015). *India moves 13 position ahead from 65th to 52nd rank in Tourism and Travel competitive index as per world Economic Forum Report*. Retrieved from http://pib.nic.in/newsite/printrelease.aspx?relid=134051

Ministry of Tourism, GoI (2016b). *India Tourism Statistics at a Glance 2014* (pp. 14-15). Retrieved from: http://tourism.nic.in/writereaddata/CMSPagePicture/file/marketresearch/statisticalsurveys/India%20Tourism%20Statistics%20at%20a%20Glance%202014.pdf.

Ministry of Tourism, GoI (2016c). *252.3% Growth in Tourists Arrival on E-Tourist Visa in January 2016 Over the same Period in 2015*. Retrieved from: http://pib.nic.in/newsite/PrintRelease.aspx?relid=136413

Mukhopadhyay, S. (2010). *Tourism Economics*, Anne Books Pvt. Ltd., New Delhi.

Narendra, K. (2014). Marketing of Tourism Products in Andhra Pradesh—A case of APTDC. In V. Babu and J. Gade, *Tourism in India* (1st ed., p. 195). Hyderabad: Zenon Academic Publication.

NDTV Profit (2015). India Moves Up in World Bank's Ease of Doing Business List. Retrieved from http://profit.ndtv.com/news/economy/article-india-moves-up-in-world-banks-ease-of-doing-business-list-1237196

NDTV (2015). Government Changes Name of Visa on Arrival Scheme to E-Tourist Visa. Retrieved from http://www.ndtv.com/india-news/government-changes-name-of-visa-on-arrival-scheme-to-e-tourist-visa-754929

Planning Commission of India,. *Skill Development and Training* (p. 89). Retrieved from http://planningcommission.nic.in/plans/planrel/fiveyr/11th/11_v1/11v1_ch5.pdf.

Suri, A. (2014). *Best Time Ever To Be An Entrepreneur In India | Entrepreneurship Blog. Beacon.wharton.upenn.edu*. Retrieved 18 February, 2016, from https://beacon.wharton.upenn.edu/entrepreneurship/2014/02/best-time-ever-to-be-an-entrepreneur-in-india/

Web Team, B. (2016). Key takeaways of Modi's speech at Make in India function. *Business Standard*. Retrieved from http://www.business-standard.com/article/economy-policy/modi-s-make-in-india-mantra-decentralisation-deregulation-tax-reforms-116021300653_1.html

WTTC (2015). *Travel and Tourism Economic Impact 2015 India* (p.1). Retrieved from https://www.wttc.org//media/files/reports/economic%20impact%20research/economic%20impact%202015%20summary_web.pdf.

www.indiahealthcaretourism.com, *India: A Premier Healthcare Destination*. Retrieved 6 February, 2016, from http://www.indiahealthcaretourism.com/india_a_healthcare_destination.php

www.narendramodi.in, (2016). *PM launches 'Make in India' global initiative*. Retrieved 18 February, 2016, from http://www.narendramodi.in/pm-launches-make-in-india-global-initiative-6644

Zee News (2014). Narendra Modi's Make in India Campaign: Five challenges. Retrieved from http://zeenews.india.com/business/news/economy/narendra-modis-make-in-india-campaign-five-challenges_109098.html

3

Strategies and Mechanisms to Recover Hospitality Industry in India

Arun Kumar Nambiar and *Balaji, B.*

The service sector in India and especially the hospitality sector have a huge potential. There seems to be service failures on various fronts in spite of the fact that the country boasts of trained manpower, incredible tourism products, well connected places and enviable heritage. A doctoral-level research was undertaken to ascertain the causes of service failures based on "moments of truth" and in the process hotel managers across star categories were interviewed. The strategies to recover from such failures have been categorised and presented. The changing trends in hospitality industry are also discussed.

I. Introduction

The service sector consists of the "soft" parts of the economy, i.e. activities where people offer their knowledge and time to improve productivity, performance, potential, and sustainability. Perishability is an important characteristics of the tourism industry. The products/services in the tourism industry are consumed as they are produced. For e.g.: Hotel rooms/cars cannot be warehoused for future sales. India's large service industry (web 1) accounts for 5.8 per cent of the country's GDP.

The service sector is in a state of rapid change reflecting a variety of factors from regulatory changes to globalisation and use of new technologies. The net effect is increased competition. A clear understating of the distinctive characteristics of service management, free of traditional misconceptions, is needed if service businesses are to succeed in the future.

There are three types of services marketing (Jha, 2010):

(a) External services marketing (relationship between company and market);
(b) Internal services marketing (relationship between company and employees); and
(c) Interactive services marketing (relationship between employees and market)

All the three are equally important in service delivery and the services marketing mix (Raghu and Venugopal, 2010) comprises: (a) Product, (b) Place, (c) Price, (d) Promotion, (e) People, (f) Process and (g) Physical evidence.

II. Hospitality

Hospitality (web 2) is the relationship between guest and host, or the act or practice of being hospitable. Specifically, this includes the reception and entertainment of guests, visitors, or strangers, resorts, membership clubs, conventions, attractions, special events, and other services for travellers and tourists. The word *hospitality* derives from the Latin *hospes*, which is formed from *hostis*, which originally meant "to have power". The meaning of "host" can be literally read as "lord of strangers". *Hostire* means "equalize or compensate".

The World Tourism Organisation's (UNWTO, 2010) key trends for 2009 were:

(a) Under the impact of the worldwide financial crisis and following economic recession, international tourist arrivals declined by 4.2 per cent in 2009 to 880 million.
(b) International tourism receipts reached US$ 852 billion (611 billion euros) in 2009, corresponding to a decrease in real terms of 5.7 per cent on 2008.
(c) Growth returned to international tourism in the last quarter of 2009 after 14 months of decline.

According to the August 2010 Interim Update of the *UNWTO World Tourism Barometer*, worldwide international tourist arrivals increased by 7 per cent between January and June 2010 compared to the very depressed levels of the same period of 2009, thus continuing the recovery trend that started in the last quarter of 2009. In the second half of the year, the rate of growth is likely to slow. For the full year 2010 UNWTO projects a growth in international tourist arrivals of between 3 per cent and 4 per cent.

III. Trends Influencing Hospitality in India

The trends that are influencing the hospitality industry (Khanna and Thasani, 2010) in India and the key game changers are summarised:

(*i*) *The Indian Economy*: FDI growth, growth of GDP at more than 7 per cent, resilient economy, exponential service sector growth.

(*ii*) *The Maturing of Indian Hotel Markets*: Emergence of secondary and tertiary cities, micro-markets, improved infrastructure, development of India's image, niche tourism like medical tourism, religious circuits, adventure tourism etc.

(*iii*) *Hotel Brand Growth in India*: Entry of most major international brands, growth of the Indian middle class, educated and well exposed Indian audiences, expected emergence of branded budget and economy hotels.

(*iv*) *India–The MICE Business Opportunity*: Growth of science and technology related industries, manufacturing sector, expected emergence of dedicated convention centres in more cities.

(*v*) *Hospitality Marketing Trends*: Broadening of the playing field with entry of many domestic and international hotel chains, well educated, travelled and experienced customer base, accommodates customer needs and experiences, consistent delivery of brand promises, online channels like Web 2.0 and social networking.

(*vi*) *Hotel Development Costs*: Likely rationalisation of land costs, increased import of material from global sources, expected rationalisation of costs, with government intervention in relaxing the license process.

(*vii*) *The Debt, Equity and Valuation Paradigms*: Expected rise in valuations and sale/purchase of hospitality assets, strong likelihood of infrastructure status for hospitality, increased possibility of securing debt at reasonable rates and for extended periods, growth of private equity investments and hospitality funds, expected rationalisation of asking price of hotel assets

(*viii*) *Food and Beverage (F&B) Concepts*: Rapid growth of standalone restaurants, fine dining experiences, entry of restaurant-focused funds, focus on Interior design.

(*ix*) *Manpower—The Human Element*: Continued good-quality talent crunch, increasing growth opportunities for the global Indian to relocate to India, continued hiring from and attrition to related service sectors, expected offerings of Employee Stock Options and competitive Healthcare plans by more hotel chains, innovative HR practices.

(*x*) *Technology and Hospitality*: Continued significant contribution of third party travel websites to hotel reservations, increasing role of websites in the overall sales and marketing strategy, increasing reliance on search engine optimisation, web advertising and e-marketing.

(*xi*) *Financial Crisis*: In the first half of the year 2009-10, the Indian hotel industry (FH & RA, 2010) felt the effects of the global financial crisis, coupled with the Mumbai terror attack, which took place in the previous year.

(*xii*) *Expenditure*: With most organisations curbing expenses related to travel and entertainment, the hotel industry suffered from a decrease in commercial travel and decline in revenues from meetings and conferences as well as corporate events and get-togethers. However, towards the end of the year, strong domestic demand, coupled with increased global confidence in the business environment in India helped in improving occupancies and average rates. Overall, the average occupancy across India declined by approximately –3 per cent, with some cities witnessing declines of up to –15 per cent, reflecting decreased travel by corporations, re-negotiation of corporate contracts, and decreased leisure travel. However, the average rates witnessed an increase of approximately 8 per cent.

The increase in departmental and fixed expenses as a percentage of revenue, coupled with a decrease in top-lines lead to a decline in net income percentages of approximately 11 per cent in 2009-10 over 2008-09. The PAR increase in property operations and maintenance costs, along with the POR increase in food and beverage expenses is responsible for the reduction in bottom lines.

(*xiii*) *Trends in Major Cities*: The hotel industry suffered in 2008-09 and 2009-10, with erosion of occupancy and rates in most major markets, as a result of decreased travel by corporations, slowdown in the global economic growth, and the terror attack in Mumbai. However, the last quarter of 2009-10 begun to show signs of recovery, with positive business sentiment and increased investor confidence in the country. With renewed interest in India as an emerging market, we expect to see launch of new projects, expansion of existing business units, and a revival in commercial travel in the next two years. The government's focus on infrastructure development, coupled with the above trends, will help in reviving the hotel industry in the coming years.

(*xiv*) *In Sync with Nature*: Few subjects have been able to draw the type of focused attention in recent years that the subject of sustainable development has. Now, more than perhaps ever before, there appears to be a clear consensus among the various stakeholders in our global society—be they our governments, civic administrations, international banks and partnerships, or industry at large—that yes, our way of life is putting an increasing burden on the planet, and that this concern is too important to not be adequately addressed.

(*xv*) *Energy Efficiency*: The need to meet guest expectations on all fronts together with the pressure of rising energy costs has led hotels to adopt a more holistic approach to energy management. Hotels have incorporated ample open space and large terraces into its building design, thus eliminating the need for daytime lighting in the lobby and in several of the hotel's public areas. Back-of-the house areas such as the kitchens have been placed in the south-west portion which receives most of the strong daytime sun; the guest rooms, on the other hand, are located in the cooler north-east portion of the building, allowing guests to enjoy an ambient in-room temperature without a great load on the hotel's air conditioning system. Entire requirement of hot water is met through photovoltaic panels, and this accounts for 35 per cent of this hotel's energy consumption.

(*xvi*) *Water Conservation*: Popular conservation techniques in India and worldwide include low-flow plumbing, rainwater harvesting with the collected rainwater passed though filtration beds and emptied out for ground recharge, xeriscape landscaping, drip irrigation, and the reverse osmosis/UV filtration of grey water and its subsequent reuse in gardening and as flush water in toilets.

(*xvii*) *Solid Waste Management*: The waste generated by hotels is an area that offers vast potential for better management. Several

ECOTEL certified hotels in India have already taken a lead in this area, through the meticulous segregation of waste into four categories: wet garbage (food waste), dry garbage (most types of chapter), dry garbage (other recyclables) and non-recyclables. Food waste is composted on-site, while waste kitchen oil is given to outside agencies to be used in manufacturing soap and detergents. In cities where municipal recycling centres exist, ECOTEL's sell items such as chapter, aluminium and glass to the appropriate vendors to be sent forward to such centres. These practices have brought about a drastic reduction in the volume of actual waste.

IV. Service Failure

Service failure is defined as a mistake or error that occurs during the service delivery, causing dissatisfaction of customers (Lewis and Spyrakpoulus, 2001).

Based on the service provider's behaviour when service failure occurs, Bitner *et al.* (1990) created three classifications for service failure: (a) service delivery failure, (b) needs for customised service, and (c) employee action.

Service failure occurs when a service provider cannot deliver service that meets the customers' expectations (Alexander, 2002). Service failure can be identified through customer and service providers using the following four causes: (a) an improper service provider response to a service delivery system; (b) an ineffective response of the service provider to customer requests; (c) unwanted service provider actions; and (d) inappropriate customer behaviour. Among these four areas, the most significant finding was that service provider feedback is important to customer assessment. Contentment can happen after dissatisfaction with service when customers have a chance to express their feelings and receive an apology and corrective action from the service provider.

On the other hand, customers who receive poor or failed service from a company may not stop using the service but are likely to give a negative word-of-mouth reports that can damage the company's image (Heung and Lam, 2003).

Costs of service failure have been identified as decrease in customer assurance (Boshoff, 1999), negative referrals (Bailey, 1994), customer defection (Keaveney, 1995), loss of profitability (Armistead *et al.*, 1995), decline in employee morale and performance (Bitner *et al.*, 1994).

Keaveney (1995) proposed eight major causes of switching behaviour of customers: (a) unreasonable price, (b) inconvenience (location, hours, wait times), (c) core service failure, (d) service encounter failures, (e) service failure response, (f) competition, (g) ethical problems, and (h) involuntary switching.

Lovelock *et al.* (2001) stated that when service failure occurs customers respond in four major ways:

(a) Customers may do nothing but reputation of the service provider is decreased in their perception and will consider switching to other providers if it happens again.
(b) Customers may complain to external agencies about the service failure.
(c) Customers may take specific action with a third party.
(d) Customers may switch and may simply not use the service again.

Armistead *et al.* (1995) studied service failure in the airline industry and described three types of service failure:

(a) Error of service providers like loss of baggage during transit.
(b) Error of customers like passengers forgetting their passport or ticket.
(c) Error of related organisations like strike of staff.

Lewis and Spyrakopoulous (2001) studied perceptions of customers on service failure and service recovery strategies in retail banking. Subsequently, they classified 11 types of service failures and grouped them into 5 categories: (a) Banking procedures, (b) Mistakes, (c) Employee behaviour and training, (d) Functional/technical failure, and (e) Actions or omissions of the bank that are against the sense of fair practices.

V. Service Recovery

Service recovery is referred to as the feedback delivered to customer by a service provider following a service failure (Alexander, 2002). It refers to steps that are intended to identify and correct service failures or quality problems (Simon, 2004). It can be recognised as a crucial determinant of customer satisfaction and retention (Matilla, 2001). It has two dimensions: technical and functional as per Parasuraman *et al.* (1988). Gronroos (1988) noted that actions and activities that the service industry and its providers execute in service recovery include the need to "rectify, amend and restore the loss experienced" by customers from insufficiencies in service performance.

Lewis and McCann (2004) categorised service recovery strategies as: (a) apology, (b) correction, (c) empathy, (d) compensation, (e) follow-up, (f) acknowledgement, (g) explanation, (h) exceptional treatment, and (i) managerial intervention.

Lewis and Spyrakopoulus (2001) categorised service recovery strategies as: (a) correction, (b) exceptional treatment, (c) explanation, (d) apologies, (e) compensation, (f) re-direction of the complaint, and (g) no response.

Service recovery is the process of dealing with a situation whereby a customer has experienced a failure in the firm's offering. Service recovery aims to return the customer to a state of satisfaction. Service recovery techniques may include providing customers with explanations about the service failure, apologising, empowering staff to resolve problems on the spot, making offers of compensation, and being courteous in the process (Bitner, 1990; Goodwin and Ross, 1990; Hoffman *et al.*, 1995; Sparks and Callan, 1996; Blodgett *et al.*, 1997). As many of these activities fall into the domain of the front line service provider, customers tend to base their service evaluations largely on the behaviour of the provider (Surprenant and Solomon, 1987).

The importance of the manner in which the service breakdown is recovered is still unclear. Front line service providers do not always know how far they should go with their attempt to recover the problem, whether they should express a considerable amount of concern, whether they should compensate the customer or follow company policy or do something special for the customer.

VI. Research Findings

One part of the doctoral-level research aimed at ascertaining the causes of service failure in order to recommend service recovery strategies for the hospitality industry. The managers of various categories of hotels at Bangalore were interviewed by means of unstructured format wherein their observations of service failures and causes were compiled. Service recovery strategies were also ascertained from them.

The responses of 32 hotel managers at Bengaluru have been categorised into the following:

(a) Recovery from Operations Service Failure

- Enhancing the internal infrastructure.
- Improving quality of roads, national as well as State Highways linking airports and rail heads to important tourist destinations.
- Luxury Trains to trudge across important heritage locations.
- Introduction of *Bharat Darshan* Trains—a semi-premium category to link important locations.
- Review the worldwide trends at regular intervals and implement new concepts.
- Research and find acceptability of new/emerging concepts and find out whether it would be feasible in India.
- Start huge "Duty Free" Shopping Arenas at Delhi, Kolkata, Mumbai, Bangalore, Hyderabad Airports.
- Night Entertainment—Increase timings of Pubs and Bars at important tourist locations.
- Curb violence in the name of moral policing.
- Curb crime like rape, murder.
- Involve the different Governing Bodies/Ministries and delegate responsibilities with the PMO for regular updation and status reporting.
- Classification like Classic Destinations, Emerging Destinations, Sport Activities, Trendy Products and Special Product of the Year.

(b) Recovery from Internal Marketing Service Failure (Service Provider–Employees)

- Training to inbound tour operators, outbound tour operators, travel agents, adventure tour operators, hotels, guides, government officials, NGOs.
- Developing Human Resource in Travel and Tourism.
- Development of skills in multiple domain.
- Improved internships and dedicated projects.

(c) Recovery from External Marketing Service Failure (Service Provider–Market)

- Setting up a centralised tourism repository.
- Linking the information to Incredible India website.

- Regular review and updation of the website, flashing information in case of an emergency/important developments.
- "Visa on Arrival" facility.
- Increasing off-peak Tourism activity.
- Develop/co-ordinate a major out of season country wide festival (may be cuisines/shopping fiestas/festivals) annually to increase flow of tourists.
- Developing Concept of Medical Tourism, Rural Tourism, Cruise Tourism, Religious/Buddhist Tourism, Tribal Tourism, Wildlife Tourism, Adventure Tourism, Ecotourism.
- Developing Concept of "Responsible" Tourism.
- Developing Concept of Meetings, Incentives, Conventions and Exhibitions (MICE) Tourism.
- Ensuring high quality of service amongst all stakeholders.
- Motivating stakeholders to promote a positive, quality image of India.
- Encourage higher standards of customer care and welcome—*Atithi Devo Bhavah* campaigns.
- Pay requisite attention to Domestic Tourism as well.
- Implement special incentive programme for the domestic tourists in the off-season.
- Involve Community participation.
- To set up a "One Window Outlet" for providing better service to foreign tourists.

(d) Recovery from Interactive Marketing Service Failure (Employees-Market)

- Enhance visibility/signage within the Airport (prior to exit from the premises).
- Demarcation of services like Radio Taxis, Prepaid Taxis, Auto, Transfer to Hotels/Business Centres/Cafeteria/Shopping Arcades.
- Prepaid Taxi Challans to print the registration number of the Taxis to help out the Tourists.
- Setting up 60/80 Business Hotels with all modern amenities and facilities within the Airport premises to help Business visitors.
- Ensuring Accommodation which meets market demand.

VII. Conclusion

The suggested service recovery strategies in Hospitality industry in India are by no means exhaustive. Service sector phenomena change with time and so do expectations and perceptions of consumers. India has a golden treasure and all that the nation needs is creative vision, diligent implementation and sustainable development.

REFERENCES

Alexander, E.C. (2002). Consumer actions to unethical service recovery, *Journal of Business Ethics*, 36 (3): 223–237.

Armistead, C.G; Clarke, G; Stanley, P. (1995). *Managing Service Recovery*, Cranfield School of Management, U.K.

Bailey, D. (1994). Recovery from customer service shortfalls, *Managing Service Quality*, 4 (6): 25–28.

Bitner, M.J. (1990). Evaluating service encounters: The effect of physical surroundings and employee responses, *Journal of Marketing*, 54:69–82.

Bitner, M.J.; Booms, B.H.; Mohr, L.A. (1994). Critical service encounters: The employees' viewpoints, *Journal of Marketing*, 58 (4): 95–106.

Blodgett, J.G., Hill, D.J., Tax, S.S. (1997). The effects of distributive, procedural and interactional justice on post-complaint behaviour, Journal of Retailing, 73: 185–210.

Boshoff, C. (1999). RECOVSAT: An instrument to measure satisfaction with transaction-specific service recovery, *Journal of Service Research*, 1 (3): 236–249.

FH and RA (2010). Indian Hotel Industry Survey 2009-10, VHS.

Goodwin C., Ross I. (1990). Consumer evaluations of responses to complaints: what's fair and why?, *Journal of Consumer Marketing*, 7: 39–47.

Gronroos, C. (1988). Service quality: The six criteria for good perceived service quality, *Review of Business*, 9 (3): 10–13.

Heung, V.; Lam, T. (2003). Customer complaint behaviour towards hotel restaurant services, *International Journal of Contemporary Hospitality Management*, 15 (4/5): 283–289.

Hoffman K.D.; Kelley, S.W.; Rotalsky. H.M. (1995). Tracking service failures and employee recovery efforts, *Journal of Services Marketing*, 9: 49–61.

Jha, S.M. (2010). *Services Marketing*, 6th edition, Himalaya Publishing House.

Keaveney, S.M. (1995). Customer switching behaviour in service industries: An exploratory study, *Journal of Marketing*, 59: 55–68.

Khanna, Achin; Thasani, Manay (2010). *Ten Trends Influencing Hospitality in India: How the Game is Changing*, HVS.

Lewis, B.R.; McCann, P. (2004). Service failure and recovery: Evidence from the hotel industry, *International Journal of Contemporary Hospitality Management*, 16 (1): 6–17.

Lewis, B.R.; Spyrakopoulous, S. (2001). Service failure and recovery in retail banking: The customer's perspective, *International Journal of Bank Marketing*, 19 (1): 37-47.

Lovelock, C.H.; Patterson, P.G.; Walker, R.H. (2001). *Service Marketing: An Asia-Pacific Perspective*, Pearson Education, U.K.

Matilla, A. (2001). The effectiveness of service recovery in a multi-industry setting, *Journal of Services Marketing*, 15 (6/7): 583–596.

Parasuraman, A., Zeithaml, V.A. and Berry, L.L. (1988). SERVQUAL: a multiple-item scale for measuring consumer perceptions of service quality, *Journal of Retailing*, 64: 12-37.

Raghu, V.N.; Venugopal, Vasanthi (2010). *Services Marketing*, Himalaya Publishing House, Mumbai.

Simon, J.V. (2004). Reliabiliity-based analysis of service recovery, *The International Journal of Quality and Reliability Management*, 21 (1): 11–31.

Sparks, B.A.; Callan, V.J. (1996). Service breakdowns and service evaluations: the role of customer attributions, *Journal of Hospitality and Leisure Research*, 4: 3–24.

Surprenant, C.F., Solomon, M.R. (1987). Predictability and personalisation in the service encounter, *Journal of Marketing*, 51: 86–96.

Web 1 accessed at http://indiabudget.nic.in/es2009-10/chapt2010/chapter.zip accessed on November 22, 2010.

Web 2 accessed at http://en.wikipedia.org/wiki/Hospitality on September 10, 2010.

World Tourism Organisation (2010). *UNWTO Tourism Highlights*.

4

Initiatives for a Better Tourism Order

The Case of Sri Lanka

M.R.B. Anantha Padmanabha and *M.R. Biju*

Tourism is one of the fastest growing industries globally, including in the developing world. It has grown faster than world gross domestic product since the 1950s with expenditure on tourist goods and services representing some 8 per cent of total world export receipts and 5 per cent of world GDP. Wen and Tisdell rightly observed that this is due to rising global incomes, increasing leisure time, a rising world population, fall in real transport costs, reduced travel time and globalisation. Many developing countries have recognised the possible contribution that this industry can make to economic development and have included it as an integral part of their development strategies. As a result, over the last two decades, an extensive body of literature on issues surrounding this industry in developing countries has been built up. Employment generation, foreign exchange earnings and community welfare are aspects of tourism-induced development considered in most of the relevant literature.

However, the possible contribution of the tourism industry is heavily influenced by international economic and political stability, as well as by terrorist threats and civil unrest in the tourist destination. There is a widespread view among the tourism analysts that international visitors are very concerned about their personal safety and thus this industry can only thrive under peaceful conditions.

Further, tourism is one of the major foreign exchange earners and main growth sector for many countries especially the small islands which are rich with required natural and cultural resources. The world tourism market has grown at an average of 3.7 per cent over the past five years and is projected to grow by an average of 4.9 cent over the next five years, with Asia and the Pacific regions recording the fastest growth rate. According to World Travel and Tourism Council Travel and Tourism activity was hit hard by the global slump, Even so, the sector worldwide still provided over 235 million jobs last year.

Tourism remains the fastest growing service industry in the economies of most of developing countries. Hence, more research has gone into the operations of the sector in order to examine its economic significance and potential. It is known that the industry provides an important impetus to growth in other sectors such as agriculture, transportation, retailing and manufacturing and is, therefore, seen as a key component of economic development. It plays a major role for the generation of foreign exchange which directly facilitates the improvement of foreign reserves of said economies. Similarly, the sector has shown greater improvements in employment generation both directly and indirectly. Revenue accruing to tourist sites, and increase in number of hotels and similar establishments and other tourism supply establishments.

Against this backdrop, this chapter attempts to present :

- Sri Lanka's comparative position in global tourism market;
- The composition of its tourists arrivals by area of origin, the extent of foreign earnings;
- The extent of employment generation by this industry;
- Regional aspects of the tourism sector;
- Several discussion on the current trends and future prospects;
- The hurdles that have hindered the growth and development hospitality sector etc.; and
- An attempt has also been made to explore the recent phase especially after the end of civil war.

Tourism in Sri Lanka

Tourism in Sri Lanka is growing rapidly for centuries. Sri Lanka has been a popular place of attraction for foreign ,travellers. The famous Chinese traveller Fa-Hiuen arrived in Sri Lanka in the late 4th century. In the twelfth century, Italian explorer Marco Polo claimed that Sri Lanka to be the "best island of its size in the world". In view of its fascinating scenic beauty and rich cultural heritage, Sri Lanka is one of the best tourist destinations in the world.

In 2012, "post office worldwide" holiday costs barometer named Sri Lanka as the best valued destination for holidays. In 2013, the popular travel guide book *Lonely Planet* named Sri Lanka as the best travel destination for 2013. According to the *Travel and Tourism Competitiveness Report 2015* Sri Lanka is at 63 out of 141 countries.

After Sri Lanka's independence the promotion of tourism was again considered by re-establishing the Ceylon Tourist Board which took over the function of the Tourist Bureau. More formal recognition for the country's tourism sector was given with the enactment of Act No. 10 of 1966. This provided the legislation for the establishment of Ceylon Tourist Board. Since then the Ceylon Tourist Board has functioned as the state agency, responsible for development and promotion of the tourism sector in Sri Lanka.

In October 2007, according to Section 2 of the Tourism Act No. 38 of 2005, the Sri Lanka Tourist Board (Act No. 10 of 1966) was replaced by the Sri Lanka Tourism Development Authority (SLTDA).

Trends and Patterns of Inbound Tourism to Sri Lanka: An Overview

1. Early Phase

Sri Lanka's economy began to assume its modern form in the 1830s and 1840s, when coffee plantations were established in the Central Highlands by the British. When coffee fell victim to a leaf disease in the 1870s, it was quickly replaced by tea, which soon covered more land than had coffee at its height. Coconut plantations also expanded rapidly in the late nineteenth century, followed by rubber, another cash crop introduced in the 1890s. At independence in 1948, these generated over 90 per cent of export proceeds. However, the economy gradually became more diverse after the late 1950s, partly as a result of government policies that encouraged this trend. This was because successive administrations tried to reduce the country's dependence on plantation agriculture because of a long-term decline in their value relative to the cost of imports.

2. In 1960s and 1970s

Much of the diversification of the economy, especially in the 1960s and the early 1970s, took the form of import substitution. This involved producing for the local market goods that the island could no longer afford to import. The Sri Lankan economy was further diversified with the introduction of liberalised economic policies in 1977 which promoted a number of non-traditional export sectors such as tourism, textiles, garments, refined oil, and processed agricultural products. Of these non-traditional sectors, tourism was recognised as the potential growth sector by the architects of these new economic polices.

3. Establishment of Sri Lanka Tourist Board

Foreign tourist arrivals in Sri Lanka expanded rapidly after 1966 with the establishment of Sri Lanka Tourist Board (the primary agency of charge in promotional and organisational responsibilities of the tourist industry in Sri Lanka, but eventually reached a ceiling of under 4,50,000 inbound tourists per year. The period 1967-76 witnessed an increase of 19 per cent on average per annum in the total overseas visitors to Sri Lanka and this was further increased (by 23% on average per annum) between 1977-1982 with Sri Lanka's introduction of open economic policies.

However, national security issues related to ethnic conflict have caused major fluctuations in tourist arrivals since 1983. This was further exacerbated by the internal uprising of 1987/1989 in the south. The 1982 height of 4,07,230 foreign visitors arriving in Sri Lanka was matched only in 1994 with 4,07,511 arrivals and subsequently in 1999 with 4,36,440 arrivals. The number of tourist arrivals between 1983 and 2002 have proven to be relatively volatile. However, during this period, the average length of tourist stay has been relatively stable at about 10.1 heights.

4. Sri Lanka's Position in the International Tourism Markets

According to WTO, the number of international arrivals globally has grown continuously since 1990, (except for a decrease of 0.5% in 2001 as a consequence of terrorist attacks in the US). It reached a height of 702.6 million arrivals globally in 2002, the latest year for which data are available. During this period, the largest proportion of international tourist arrivals were recorded in Europe and the Asia-Pacific region continued its position as the world's third largest international tourist market with a vigorous performance in 2002 of an increase of 10 million tourist arrivals. However, international tourist arrivals in the South Asian sub-region during this period did not show a significant improvement and its global share has fluctuated between 3.2 and 5.9 of the total international tourist arrivals. The situation in Sri Lanka reflects this with its share in the global market fluctuating between 0.065 and 0.055 per cent of the total international tourist arrivals. Furthermore, its share in the South Asian sub-regioı leclined continuously until 2001.

5. Composition of the International Tourist Arrivals in Sri Lanka

Sri Lanka relies heavily on Western European markets, specially the United Kingdom and Germany who alternate between first and second place as major source nations for tourist arrivals between 1991-2001. However, in 2002, India became the largest single source of arrivals in Sri Lanka. During this period, France, Japan, Italy, USA and the Netherlands also become strong source markets. The Sri Lanka Tourist Board Marketing Plan for 2000 listed Russia, Poland, Switzerland, Australia Singapore, and Canada as potential markets (see Sri Lanka Tourist Board, 2000).

6. Foreign Earnings by the Tourism Industry in Sri Lanka

Tourism is currently one of Sri Lanka's top five exports with foreign earnings from tourism contributing US$ 253 million in 2002 (Sri Lanka Tourist Board, 2003). This marks an increase of 20 per cent from 2001 (US$ 211.1 million) but is still less than the level of revenue earned in 1999. A similar fluctuation could be seen in tourism earnings in Sri Lanka since early 1980s to that in arrivals. For example, between 1980 and 1982 tourism earnings increased by 15 per cent per annum on average and this declined by 17 per cent per annum on average between 1983 and 1985. Then annual tourism earnings increased by 27 per cent per annum average between 1990 and 1994. This subsequently declined by 12.5 per cent per annum on average between 1995 and 1996. In 2002, foreign exchange earnings increased by 28.3 per cent from Rs. 18,863.3 millions in 2001 to Rs. 24,202.0 million in 2002.

7. The Generation of Employment by the Tourist Industry in Sri Lanka

The view is often held that tourism is, in general, a labour-intensive industry and is capable of providing employment opportunities for a large number of poorly educated or unskilled workers, a characteristic that applies to many rural areas in the developing countries. The situation in Sri Lanka is illustrative. Despite the frequent fluctuations in foreign tourist arrivals in Sri Lanka, the total number of jobs generated by the Sri Lankan tourism industry has continuously increased over the past three decades. At present, this industry provides a total of 93,170 jobs. Of these 38,821 or 41.6 per cent are through direct employment and accounts for about 15 per cent of the total employment generated by the service sector in Sri Lanka.

8. The Expansion of Tourism Accommodation Facilities in Sri Lanka

According to ADB.(1998), until the early 1980s, the Hotel Corporation, (a semi-privatised formerly state owned body) owned and controlled 76 per cent of tourism accommodation in the country. During this period (between mid-1960s and early 1980s) the expansion in the tourism accommodation facilities resulted largely from state investments. However, with the introduction of liberalised economic policies in 1977, significant amounts of national and international investments were made in the construction of tourism accommodation, particularly in Colombo and the Southwest coast. As a result, at present most accommodation for tourists in Sri Lanka is in the private sector and it controls a large part of the inbound tourist market (Sri Lanka, Tourist Board, 2003).

9. Regional Aspects of Tourism Industry in Sri Lanka

Unquestionably Sri Lanka's diverse combination of tourism attractions, including fine beaches, world class historical sites, wildlife resources, hospitable people, tropical climate and its relatively compact area ensure it as a destination well suited for tourism/recreation activities at the local/regional level. However, at present, the greatest concentration of the tourism facilities, particularly the accommodation establishments, is in the Southwest followed by the Colombo and Colombo District.

Currently, wildlife tourism product are not widely promoted by the Sri Lanka Tourist Board and international tour operators as a "must see" part of Sri Lanka's product mix, although the potential is widely acknowledged (Wickremasinghe and Santhiapillai, 2000). However, analysis of secondary data on the visitors to five selected national parks reveals that there is great potential to develop nature/wildlife-based tourism at the local/regional level. The next section presents an analysis of the economic contribution that tourism could make to regional economic development using the Pinnawala Elephant Orphanage as a case study.

There are several reasons why foreign tourism industry in Sri Lanka has not yet spread significantly outside the Colombo and Southwest coast resort regions and is unable to utilise its local and regional tourism potentials. First, as in many developing countries, the tourism industry in Sri Lanka is handled by a small number of mainstream hotel owners who are also tour operators and they are in turn part of larger groups and trading houses. Consequently, the supplementary tourism establishments outside the mainstream operators, particularly at the regional level, do not get enough business to run them profitably. This hinders investment in the local and regional tourism business. Secondly, for long-haul, extra regional tourists, reports of instability in any destination can be extremely damaging in terms of influencing a decision to travel outside the Colombo and South coast resort regions, such as visiting Anuradhapura in the ancient city resort region. Media reports in the tourists' home country can be overstated in the desire to attract readers. This can be particularly discouraging to prospective tourists, particularly non-package tourists who do not have first-hand information and experience of tourism attractions outside the main tourist regions of Sri Lanka. Finally, a further reason for the concentration of tourism in Colombo and Southern coastal regions is that Colombo is the only port of entry to Sri Lanka by air. Foreign tourists have a limited time budget and do not, therefore, tend to travel a great distance from their port of entry.

Major Tourist Destinations

Tourist attractions are classifiable as natural or anthropogenic. Natural attractions include nature spots, flora and fauna, and places with a pleasant climate. Geo-tourism sites may also be included in this category. Anthropogenic attractions include archaeological and cultural attractions, historical and religious sites, performing arts and folklore, handicrafts and artifacts.

(a) Wildlife

Despite its small size, Sri Lanka possesses high level of biodiversity and wildlife resources, and is rated among the 34 biodiversity hotspots in the world. Many species of flora and fauna are indigenous to Sri Lanka. This has made the island a country with the highest rates of biological endemism in the world. Thirteen per cent of Sri Lanka's land surface has been designated as Wildlife Protected Areas (WLPAs) which at present exceeds a total area of 8500 km^2. Approximately 7 per cent of the area is national parks, the areas allowed for the public to see and study wildlife. Sri Lanka's national parks have been become popular tourist destinations.

(b) National Parks

Adam's Bridge, Angammedilla, Bundala, Chundikkulam, Delft, Flood Plains, Gal Oya, Galway's Land, Hikkaduwa, Horagolla, Horrowpatana, Horton Plains, Kaudulla, Kumana, Lahugala Kitulana, Lunugamvehera, Madhu Road, Maduru Oya, Minneriya, Pigeon Island, Somawathiya, Udawalawe, Ussangoda, Wasgamuwa, Wilpattu, and Yala.

(c) Beaches

Sri Lanka possesses nearly 1600 km coastlines with tropical beaches which are popular among both local and foreign tourists. Most of the coastlines of the country are studded with varying coastal features such as bays, lagoons, sandbanks, and rocky headlands. Marine recreation activities, such as sea bathing and swimming, surfing, boating, snorkelling, deep-sea fishing, underwater photography, and scuba diving, can be seen at most of these beaches and related resort areas. Beaches at Tangalle, Beruwala, Mirissa, Bentota, Unawatuna Arugam Bay, Pasikudah, Uppuveli and Negombo are considered as famous tourist beaches in the country.

(d) Natural Scenic Beauty

Sri Lanka has numerous tourist attractions with areas of natural scenic beauty, primarily including mountainous terrains, agricultural landscapes, waterfalls, places with diverse climatic conditions, reservoirs, and rivers.

(e) Botanical/Zoological Gardens

The country has six botanical gardens and four Zoological gardens. The botanical gardens are maintained by the Department of National Botanical Gardens, and the zoological gardens are maintained by the Department of National Zoological Gardens. The gardens have become attractive places among local and foreign visitors.

(f) Botanical Gardens

Royal Botanical Gardens, Hakgala Botanical Garden, Henarathgoda Botanical Garden, Mirijjawila Botanical Garden, Seetawaka Botanical Garden, and Ganewatta Forest Medicinal Herbal Botanical Garden.

(g) Zoological Gardens

National Zoological Gardens, Pinnawala Elephant Orphanage, Pinnawala Open Zoo, and Ridiyagama Safari Park.

(h) Heritage

Heritage tourism involves visiting historical sites. Sri Lanka is very rich in pre-historic, proto-historic, and historic monuments, which bespeak its ancient civilisation and culture. Mainly Buddhism has influenced in moulding the cultural heritage of the country. The historic period of Sri Lanka proper starts at *circa* 236 B.C. with the introduction of Buddhism to the country by the missionaries sent by the Indian empire Asoka. The UNESCO has declared six archaeological and two ecological World Heritage Sites in the country. Besides the World Heritage Sites the Government of Sri Lanka has declared a number of archaeological protected sites and monuments within the country.

(i) World Heritage Sites

Anuradhapura, Central Highlands of Sri Lanka, Dambulla cave temple, Galle, Polonnaruwa, Sigiriya, Sinharaja Forest Reserve, and Temple of the Tooth.

(j) Archaeological Protected Monuments

Nuwara Eliya District, Matale District, Kandy District, Ampara District, Trincomalee District, Batticaloa District, Anuradhapura District, Polonnaruwa District, Kurunegala District, Puttalam District, Kilinochchi District, Mannar District, Mullaitivu District, Jaffna District, Vavuniya District, Kegalle District, Ratnapura District, Galle District, Matara District, Hambantota District, Badulla District, Monaragala District, Colombo District, Kalutara District, and Gampaha District.

(k) Pilgrimage

Sri Lanka is well known for its rich Buddhist culture as well as other religions. Being a religious country, Sri Lanka has many places with religious and historic significance, which attract tourists from all-over the world. Anuradhapura, Temple of the Tooth, Sri Pada, Shrine of Our Lady of Madhu and Kataragama, are a few famous religious sites in the island that attract a large number of tourists.

The foot pilgrimage called *Pada Yatra*, which is one of Sri Lanka's oldest traditions, has been practiced for centuries, where the local people from Jaffna come along the East Coast to Kataragama shrine.

(l) Related Attractions

Buddhist Vihara in Sri Lanka, Hindu temples in Sri Lanka, Atamasthana, and Solosmasthana.

(m) Sports and Adventure

Sports tourism is defined as either people being involved in, observing or participating in a particular sporting event for leisure. Sri Lanka is also a destination for sports such as cricket, rugby, golf and surfing. Except cricket, the contribution to the tourism sector from other sports are still at a very low level. Apart from mainstream sports events, adventure sports are also included in sports tourism. Trekking, hiking, diving, rock climbing, deep sea fishing, whale watching and hot air ballooning are some of the adventure sports those can be found in Sri Lanka.

(n) Cultural Tourism

Cultural tourism includes tourism in urban areas, particularly historic or large cities and their cultural facilities such as museums and theatres.

(o) Museums and Theatres

Currently four national museums and 26 archaeological museums have been established in Sri Lanka. National museums are maintained by the Department of National Museums and archaeological museums by the Department of Archaeology. Besides the museums, a large number of theatres also can be found in Sri Lanka.

(p) Festivals

Sri Lanka is a multi-cultural country with several festivals celebrated by various communities. Sinhala and Tamil New Year celebrations, Vesak Festival, Christmas, Ramadhan festival, Thai Pongal, and the Galle Literary Festival are a few of the major festivals.

(q) Performing Arts

There are three main traditional dance forms in Sri Lanka: Kandyan dancing, low country dancing, and Sabaragamuwa dancing. Though not unique to Sri Lanka, '*Bharatanatyam*', which originated from India is also popular in Sri Lanka particularly among the Tamil community.

(r) Food

The cuisine of Sri Lanka has been influenced by many historical, cultural, and other factors. Rice is the main staple diet of the country. Other staples include hoppers, string hoppers, and pittu.

Being one of the largest producers of tea in the world Sri Lanka is best known for the production of unorthodox tea. Tea was introduced to the country by the British who called the country "Ceylon". Pure Ceylon tea is considered some of the finest tea produced anywhere in the world.

(s) Handicrafts

Handicrafts available in Sri Lanka include wood carving, silverware, brass castings, ceramic ware, bamboo products, pottery, *batiks*, lace works, cane works, costume jewelry, lacquerware, wooden masks, coir goods, handlooms, and ivory products.

(t) Related attractions

Museums in Sri Lanka, Theatre of Sri Lanka, Festivals in Sri Lanka, Esala Perahera, Dances of Sri Lanka, Sri Lankan cuisine, Sri Lankan sweets and desserts.

Six Regions

Currently, Sri Lanka Tourism Development Authority has classified Sri

Lanka into several resort regions suitable for tourism development.

- **Colombo and Greater Colombo Resort Regions:** The Colombo and Greater Colombo Resort Region spreads along the Mount Lavinia in the south to Negambo in the north. Colombo city is the main part of the zone, and is the centre for business activities, conferences and sport events in the country. Colombo serves as both a gateway and stopover point for international tourists.
- **South Coast Resort Regions:** The south coast zone extends from Wadduwa to Tissamaharama. The zone has been divided into two main regions. The first region extends from Wadduwa to Galle. Coastal areas like Kalutara, Beruwala, Bentota, Dedduwa, Madu Ganga, Balapitiya, Ahungalla, and Hikkaduwa are included in this region. The second region, extending from Galle to Tissamaharama, includes Unawatuna, Koggala, Weligama, Mirissa, Matara, Tangalle and Hambantota areas as sub-points of the zone.
- **East Coast Resort Regions:** The East Coast Resort Region extends from Kuchchaveli in the north to Pottuvil in the south. The main tourism zones in this region are Arugam Bay, Pasikudah, Trincomalee and Nilaveli.
- **West Coast Resort Regions:** The West Coast Resort Region extends along Kalpitiya, Marawila and Waikkala areas.
- **High Country Resort Regions:** Nuwara Eliya, Bandarawela and Maskeliya are included for the High Country Resort Region.
- **Ancient Cities Resort Regions:** This region has five world heritage sites, namely Anuradhapura, Dambulla, Kandy, Polonnaruwa and Sigiriya. Other regions include Habarana, Giritale, Matale and Victoria.

Tourist Arrivals—Current Trends

When the government decided to develop the tourism sector as a separate sector of the country's economy by establishing the Ceylon Tourist Bureau in 1966, there were 18,969 foreign tourist arrivals in Sri Lanka. There was an upward trend of tourist arrivals until 1982, with the exception of 1971. Between 1976 and 1982, tourist arrivals had increased 24 per cent per year. The tourist traffic in 1982 showed that there was a remarkable growth in number of tourists, with 4,07,230 arrivals. However, with the beginning of the civil war in 1983, the growth of tourist arrivals declined and stagnated to around 3,00,000-5,00,000 arrivals annually.

The civil war that had lasted over 25 years was ended in 2009 as LTTE separatists were defeated by government forces. In 2009 the tourist arrivals numbered 4,48,000, and in 2015, 17,98,380, showing over 300 per cent growth in six years.

Most visitors arriving to Sri Lanka on a short term basis in 2016 were from the following countries:

Rank	*Country*	*Number*
1	India	3,56,729
2	China	2,71,577
3	United Kingdom	1,88,159
4	Germany	1,33,275
5	France	96,440
6	Maldives	95,167
7	Australia	74,496
8	Russia	58,176
9	United States	54,254
10	Canada	44,122
	Total foreign	**20,50,832**

Source: Govt. of Sri Lanka, Tourism Statistics, 2017.

Sri Lanka's tourism industry in the past two decades has experienced testing times. The industry has clearly shown resilience in the face of numerous challenges. Today, Sri Lankan tourism has made a strong comeback. The most encouraging happening is the new peace scenario. The peace initiatives launched by the government in late 2001 and the announcement of the peace agreement have ended the uncertainties that prevailed in the past. This has boosted the confidence of the industry and created new options for developing the industry and attracting more visitors. The Northern and Eastern beaches and other exotic attractions, once closed for tourism purposes, will soon become available again. With this option, Sri Lanka will once again become an all-year-around destination and will have the ability to address seasonality gaps. New investment opportunities are being explored to develop this region in a systematic and planned manner (Central Bank of Sri Lanka, 2002).

According to the Sri Lanka Tourist Board (2003), the total number of tourists arrival in Sri Lanka for the year 2002 was 3,93,171, a more than 16.7 per cent increase when compared to the tourists arrival in 2001. A total of 37,782 tourists arrived in Sri Lanka in October 2003, which shows an increase of 27.1 per cent compared to the corresponding month in 2002. During the same month, tourist arrivals from Western Europe rose 14.62 per cent compared to the same month in 2002. Tourist arrivals from East Asia and South Asia recorded increases of 74.4 per cent and 76.2 per cent respectively when compared to the figures of July 2002. Arrivals from India showed an increase of 116.2 per cent during the same month. Arrivals from Japan, too, increased by 94.3 per cent in the same month in comparison to the year 2001. In the year 2001, gross earnings from tourism were US$ 211.1 million and in 2002 it went up to US$ 253 million.

No doubt tourism has a great potential in Sri Lanka and is one of the fastest growing sectors internationally. However, the tourism industry in Sri Lanka had been beset with many problems. The number of flights and the range of airlines serving the country, especially from western countries, needs to be increased. Another constraint already experienced is inadequate accommodation, particularly at the regional level. There is an imbalance in the tourist accommodation available in the country. Most tourist accommodation is in Colombo, and Southern coastal resort regions. The room availability in other regions is inadequate. No such facilities are available at all in the Eastern coastal regions. Quality accommodation, in particular is in short supply in many areas. The improvement of road conditions could enhance the comfort and safety of tourists and reduce travel time from one destination to another. At present the access to many tourist destinations and hotels is very poor. There are two aspects of development of the industry that must be kept in mind. Increased tourist traffic should not lead the industry into excessively increased room rates and excessive meal charges. It must always be remembered that tourism is internationally very competitive. It is easy to make the mistake of raising prices so much that could undermine the international competitiveness of the industry.

Though the Government stepped in and set up machinery such as a Tourist Board, a Hotels Corporation, a Hotels School and even a Tourism Ministry to co-ordinate all tourism development activities, this was not sufficient to ensure adequate development of Sri Lanka's strides for the tourist industry. From the beginning, the tourist industry in Sri Lanka had been heavily dependent on state assistance. Not only was there direct investment by the Government (the first Five Star Hotel was put up by a Government Corporation), but there were constant 'aid packages' to keep the industry going. While there has recently been increasing private investment, it has not been large. Foreign participation had been more in management than in direct investment.

After the tourism industry gained some momentum in the 1970s up to the early 1980s, the next two decades became catastrophic, due to the deterioration in the law and order situation in the country. This was because of the "ethnic disturbances", triggered off by the riots in 1983. Since then, there had been continuous breakdowns in the law and order situation, with the LTTE not only taking over certain parts of the country, including the beautiful eastern coast, but also carrying out attacks in the heart of the capital city, Colombo. Though tourists were not particularly targeted in these attacks, there had been direct impact on tourist traffic due to their assaults on economic targets like the Central Bank of Sri Lanka. The worst was the attack on the one and only International Airport in the country, the Colombo Airport, in August 2001. Tourism being understandably sensitive to these developments, even the modest gains in tourism in the past decades were lost.

Fortunately, at present, the main impediment to tourism development in Sri Lanka is being tackled. There was evidenced a 'cease-fire' between the forces of the Government and LTTE, commencing in November/December 2001, followed by a formal Memorandum of Understanding. Since then, there has been no fighting between these groups. Discussions have been proceeding between the two parties to the conflict for over one year, aimed at a permanent solution and a sustainable peace. Though these talks have since stalled, the effort to resume them continues, with foreign facilitation. This has had a salutary effect on tourism and both investment and tourist arrivals have improved, as shown elsewhere in this chapter.

Supplementing the prospects created by the improved law and order situation in the country are the positive steps taken by the Government to provide leadership, develop professionalism in the tourism industry and build on its existing infrastructure. The latter effort, is based on direct partnership with the private sector. The Government, is withdrawing from its existing direct involvement in tourist businesses (by privatisation of state-owned tourist facilities) to make way for the private entrepreneurs. There is also increasing foreign participation in the Sri Lankan tourism industry. With improved law and order in Sri Lanka, tourism is poised to make an expanding contribution to Sri Lanka's economic development. In addition, peace is likely to facilitate greater decentralisation of Sri Lanka's tourism industry and encourage regional economic development. As the case study of Pinnawala Elephant Orphanage illustrates, much scope exists for stimulating economic decentralisation and regional development as a result of suitable tourism ventures. There are now good prospects that tourism will be able to make a sustained and growing contribution to Sri Lanka's economic development and that an improved balance will be achieved in its regional distribution of tourism.

Given its natural advantages, the tourism sector is viewed as one of the most important engines of growth and development in the Sri Lankan economy and as such, is a key focus in the Government's industrial strategy. Tourism main supporting sectors account for more than 8.0 per cent of GDP. In relation to employment, agriculture transport, storage and communication, construction, and distribution are the primary beneficiaries from a dollar spent within the tourism industry. Further, these sectors account for over 7.0 per cent of the employed labourforce. However, the descriptive analysis points to the continued low and declining impact of the industry on the overall economy in particular in the context of other countries like Thailand, Malaysia and Kenya. However, the investment share for tourism sector being high the unstable political situation could be the closest reason for this less performance in the case of comparison.

In short, with the end of civil war, no doubt the expected boom in the industry over the years to come will have a noticeable impact. It has to be kept in mind that there is a strong relationship between the political stability and macro-economic performance in particular with reference to the tourism sector. It is highly recommended to maintain a stable political situation of the country in order for industries like tourism to flourish in the days to come.

REFERENCES

Andriotis, K. (2002). "Scale of Hospitality Firms and Local Economic Development: Evidence from Crete", *Tourism Management*, Vol. 23: 333-341.

Asian Development Bank/ADB (1998). Biodiversity Conservation Project, Sri Lanka PPTA No. 2942-SRI, Asian Development Bank, Manila, Philippines.

Central Bank of Sri Lanka (2002). *Annual Report*, Central Bank of Sri Lanka, Colombo, Sri Lanka.

Dabour, N. (2003). "Problems and Prospects of Sustainable Tourism Development in the OIC Countries: Ecotourism", *Journal of Economic Co-Operation among Islamic Countries*, Vol. 24: 25-62.

Harrison, D. (2001). *Tourism and Less Developed World*, CABI Publishing, Wallingford, UK.

Lakshman, W.D. (1997). *Dilemmas of Development : Fifty Years of Economic Changes in Sri Lanka*, Sri Lanka Association of Economists, Colombo.

Clem Tisdell and Ranjith Bandara (2004). *Economics, Ecology and The Environment, Working Chapter No. 94*, The University of Queensland. ISSN 1327-8231.

Wikipedia.org–*Tourism in Sri Lanka*.

Ruwan Ranasinghe and Ravindra Deyshoppriya (2010). *Analysing the Significance of Tourism on Sri Lanka Economy : An Econometric Analysis*, ICBI 2010, University of Kelaniya, Sri Lanka.

WTO (2003). *Tourism Highlights*, Madrid.

WTTC (2003). *Travel and Tourism : A World of Opportunities*, Sovereign Court London, UK.

5

Human Rights and Tourism

Third World Perspective

Shan Eugene

Human Rights as a Concept

Human rights are basic principles aimed at ensuring equality and dignity for all. The Universal Declaration of Human Rights embodies the international consensus on human rights and forms the cornerstone of today's human rights law.[1] This law places obligations on states to respect, protect and fulfil the human rights of individual citizens, and these include Civil and Political rights such as the right to association and to participate in civil society, as well as Socio-economic rights such as the right to housing and to health. Although tourism was not widely perceived as an area where the human rights declaration could find application, its ramifications for tourism are far and wide. In fact, a few of the articles of the UDHR are more direct in their application to tourism human rights than to any other sector—for instance, Article 13, and Article 24. Article 13 is very important for tourism as it declares the right to freedom of movement and residence within the borders of each state.[2] No regulations, including unfriendly visa regimes or poor relationships among countries, should be an insurmountable burden upon the one who wants to globetrot. The right to leave a country is juxtaposed with the right to return—which is the spirit of tourism. When Article 13 is read with Article 24, a fuller implication upon tourism becomes clear. Article 24 says that everyone has the right to rest and leisure, including reasonable limitation of working hours and periodic holidays with pay.[3] UDHR speaks of the role of Human rights protection in strengthening the development of friendly relations between nations; similarly, one of the goals of tourism is achieving international peace and harmony.

A human rights approach to tourism is integral to true sustainability. It is in keeping with emerging international business and human rights norms, standards and practices, especially the United Nations Guiding Principles on Business and Human Rights. Although human rights is an area of inquiry that can potentially address a lot of issues associated with tourism, not more than a handful of studies have been conducted relating the two.

.Sex-tourism—who has not heard about it? We see documentaries about it, we hear it is a plague in Thailand, Vietnam and many South-east Asian countries, and we award humanitarians who stand against it. Sex-tourism is one of the worst aspects of the industry where violations of human rights occur. The commercial sexual-exploitation of children through Child-Sex-tourism (CST) violates their fundamental rights and prevents them from leading the "productive, rewarding and dignified lives" to which they are entitled. Some psychological effects associated with the prostitution of children are post-traumatic stress disorder, lowered self-esteem and problems in interpersonal relationships. There is also a risk that young prostituted girls becoming pregnant and giving birth to premature babies and other complications. Furthermore, children who are taken to foreign countries may not know the local language and, therefore, will have more difficulty in negotiation safer-sex practices.

Paedophilia is becoming increasingly rampant in the Indian tourism sector, says a new study conducted by the Indian Institute of Social Sciences. Hoteliers and shack-owners act as agents, luring young boys and girls into the sex trade.[4] It takes place all-around the world but several countries have become preferred destinations for sex-tourists, such as Brazil, Costa Rica, Cuba, the Dominican Republic, Russia, Kenya, the Netherlands, the Philippines and Thailand.

Tourism in the Third World

Tourism is a truly global business that turns everything on Earth—even the most sacred domains—into commodities. Most travellers would not want to wake up to the fact that they are just feeding a multi-billion-dollar industry and contributing to unsustainable patterns of consumption and production. But there is little awareness that as always, it is the poor who have to pay for the social and environmental costs of excessive tourism.

Third World countries justify the promotion of Tourism as a driving force for economic development. Tourism is about the transitory movement of people across the varied range of geographic and cultural products for the direct experience of these products and the mental transformation in those who travel in that process.[5] The tourism industry's product, which is used as a trade export item at international level, is the live assemblage of natural and human resources, wildlife, culture, history and heritage and social exchange.

Tourism promotion in magazines and newspapers promises would-be vacationers more than the sun, sea and sand; they are also offered the fourth 'S'–Sex. Resorts are advertised under the labels of 'hedonism', 'ecstanism' and 'edenism'.[6] Though tourism is not the cause of sexual exploitation, it provides easy access to it. Tourism also brings consumerism to many parts of the world. The lure of this easy money has caused many young people including children, to trade their bodies in exchange for bikes, dresses, electronic gadgets etc.[7] In other instances, children are trafficked into the brothels on the margins of the tourist areas and sold into sex-slavery, very rarely earning enough money to escape.

It is high time to stop treating Tourism as a 'holy cow' to be protected, nurtured at all costs. Concepts of 'new tourism' such as community-based ecotourism are projected as ways to reform mass tourism, which is increasingly dreaded because of its negative impacts. In one way, tourism helps to develop states' economy while in another way it violates the basic rights of people. The concept of tourism in the form of a master-servant relationship is the major reason why human rights of residents are violated.[8] Child-sex tour operators are more likely to be individuals looking for other individuals with similar sexual interests, with profit as a secondary motive, than organised commercial ventures.

In the specific case of Tourism, some noted advocacy groups include end child prostitution in Asian tourism, ecumenical coalition of churches for tourism etc. With the exponential rise in the tourism industry, However, comes the growth of a darker, more clandestine phenomenon—child-sex-tourism (CST). It is part of the multi-billion-dollar global Sex-tourism industry, and is a form of child prostitution within the wider issue of commercial sexual exploitation of children, who are under 12 years and thus a violation of human rights.[9] Paedophiles use the internet to plan their trips by seeking out and trading information about opportunities for child sex-tourism and where the most vulnerable children can be found in areas of low income. Abject poverty often contributes to the sale of children for prostitution.[10] In fact sex-tourism is sometimes readily encouraged by governments that depend on the sex-industry for revenue.

While Asian countries including Thailand, India and the Philippines, have long been prime destinations for child sex-tourists, in recent years, tourists have increasingly travelled to Mexico and Central America for their sexual exploits as well.[11] Compared to our South-east Asian neighbours where exploitation of girls is a problem, in Sri Lanka it is boys who are vulnerable than girls.

Sex-tourism is not a subject that is widely discussed in India and that is probably because we Indians do not like talking about sex. In fact one of the reasons for the flourishing Child sex-tourism in the country is thought to be caused by the lack of awareness amongst citizens. The other cause is our weak justice system and the apathetic attitude of the administration. Sex-tourism in India has assumed serious dimensions; because of the lack of open protests by the public and slender chances that the abusers will be caught or punished. While Goa has been the "sex destination" of foreign tourists for a long time, a growing number of cases have been reported from the beaches of Kovalam in Thiruvananthapuram (Kerala), Puri in Odisha and Digha in West Bengal. In places like Alleppey (Kerala, India), foreign tourists stay in houseboats, making houseboat Sex-tourism a new and thriving concept. These houseboats are considered relatively safer than other places as there are hardly any raids on houseboats. "Mostly the tourists are top class executives who come here in search of houseboats and backwater tourism as they find the houseboats safe with no interference from outside and police and the study conducted by National Human Rights Commission finds that Kerala especially Alleppey is becoming the hub of Sex-tourism", says Saveen V.S., an Officer in Sexual Health Project, Alleppey.[12] And it is not just the major tourist centres like Goa and Kerala which are child-sex destinations, but the whole country! Religious tourist spots in Tamil Nadu and Odisha which attract a huge number of tourists yearly also get sex-tourists. What is shocking is that child-sex-tourists often pose as donors to childrens' homes and information on these "childrens homes" has been given in the famous travel guide—Lonely Planet! One such 'home' mentioned in the Lonely Planet was shut down in Mamallapuram after investigations.[13]

While much of the initial international attention on Child-Sex-tourism focused on Thailand and other countries of South-east Asia, there is no continent or region, unaffected by the child-sex trade.[14] As countries develop their economies and tourism industries, child-Sex-tourism seems to surface. In Africa many countries are faced with a rising child prostitution problem, partly due to poverty, migration from rural to urban areas, and...the advent of tourism.[15] In Zimbabwe, the problem is related to sex trade at the border. Sudan, Kenya and Libya are also facing the same challenge. Algeria has been reported as a place of transit for traffickers. In Mauritania, there are reports of foreign pedophiles at work and an increase in boy prostitutes.[16] Brazil is considered to have the worst child-sex trafficking record after Thailand. In Brazil, street kids in the tourist-resort areas of Brazil are being exploited in massage parlours and clubs. Although surveyed establishment serve mostly local patrons, there are reports of an increased demand for child prostitutes from visiting businessmen, developers and tourists in a child-sex trade operating outside the local brothels. Costa Rica has emerged as a new 'hot spot' for the sexual exploitation of minors, with internet sites promoting the country as a paradise for Sex-tourism. Some of these sites offer "all-inclusive sexual holiday packages".[17] And in India, mostly local clients or West Asian businessmen patronize prostituted children. Therefore, it is difficult to precisely measure the exact number of children affected by sex-tourism. Boy prostitution and the growing pedophile child-sex industry are considered imported social problems catering to foreign tourists.

Many governments have enacted laws to allow prosecution of its citizens for child sexual abuse committed outside their home country, but all in vain. Its worldwide growth demonstrates the need for national and international initiatives that form a comprehensive response to the prostitution of children.

The Sex-Tourists

Sex-tourism includes domestic sex-tourism, which is travel within the same country, or international sex-tourism, which involves travel across national borders. Sex-tourism benefits not only the sex industry but also the airline, taxi, restaurant and hotel industries. Child-sex-tourism (CST) is a shameful assault on the children and a form of violent child abuse. Child-sex-tourists are generally men, although women have been known to employ foreign prostituted children as well. Some sex-tourists travel from their destination countries to another solely for the purpose of committing a sexual act with a child. Other travel for business or vacation, but then become tempted by the availability of prostituted children or attracted by offers from tour operators and local establishments.[18] Some child-sex-tourists are service men based away from home, who have taken up residence in a foreign country.

Sex-tourist, defined as "those who travel to a country for the sole purpose of having sex" see it as an opportunity, or even an entitlement, to have sex available for less money than they would pay at home.[19] There are sex-tourists who travel from poorer countries such as India, Argentina, Mexico and a number of affluent sex-tourist destinations exist in places such as Amsterdam, Las Vegas, New Orleans etc. There has been a spate of incest cases reported from throughout the world like Austria, Italy and India. Tourists engaging in CST often travel to developing countries for anonymity and the availability of children in prostitution is typically fuelled by weak laws, corruption, and poverty.

Sex-tourism is an integral part of commodification of body, culture and place on which the tourism industry is based.[20] However, the commodification of sexuality is wider than just individuals. Sites of seduction are created where the tourist and the investor are to be seduced.

Pedophiles, which make up a large group of the sex-tourists that exploit children, mainly under 12 years, keep track of news articles that mention the locations of kids and schools in particularly poor areas. They then share their stories and plan sex-tours, said Carol Smolenski, the executive director at ECPAT-USA, the U.S. branch of an international network that combats child-sex-tourism.[21]

In general, child-sex-tourists travel to poorer countries from economically developed ones. They often exhibit indifference or ignorance to the harmful consequences suffered by the prostituted children and perpetuates the view of children as economic commodities. Child-sex-tourists also benefit from local citizens' reluctance to report these kinds of crimes.

Factors Supporting Child-Sex-Trade

The most significant societal factor that pushes children into this trade is poverty. Poverty often correlates with illiteracy, limited employment opportunities and bleak financial circumstances for families. They are lured away from broken homes by 'recruiters' who promise them jobs in a city and then force the children into prostitution. Secondly, the Internet has also facilitated the recent rise in child-sex-tourism by providing a convenient marketing channel.[22] Websites provide potential child-sex-tourists with pornographic accounts written by other child-sex-tourists. Thirdly, national governments in countries which are struggling economically have become increasingly tourist-oriented in their search for profitable sources of income. These governments sometimes turn a blind eye to the sex-tourism industry, thus allowing the industry to perpetrate sexual exploitation upon children in order to encourage tourism in their country.

Legal Perspective

The response of destination countries to the epidemic of child-Sex-tourism has been ineffective. Although many of the countries have passed legislations that criminalises sexual exploitation of children, these laws often remain un-enforced against tourists. Efforts to combat child sexual exploitation often run into conflict with foreign governments' efforts to promote the international tourism industry. The United States has risen to take legislative steps against the growing evils of child-sex-tourism.

But from a legal perspective, Sweden is one of the countries that has extra-territoriality components embedded in its penal code, providing protection to victims who are younger than 15 years (3 years below the age of consent under international standards, 18 years).[23] The cornerstones of Swedish policies against prostitution and trafficking in human beings is the focus on the root cause, and the focus on addressing the demand. Swedish actions in the areas of prevention of CST and trafficking resulted in important examples of good practices, in the policy-making arena. Empirically, the model launched in Sweden (Code of Conduct for the tourism industry) has become a standard internationally recognised by UNICEF, OSCE, ILO and UNWTO for the protection of children by the tourism industry. Queen Silvis of Sweden has played an important role as a supporter of the cause, both in the organisation of world congresses, as well as in the promotion of tourism private section action.[24]

ECPAT (End Child Prostitution, Child Pornography and the Trafficking of Children) works around the world in an effort to tackle child-sex-tourism and to hold offenders to account.[25] Its Code of Conduct for the Protection of Children from Exploitation in Travel and Tourism–launched jointly with the UNWTO and a number of tour operators in 1998–is an instrument of self-regulation and corporate social responsibility designed to raise awareness and enhance protection for children. ECPAT states that children who are kept in brothels under unimaginably inhumane conditions are not the only ones who suffer sexual exploitation; but also those who have jobs that require personal contact with tourists are often exposed to similar abuses and infringement of their rights.[26] Thus over recent years, the international campaign ECPAT, has drawn worldwide attention to the issue of commercial child-sex exploitation. In 2000, ECPAT international created a Code of

Conduct for the Tourism Industry to protect children from "sexual exploitation" (UNEP, 2002).[27] The World Tourism Organisation, the International Air Transport Association and some trade unions have also introduced action programmes against child-sex-tourism.[28] These are just initiative examples, although the journey towards its elimination is unlikely to be completed in the short run.

World Tourism industry has a great influence and ability to discourage and act against child-Sex-tourism. The Tourism Bill of Rights and Tourist Code adopted in 1985, established standards of conduct for states, tourism professional and tourists on the issue of sexual exploitation. The Universal Federation of Travel Agents' Associations has produced a Children's and Travel Agents' Charter that pledges to give assistance to various organisations concerned with the welfare of child victims of sex-tourism "to help restore the dignity—physical, and mental health to such children".[29] The tourism industry is also actively working to eradicate sex-tourism by distributing pamphlets and information discouraging sex with children.

Eventhough tourism policies and government efforts have been made in order to deal with such underhand producers, sex-tourism continues as a potential force that is promoted by certain unlawful agencies and individuals. This is an emerging trend in tourism industry of the Third World countries and it has a negative impact upon the promotion of health and heritage tourism which is an attractive area of tourism in countries like India. Of course, laws and tourism plans would not make a difference if enforcement is lax.

Legalisation or decriminalisation of the industry is not seen as an answer to all the problems, but seen as a means of securing better support mechanisms in terms of health, protection and self-assessment by those men and women who work as sex-workers. Programmes and initiatives under the auspices of international organisations help raise the level of awareness regarding child-Sex-tourism and promote action on both national and international levels.[30]

Need of Human Rights in Tourism

Tourism is one of only of a few industry sectors that continues to see growth, and with this growth comes the need for responsibility—a responsibility to ensure all those involved understand and actively support basic human rights. Regarding the content of existing Child-sex-tourism and trafficking programmes in tourism, it is significant observing that they concern corporate behaviour, and have an entirely voluntary character. In many circumstances new challenges were encountered which included—reluctance of governments to acknowledge the existence of problems, lack or insufficient numbers of skilled trainers, low capacity of local law enforcement, corruption and weak legal systems in tourist destinations and particularly in developing countries. There are many reasons why children do not report sexual offense, including the sensitive and intrusive nature of the offence, coercion by the offender, lack of witnesses to support allegation, fear of retribution and the victim's fear of the consequences themselves, their family and perhaps even the perpetrator.[31] There are other problems related to our laws :

1. No special police unit to trace missing children or pedophiles specifically.
2. Corruption amongst lower ranks of the police force.
3. Indian pedophiles deported to India from foreign countries are free. They cannot be prosecuted in India for a crime committed abroad.

And we need to remember that it is never just foreigners who are the 'market' for these children, whether in India or other underdeveloped countries; there is a domestic market too.

In the name of development, human rights are often neglected and Tourism is no exemption from this. For meeting the needs and interests of the tourists and businessmen, local communities suffer severely. The inequalities and exploitation of the poor by the powerful is inherent to the worst form of tourism practices. This results in serious violation of human rights of the local communities.

The responsibility for curbing child-sex-tourism cannot rest solely with the destination countries. Sending countries must also act to punish those who travel to sexually exploit children. The German and Swedish statutes extend the reach of domestic laws through extra-territorial jurisdiction (i.e. to hold nationals accountable for actions committed abroad that would violate domestic laws if committed within the sending country). Countries should tighten their national laws against child-Sex-tourism and should include certain provisions like :

- Age of protection.
- Extra-territorial and universal jurisdiction.
- Prohibitions against travel to engage in criminal sexual acts with minors.

— Provisions aimed at sex-tour operators.
— Provisions aimed at traffickers and procurers.

In addition to national and international legislations, child-sex-tourism can be combated through innovative and comprehensive law enforcement initiatives, because collaboration is essential to comprehensive responses and mutual co-operation between other countries can aid in such enforcement. General co-operation and intelligence sharing between the police and other human rights agencies is an important step towards combating the growing problem of child-sex-tourism. Strong partnerships between governments, international organisations and all sectors of society are essential. CST has to become high priority for our government, and it is as important to fight CST as it is to fight terrorism. It is childrens' minds we are talking about here, minds that can be damaged forever, therefore, I call it "soul murder".

Tour operators must incorporate the principle of human rights due diligence into their business policies. Tour operators must acknowledge their responsibility and must cooperate with governments and other stakeholders in certain destinations. National and International hotel and tourism associations should create incentives and sanctions for their members to fulfil and continue to develop human rights standards. A hotline to which visitors can call to provide information to authorities on sex-tourists should be available to the citizens.

The key to efficiently fight child sex-tourism is to raise awareness—both amongst tourists (with a phone number to call if suspicious) and amongst families. What is most difficult is, to control the issue at the grassroots level, as many abusers stay in family homes, where parents may even agree to the abuse, in exchange for money.

Some say that sex-tourism is about sex, but in reality it is about power and opportunism. While it is true that sex-workers make more money than working in the market, there are other, more effective ways to improve the lives of people, besides buying sex from them. Perhaps as tourists and as people, before we depart, we might care to ponder not only others' choices, but also our own and what we want to make of them.

NOTES

1. Chauhan, S.R, and Chauhan, N.S. (2012), *Tourism and Human Rights*, Global Vision Publishing House, New Delhi, p. 5.

2. Donnelly, J. (2003), *Universal Human Rights in Theory and Practice*, Cornell University Press, USA, p. 47.
3. While leisure and recreation have been included as rights, tourism does not figure explicitly.
4. *Source*: http://www.newindpress.com/, January 16, 2006.
5. Chauhan, S.R. and Chauhan, N.S., *Tourism and Human Rights*, *op. cit.*, p. 23.
6. Harshada, S. Rathod, "Tourism—A Remedy to eradicate social evils in India", (ed.) Tapan, K. Panda, Sitikantha Mishra and B.B. Parida (2004), *Tourism Management* (*The Socio-economic and Ecological Perspective*), University Press India (Pvt.) Ltd., Hyderabad, p. 130.
7. Chauhan, S.R. and Chauhan, N.S., *Tourism and Human Rights*, *op. cit.*, p. 127.
8. *Ibid*., p. 25.
9. Cooper, C. (2004), *Tourism : Principles and Practices*, Prentice Hall, United Kingdom, p. 35.
10. Barry (1995), *The Prostitution of Sexuality*, New York : New York University Press, p. 40.
11. Sudheer, S.V. and Anil Kumar, K., "Impact of Negative factors of Tourism on the host community", (Eds.), M. Sarngadharan, G. Raju (2005), *Tourism and Sustainable Economic Development* (*Indian and Global Perspectives*), New Delhi : New Century Publishers, p. 312.
12. *Source*: http://www.nchro.org
13. *Source*: http://www.tourismconcern.org.uk/tourismwatch-southindia/index.php/reports/
14. Bellamy, C. (2005) State of World's Children 2005. UNICEF. Accessed at http://www.unicefusa.org/site/pp.asp?c=duLRI8O0H&b-262152 (August 2005)
15. *Ibid.*
16. *Ibid.*
17. Burgess and Clark (Eds.) (1984), *Child Pornography and Sex Rings*, Lexington, MA: DC Health Company, p. 60.
18. Cooper, C., *Tourism : Principles and Practices*, *op. cit.*, p. 50.
19. *Ibid.*
20. Harshada, S. Rathod, "Tourism—A Remedy to eradicate social evils in India", (Ed.) Tapan, K. Panda, Sitikantha Mishra, B.B. Parida (2004), *Tourism Management* (*The Socio-economic and Ecological Perspective*), Universities Press India (Pvt.) Ltd., Hyderabad, p. 119.
21. *Ibid.*
22. Sudheer, S.V. and Anil Kumar, K., "Impact of Negative Factors of Tourism on the Host Community", (eds.), M. Sarngadharan, G. Raju (2005), *Tourism and Sustainable Economic Development* (*Indian and Global Perspectives*), New Delhi : New Century Publishers, p. 338.
23. *Ibid.*

24. Putting Tourism to Rights : A challenge to human rights abuses in the tourism industry, A report by Tourism Concern, Jenny Eriksson, Rachel Noble, Polly Pattullo and Tricia Barnett, CAFOD and the Joel Joffe Trust, referred www.tourismconcern.org.uk
25. *Ibid.*
26. The countries that are signatories to the Code are USA, UK, Sweden, Denmark, Germany, Romania, Bulgaria, Japan and Thailand.
27. *Source*: http://www.unep.org (2005).
28. *Source*: http://www.ilo.org (2001).
29. http://www.uftaa.org/index.php?option=com_content&view=article
30. In 1996, the First World Congress Against Commercial Sexual Exploitation of Children was convened in Stockholm, Sweden as a forum to develop strategies for an international response.
31. Cooper, C., *Tourism : Principles and Practices*, *op. cit.*, p. 100.

6

Unemployment Problem and Tourism Industry in India

A Qualitative Study

Amit K. Chakrabarty

Introduction

In ordinary parlance unemployment is a situation of individuals' joblessness at the prevailing wage rate. Lord Keynes expresses that unemployment is the result of deficiency in effective demand in advanced economies. Machine becomes idle as a result of deficiency in effective demand. In consequence of machines' idleness demand for labour falls. It implies that there exists a positive correlation between effective demand and employment. According to Lord Keynes, unemployment may be arrested by keeping the level of effective demand sufficiently. This type of unemployment shown in the advanced countries is termed as cyclical or frictional unemployment by Keynes. In developing or underdeveloped economy Like India, cyclical or frictional unemployment is not more serious. Such type of countries are suffering from the problem of chronic underemployment or disguised unemployment in the rural sector and also suffering from the urban unemployment among the educated class. It should be noted that unemployment problem in underdeveloped or developing countries is not the consequence of deficiency of effective demand but due to shortage of capital equipment or other complementary resources. To combat the situation, the economy should create higher rate of saving for capital formation by managing resources tactfully.

Tourism is one of the fastest growing industries in the world presently.

It has become one of the most significant industries across the world. Now, its position in respect of world is just below the oil and automobile industries. Tourism industry creates sufficient employment opportunity and brings foreign currency. The receipt from international tourism provides a valuable source of earnings from many countries both developed as well as developing. Tourism provides more sizeable earnings than primary products. The income from tourism tends to increase at a higher rate than merchandise export and it is an assured change of financial flow from developed countries to developing countries, raising the latter's export earnings and rate of economic growth.

The income from foreign tourism in the form of foreign exchange adds to the national income and as invisible export, reduces the loss in the overall financial position. The invisible which come from transport and shipping, banking and insurance, income on investments etc., utilised by tourists visiting the host country, influence the balance of payments of the country.

The foreign exchange earnings from tourism which were estimated at Rs. 1063 crores in 1981 increased to Rs. 1189 crores in 1985, Rs. 1856 crores in 1987, Rs. 2456 crore in 1990, Rs. 3249 crores in 1995, Rs. 4105 crores in 2000 and Rs. 5238 crores in 2004.

Tourism facilities such as hotel, public transport, museums, clubs, and sports complexes, National parks are also used by domestic tourists and visitors although a significant portion of the costs is borne by foreign tourists. Tourism also contributes to tax and indirectly through property profits and income taxes. Tourism provides employment. Tourist expenditure not only supports the tourist, but also helps indirectly to support many other industries, which supply goods and services to the tourist industry. Thus, the money spent by the tourists after a series of transfer over a period passes through all sectors public utilities, primarily made available for foreign tourists are widely by other sectors of the economy.

Another important economic effect of tourism is related to regional development of isolated and economically underdeveloped areas. Many of such regions having high scenic beauty and culture attractions can become areas of great interest for tourists bringing property to the local people. Khajuraho which is now an internationally famous spot was a remote an unknown small village about 20 years ago. The development of Khajuraho as a world famous tourist resort has resulted in the acceleration of many economic and social activities, providing employment and prosperity to a large population of the area. Similarly, with a view to bring development and prosperity, a number of under-developed regions have been developed for attracting tourists.

Another major direct economic effect of tourism is related to employment. Most of the developing countries are facing problems of unemployment and underunemployment. The tourist industry is a valuable source of employment to a large number of people from the unskilled to waiter, cooks, managers, executives in hotels, roads, airports, water supply and other public utilities, the basic infrastructures for tourism promotion creates jobs for thousands of skilled and unskilled workers.

Review of Literature

Fazili and Ashraf (2004) suggest that for development of tourism industry in India required establishment of a National Tourism Board, which can only overcome the conflicts between various agencies involved in this industry. Konar (2004) opines in his study that as a labour intensive industry (employment multiplier is 2.36) tourism in India has a great potentiality to absorb many unemployed people. He also argued that the development of this industry mainly depends on country wide infrastructural development. Anbuselvam and Namasivajam (2005) think that foreign tourist arrivals in terms of share in the national arrivals is encouraging, there is scope for improvement matching the potential. Barai and Rao (2005) emphasize on medical tourism in their study because many foreign tourists come India to treat and check their health. So development of tourism industry includes also improvement of medical infrastructure. Sathyanarayana and M.V. Raghavalu (2005) explain in their study that the development of tourism industry means adequate hotel accommodation, better transport facilities, medical and communication facilities at multi-languages to allocate the huge budgetary allocations. The Central and State Governments should allocate huge budgetary allocations for this industry, to solve the problem of unemployment. Sinha (2008) argues that since tourism is a multidimensional activity, and basically a service industry, it would be necessary that all wings of the Central and State Governments, private sector and voluntary organisations become active partners in the endeavour to attain sustainable growth in tourism if India is to become a world player in the tourist industry. Patel (2012) thinks that the development of tourism is a very complex process of interaction among many players, who have shared the responsibility concerning the environmental, social and economic sustainability of this lucrative sector. Dayananda (2014) supposes that tourism has become one of the major sectors of the economy, contributing to a large proportion of the National income and generating huge employment opportunities. It has become the fastest growing service industry in the country with great potentials for its further expansion and diversification. Tourism industry is capable to generate employment to both skilled and unskilled workers, directly and indirectly. Venkatesh and Raj (2016) recommend in their study that the effective development of the potentials in the tourism industry, government should formulate and design policies related to development of travel industry as well as travel education scenario in India.

In this chapter it has been tried to find out the causes of unemployment in India and the role of tourism industry in reducing the unemployment problem in India. It also tries to discuss elaborately the nature of unemployment problem in South Asia as well as India and also discusses about the development of tourism industry in India after independence. The purpose of this comparative analysis is to find out the role of tourism industry in India to reduce the number of unemployed people.

Objective of the Study

The objectives of this chapter are:

(a) To portray the unemployment scenario of South Asia and India, emphasising nature and causes of the problem.
(b) To discuss about the extent of unemployment in India.
(c) To review the development of tourism industry in India after independence.
(d) To analyse the role of tourism industry in employment generation as well as plummeting unemployment.

Methodology

This qualitative study is purely based on the information collected from different sources like websites, articles published in reputed national and international journals, newspapers and reputed reference books related to this field. Phase-wise discussion of different aspects relating to unemployment and tourism industry of India has been done to realize the objectives of the study. Finally, the author reaches to the conclusion and recommends something for betterment of tourism.

Discussion

Scenario of South Asia and India

Most of the countries of South Asia, *viz.* India, Pakistan, Bangladesh, Bhutan, Nepal, Sri Lanka are passing through the second stage of demographic transition. In this stage countries must suffer from the problem of population explosion, unemployment and slow rate of economic growth. Out of 1.4 billion people of South Asia, 60 per cent are in the working age group. Only 66 per cent of the total working age group participates as labourforce. Employment growth rates are lower than GDP and labourforce growth rates. Agriculture is the main occupation of the people, although it suffers from the lack of investment and low productivity. One third of the total population of South Asia is in poverty. Illiteracy in South Asia is also a matter of great concern. In South Asia major portion of the total unemployed is youth. In the year 1997, 70 per cent of the total unemployment of Sri Lanka is youth, 58 per cent of the total unemployment of India is youth and 45 per cent of total unemployment of Pakistan is youth. Declining trend of employment in public sector during the past decade dampens the prospects of employment of educated youth. Employment provided in the private sector is mostly in the semi-skilled or low-skilled section. In the year 1997, 41 per cent of the total Higher Secondary passed youth of India was unemployed. In South Asia women have limited opportunity to get themselves employed. Two third of South Asia women are engaged in agriculture and agriculture related activities. Women form the majority in the informal sector, although they are failed to get reasonable opportunity and wages. In the year 2009-2010, male and female unemployment rate in South Asian countries is shown in Table 6.1. Table 6.1 shows the highest unemployment rate (8%) of women in Sri Lanka (8%) and Bangladesh (8%), the lowest in Nepal (1%) and Pakistan (1%). In case of male unemployment, Sri Lanka and Bangladesh rate (4%) is highest and Pakistan is lowest (1%).

Table 6.2 shows overall unemployment rate of South Asian countries in the year 2013-2014. The highest rate of unemployment is 6 per cent in Pakistan and lowest in Nepal, 2.7 per cent. Unemployment rate in India is 4.9 per cent in the year 2013-2014. The unemployment rate of India has risen from 6 per cent in 1994 to 7.32 per cent in 2001 though it reduced to 4.9 per cent in 2014 (The Economic Survey of India). WTO has failed to generate more employment in South Asia because of the unilateral trade measures adapted by the developed countries.

Table 6.1: Female and Male Unemployment Rates in South Asia, 2009-2010

Countries	*Female (%)*	*Male (%)*
Bangladesh	8	4
India	4	3
Nepal	1	2
Pakistan	1	1
Sri Lanka	8	4

Source: National Labourforce and Household Survey, 2010.

Table 6.2: Unemployment Rates in South Asia, 2013-2014

Countries	*Rate (%)*
Bangladesh	4.5
Bhutan	2.9
India	4.9
Nepal	2.7
Pakistan	6.0
Sri Lanka	4.4

Source: www.tradingeconomics.com

India which is a thickly populated country in South Asia has a very large labourforce. The quality and productivity of the labourforce is poor and low. Only 8 per cent of the total workforce is engaged in the organised sector and 92 per cent is engaged in the unorganised sector. Workforce of the organised sector contributes nearly 40 per cent of national output. The status of the labour in the organised sector is reasonably good, but the working condition in the unorganised sector is extremely bad. Underprivileged workers, child labours are the majority in the unorganised sector. The fastest growing industry in India is I.T. In the year 2002-2003, it earned revenues of Rs. 11,700 crore. In the year 2004, the industry alone created 1.85 lakh jobs in Karnataka. Though the majority of the jobs are in Bangalore, the largest number of jobs were lost also in Bangalore. During the post-liberalisation and globalisation period, the number of jobless workers in Karnataka is about 3 lakh. The number of closed state-enterprises in Karnataka is 27.65 per cent of workers become contract workers in Mumbai. Employees of public sectors are forced to take VRS. The situation which implies the job security of workers is losing in India. Massive migration of labourers from rural area to urban area is a serious problem of the Indian economy. Out of total rural labourforce of Orissa, 60 per cent have migrated due to loss of jobs.

Extent of Unemployment in India

The backlog of unemployment at the beginning of the First Five Year Plan was 3.3 million to which were added 9.0 million new entrants during this period. The Plan provided additional employment to 7.0 million, thus leaving a backlog of 5.3 million at the beginning of the Second Five Year Plan. In the subsequent plans, the backlog has been continuously increasing, since the new jobs created during each plan period invariably fell short of new entrants to the labourforce. A projection of National Sample Survey (NSS) on unemployment reveals that 16 million persons were unemployed and 12 million persons were estimated to be severely underemployed during the year 1990. It implies that the total backlog of unemployed persons in the beginning of the Eighth Five Year Plan period (1992-1997) is 28 million (Table 6.3). The net additions to the labourforce during 1990-1995 had been expected to be 37 million. So, the total number of jobless persons during the Eighth Five Year Plan period (1992-1997) would be around 65 million. It is further expected that in the next five years, i.e. during 1995-2000, labourforce would increase by 41 million. Hence by the year 2000 AD, the total number of job seekers would be around 106 million. The Planning Commission, therefore, concludes, "Employment growth in the aggregate over the estimated employment of 300 million in 1990 would have to be about 4 per cent compounded per annum if the goal of providing employment for all is to be achieved by the end of the Eighth Plan and over 3 per cent per annum if it is to be attained by 2000 AD".

Table 6.3: Projection of Unemployment for 1990-2000

	Million
1. Backlog of employed in the beginning of 1990	28
2. New entrants to the labourforce during 1990-1995	37
Total unemployed for the 8th Plan (1+2)	65
3. New entrants to the labourforce during 1995-2000	41
Total unemployed for the 9th Plan	**106**

Source: Compiled from the Planning Commission, 8th FY Plan and 9th FY Plan.

As per the estimates the backlog of unemployment at the beginning of the Ninth Five Year Plan was estimated to be of the order 34-35 million. The labourforce was projected to increase by about 36 million during 1997-2002. Thus, the total number of persons requiring employment would be 70 million over the period 1997-2002.

The Tenth Five Year Plan aimed at creating 50 million jobs during the plan. The result of the 61st round of the NSSO shows that about 47 million persons were provided employment during 2000-2005. Thus, the aggregate employment generation of 47 million work opportunities during 2000-2005 was fairly close to the target of 50 million opportunities.

The Eleventh Five Year Plan (2007-2012) aimed at generation of 58 million work opportunities. The NSSO survey shows an increase in work opportunities to the tune of that 18 million under the current daily status between 2004-05 and 2009-10. However, the overall labourforce expanded by 11.7 million. That means new entrants to job markets were considerably less than the job created during this period leading to a fall in unemployment in absolute terms by 6.3 million. This lower labourforce can be attributed to the fact that more youth were busy in education and lower labourforce participation among working-age women.

Table 6.4 shows the year-wise registration, placement, notified vacancies, submission made and live register during the period 2006 to 2013. The numbers of unemployed persons (live Register) are decreasing every year during the period 2006 to 2009, but it increases gradually subsequently during the period 2010 to 2013. It was lowest in 2009 (3,81,52,200) and highest in 2013 (4,68,02,500). The nature of year-wise registration during the studied period is volatile though an increasing trend is noticed during the period 2008 to 2012. But on an average 53 lakh to 97 lakh unemployed persons register their names in each year of study as job seekers. In the year 2012, maximum unemployed persons, about 97 lakh registered their names with various employment exchanges

Table 6.4: Job-Seekers of all categories registered with the Employment Exchanges in India

(Figures in Thousands)

Year	Registration	Placement	Vacancy Notified	Submission Made	Live Reg.	% of Pl./Sub.	% of Pl./Vac. Notified	% Incr. in L.R. over Prev. Year
2006	7289.5	177.0	358.2	3029.5	41466.0	05.8	49.4	5.4
2007	5434.2	263.5	525.8	3666.1	39974.0	07.2	50.1	-3.6
2008	5315.7	304.9	571.0	3345.6	39114.9	09.1	9.1	-2.1
2009	5693.7	261.5	419.5	2589.3	38152.2	10.1	62.3	-2.5
2010	6186.0	509.6	706.9	3747.1	38826.9	13.6	72.1	1.8
2011	6206.3	471.5	819.7	5142.9	40171.6	09.2	57.5	3.5
2012	9722.2	427.6	682.8	2982.2	44790.1	14.3	62.6	11.5
2013	5969.4	348.5	510.7	3002.1	46802.5	11.6	68.2	4.5

Source: DGE & T, Ministry of Labour, Government of India, New Delhi.

of India. The placement was maximum (5,09,600) in the year 2010. The placement shows an increasing trend in year 2006, 2007 and 2008, but it decreased slightly in the year 2009. In the year 2010, placement was maximum; subsequently it decreases during the period 2010 to 2013. Number of notified vacancies increases during the period 2006 to 2011 except the year 2009. In the year 2011, number of notified vacancies was maximum (8,19,700). But after the year 2011, it decreased in every year. Year-wise figures of "Submission made" shows a volatile trend during the study period 2006 to 2013. It was maximum in the year 2011 and minimum in the year 2009. The above discussion expresses the gravity and extent of unemployment in India.

Tourism Industry and Employment Generation

Tourism is one of the fastest growing industries in the world presently. It has become one of the most significant industries across the world. Now, its position in respect of world is just below the oil and automobile industries. Tourism industry creates sufficient employment opportunity and brings foreign currency. To enhance national income, tourism plays a vital role. National integration and national understanding is maintained by the tourism industry. It plays a vital role in economic development of a nation, socio-culture and preservation of heritage. Tourism is an extremely labour-intensive industry with high linkage effect. As the world's largest export industry, tourism accounts for about 8 per cent of the total world's largest export, more than 30 per cent of the international trade in services, 10.7 per cent of the global workforce and about 12 per cent of world GDP. According to the World Tourism Organisation (WTO), in the year 2020 tourism will be an industry earning five billion dollars a day. The economies of the countries like Hong Kong, Singapore, Sri Lanka and small islands like Mauritius, Fiji, Malta largely depend directly or indirectly on this industry.

India is the sixth largest country in the world after China, Canada, Brazil, USA and Australia. The country is the mother of two primitive civilisations of the world. One is the Indus Valley civilisation and the other is the Aryan civilisation. India with her vast area, with her physical size and appearance, heritage, culture, splendid natural resources, coastlines, minerals, forest cover, old and antique buildings, the Taj Mahal, one of the seven wonders of the world, monuments, beautiful temples and mosques, forts, hill stations, scenic beauty, springs, rivers, canals, ponds, dams, flora and fauna, gardens, historical places, wildlife sanctuaries can easily find a permanent place in the firmament of the tourism industry. The Government of India recognised tourism as an industry in the year 1967, establishing a department called "Tourism and Civil Aviation Department". From this year the development of tourism in India started. The Government of India declared the year 1991 as a year of tourism, to give more impetus on tourism development. A report of the Ministry of Tourism and Civil Aviation reveals that India's gross foreign exchange earnings from tourism was Rs. 283 crores in the year 1997-78. In the year 2013, India received 5.9 per cent more foreign tourists than the previous year. Share of business still confines to only about one per cent of the world's total tourist trade. In the year 1950, the total arrival of tourists in India was 15,000. Up to the year 2013, the figure reached in 6.97 million. Now, tourism industry is the third largest foreign exchange earner by producing gems and jewellery and readymade garments in India. Most of the tourists coming to India belong to the countries–UK, USA, Sri Lanka, Germany, France, Japan, Canada, Italy, Malaysia and Singapore.

The role of tourism industry in generation of employment is very significant. Tourism is a labour-intensive industry. So, a large number of job-seekers can get employment in this industry. According to a report from the Ministry of Tourism, Government of India, number of people already employed in the industry is more than 7 million. The number is about 2.4 per cent of Indian total labourforce. People directly or indirectly depend on tourism industry in India is around eleven million. Tourism Industry creates employment especially for hoteliers, restaurant-owners, guides, local shopkeepers, merchants etc. The remarkable feature of the industry is that it employs a large number of both educated and uneducated women. Both skilled and unskilled women are employed in this industry. Women, in fact, outnumber men in hotels, airline services, travel agencies, handicraft and cultural activities. The estimated employment multiplier figure in the tourism industry is 2.36. It means direct employment of 100 persons in tourism industry which create job for 136 persons in other sectors of our economy. From the viewpoint of employment generation, this multiplier is very attractive than other industry-multiplier.

Conclusion

Unemployment problem in India is a matter of great concern like poverty, illiteracy, malnutrition etc. The nature of the problem is severe in a developing country like India. In India, the number of unemployed persons is increasing consistently. Organised sectors fail to create sufficient employment opportunity to absorb the unemployed labourforce. After independence, Government of India has taken many steps to tackle the problem. But these efforts have failed to solve the alarming problem of unemployment because the main cause behind this problem in India is population-explosion. In this context, tourism industry can play a vital role in Indian economy. Tourism industry is a labour-intensive industry and its employment multiplier is 2.36. A large number of unemployed persons can be employed by this industry. The Government should take necessary steps. for development of tourism industry. The Central and State Governments should allocate huge budgetary allocations for tourism industry. And the cooperation and co-ordination on the part of the Central and State Governments, local authorities and local people is needed for the development of the industry. The development of tourism industry mainly depends on adequate hotel accommodation, better transport facilities, medical and communication facilities etc. The Government should take necessary steps to improve these facilities for the growth of tourism industry in India.

REFERENCES

A. Ghosh (2004). "The Employment Challenges in India", *EPW*, November 27.

A.K. Chakrabarty (2006). "Unemployment Problem and Development of Tourism Industry in India", *Journal of Hospitality Application and Research (JOHAR)*, Vol. I, No. 2, July, p. 14.

A. Sinha (2008). "*Tourism Development in India*", Press Information Bureau, Government of India, p. 37.

D.N. Konar (2004). *The Scenario of Population Growth in India*, Akanksha Publishing House, New Delhi, 1st edition, p. 110.

Economic Impact, No. 29, International Communication Agency, Washington, D.C., USA, 1989/1, pp. 34-37.

Economic Survey, Government of India, Various Issues.

G. Sathyanarayana and M.V., Raghavalu (2005). "Problems and Prospects of Tourism in Backward Areas", *Southern Economist*, Vol. 44, No. 4, June 15, p.13.

http://data.worldbank.org

J.M. Keynes (1936). *General Theory of Employment, Interest and Money*.

K.C. Dayananda (2014). "Tourism and Employment: Opportunities and Challenges in Karnataka—Special Reference to Kodagu District", *IOSR Journal of Humanities and Social Science (IOSR-JHSS)*, Volume 19, Issue 11, Ver. IV, November, pp. 1-11.

M.C. Methani (1991). *Tourism, Yajona*, Vol. 35, No. 8, May 15.

M. Venkatesh and P.S.J.M. Raj (2016). "Impact of Tourism in India", *International Journal of Scientific Engineering and Applied Science (IJSEAS)*, Volume 2, Issue 1, January, pp. 167-184.

Planning Commission, Employment, Past Trend and Perspectives for 1990s.

R. Patel (2012). "India's Tourism Industry—Progress and Emerging Issues", *Artha Prabandha: A Journal of Economics and Management*, Vol. 1, Issue 5, August, pp. 1-10.

www.incredibleindia.org

www.tourism.gov.in

7

Web and Technology

Beginning of New Era of Tourism Development

Renu Malra

Introduction

In March 9, 2011, in Berlin, The Pacific Asia Travel Association (PATA) announced its forecasts of travel demand for 42-destinations. In the Asia Pacific region, annual average rate of growth in arrivals to these destinations will be up to seven per cent predicted between 2009 and 2013. While Asia is expected to receive growth with an average increase of around 7.5 per cent per annum, North America will get its share in growth with an average around five per cent and the Pacific between four-to-five per cent, between that period.

Within Asia, South-east Asia will be the fastest growing sub-region with just over eight per cent, followed by South Asia around 7.5 per cent and North-east Asia at over seven per cent (figures per annum). In terms of traffic generation, it is North-east Asia that will add an additional 65 million arrivals and the Americas will add close to 18-million more than in 2009. Table 7.1 reveals the fact that in the coming year Asian market will show the upward trend as compared to other markets.

Asians are getting wealthier, and the Asian tourism sector is one of the fastest growing in the world as also depicted from Table 7.1. Besides, they are also getting more internet punter. Even the lack of infrastructure has not been stopping them from accessing the internet through mobile phones. According to Euro-monitor International report in the year 2011

Table 7.1: Relative Market Share

	Relative Market Share			
Origin Markets	*% 2009*	*% 2011f*	*% 2012f*	*% 2013f*
Americas	21.2	20.3	20.1	19.9
Europe	9.5	9.3	9.2	9.1
Asia	63.8	65.0	65.1	65.4
Pacific	2.7	2.7	2.7	2.7
Others	2.7	2.8	2.8	2.9

Source: CED.

Online sales are a major growth catalyst, with online (8%) outpacing offline (1%) in value growth and expected to provide steady growth over the long term.

ICT plays an important role as a new method in increasing the demand in tourism industry, which in turn, results in attracting more tourists and generating more income, apart from further developing the tourism industry. According to World Tourism Organisation (WTO) statistics, Iran is among the top five (5) countries in having historical and natural resources for tourism purposes. Unfortunately, Iran has not performed well in introducing its attractions to tourists *via* ICT tools yet (I. Mohamed and L. Moradi, 2011). Innovations in tourism deviate from the dominant innovation paradigm that was shaped by the manufacturing sector. Tourism is big users of ICT developed elsewhere, but at the same time develops service innovations based on these technologies. The tourism industry presently employs ICT in pre-holiday phase to inform customers, help them to plan their trip and to book travel arrangements. ICT is heavily used during the travel (e.g. flights) and increasingly integrated in the offering during the holiday phase. ICT has already shaken up the value chain in the tourism industry and will continue to do so in the years to come (Leo, 2010).

There are currently an estimated 1.8 billion internet users globally. There has been substantial growth in all world regions, with regions like Africa and the Middle east both recording growth of over 1,600 per cent in the last 10 years. Asia and the Pacific remain in the top position with over 760 million, representing over 40 per cent of the total worldwide online population (UNWTO Report, 2011).

Further growth to 2.2 billion internet users is expected by 2013 (UNWTO Report, 2011).

- Asia will remain the biggest growth market where 43 per cent of the world's online population will reside by 2013, with 17 per cent of the global online population in China alone.

- Growth in the United States of America, Western Europe and major industrialised nations in Asia-Pacific such as Australia, Japan and South Korea will slow to between 1 and 3 per cent.
- Europe's growth will be fuelled by emerging markets. Russia and Turkey will grow by almost 8 per cent annually.
- China's online population (already the largest in the world) will rise by nearly 11 per cent each year over the next half decade. Other Asian countries with substantial online growth rates include India, Indonesia, Pakistan, and the Philippines. More mature markets such as Japan and South Korea will rise by less than 2 per cent each year.
- Brazil is currently the fourth largest market in the world in terms of number of internet users, but despite a 7 per cent annual growth rate over the next five years, it will drop to fifth position in 2010 when it is overtaken by India.
- The countries of the Middle East and Africa currently represent just 8 per cent of the global online population but over the next five years will see some of the highest growth rates, around 13 per cent. Egypt, Iran, and Nigeria are among the countries with the highest growth rates in the region.
- Online spending per capita is likely to remain highest in North America, Western Europe, and the developed markets of Asia throughout the next five years. The shifting online population and growing spending power among Asian consumers means that Asian markets will represent a far greater percentage of the total in 2013 than they do today.

Major Technology Trends in Tourism

1. Internet of Things (IoT)

Internet of Things describes a worldwide network of intercommunicating devices. Sensors and intelligence are being connected to the Internet to identify sense and communicate data promptly, includes image recognition technologies, embedded sensors and Near Field Communication (NFC) payments.

Tourists visiting the Spanish UNESCO World Heritage city of Caceres will be able to borrow an NFC-enabled phone free of charge, allowing them to get information on the city, pick up discount coupons and access museums during their stay. Google Nexus S phones will be provided to any visitor to the western Spanish city who requests one at the tourist information centre. Future plans include extending the functionality throughout the city so that visitors can also use the phones to buy goods in shops (NFC World, 2011)

2. Contextual and Social User Experience

In the USA, about 52 per cent of the 152 million adult leisure travellers–or some 79 million people—already use social media. Among airlines, AirAsia claims to have generated 13 per cent of sales through its Facebook fan page that has over a million followers (ITB, 2011). For the hotel industry, social media encompasses a range of internet based platforms, which include traveller review sites such as TripAdvisor and Yelp, online travel agencies like Expedia and Travelocity, as well as social networking sites, blogs and content sharing websites. The influence of sites that have a 'Book now' button cannot be underestimated (hotel-industry, 2011).

Moreover, TweetAFlight, is transforming Twitter into an instant sales channel for airlines. The whole process can be summed up in three words: Tweet. Reply. FLY, A trade mark given to this service.

3. Mobile Computing (Smartphone, Ipad)

About 40 per cent of international travellers own a smart phone with internet and e-mail access and other functions, of which more than 40 per cent use their devices to get destination information; 34 per cent of business travellers and 26 per cent of leisure travellers use them to make booking changes during their trip, over 57 per cent have a conventional mobile phone, nearly 2 per cent still do not have a mobile phone, more than 37 per cent of international leisure travellers are also using social networks by mobile access while travelling (WTM, 2010). Thirty two per cent of French mobile users and 28 per cent of those in the U.K. plan to book on their phone in the next year, just 20 per cent of Germans anticipate doing so (Phocuswright, 2011). Recently, Google introduced Schemer applications for the android mobile and I phones, which help in exploring new cities, a boom for tourism industry.

4. Apps Stores and Marketplace

By 2014 there will be more than 70 billion downloads from Apple and Android app stores. Closely related to mobile, advances in social media and geo-location sites and applications were cited as key areas of opportunity for travel marketers to target their customers on the move and reward loyalty. Although American sites such as Foursquare and Gowalla are fast gaining penetration in the UK and Europe. Google, Goggles and Layar are driving the trend towards augmented reality. Travel companies are keen to find out more about this area of new technology and opportunities that it presents for their brand (European Travel Commission). Tripwolf, one of the most famous mobile travel guides, has advantages like offline availability, the individual city guides, the maps, and even the augmented reality view can be made completely offline available. This is one of the critical success factors for mobile travel apps, since roaming costs for data connections can be extraordinary high.

5. *Gamification*

The trend in online games, already popular in the entertainment industry, is set to extend to the travel industry. The WTM Global Trends Report 2011 reveals the "gamification of travel" is already taking hold with companies and tourism organisations including Lufthansa and Tourism Ireland using gaming techniques to create brand awareness and build loyalty. Last year Tourism Ireland unveiled its Ireland Town game on Facebook giving it the potential to engage with more than 62 million people. The report, carried out in conjunction with Euromonitor, also highlights campaigns such as Nothing Like Australia with Australians encouraged to upload a photo and share their holiday experiences with the world. The experiences were then used to create an interactive map.

According to Gartner, by 2015 more than 70 per cent of Forbes Global 200 companies will have at least one gamified application. The WTM Euromonitor research also reveals location-based social networks such as foursquare will start to target travellers with local deals while airlines will launch games based on status levels (Tnooz, 2011).

Web and technology are shaping the new form of tourism industry, either it is internet booking, social media, mobile technology and apps or gamification, everything is playing a tremendous role in determining the industry. Facebook is the leading social network in the US, but it is experiencing rapid growth throughout Europe. According to comScore Facebook is the most popular social network in 11 out of 17 European countries.

REFERENCES AND WEB SOURCES

http://econsultancy.com/us/blog/7053-eight-reasons-why-2011-is-the-year-of-mobile-commerce http://new.amadeusblog.com/wp- content/uploads/2012/01/From_chaos_to_collabouration.pdf

http://econsultancy.com/us/reports/mobile-e-commerce-best-practice-guide

http://www.travelweekly.com/Travel-News/Travel-Technology/Preview-2012—Technology/

http://gisfi.org/Internet%20of%20Things%20-%20abstract.pdf

<http://www.nfcworld.com/2011/04/17/37061/spanish-city-to-lend-nfc-phones-to-tourists/

http://www.newmediatrendwatch.com/regional-overview/103-europe?showall=1

http://www.forbes.com/sites/ciocentral/2011/12/14/5-app-trends-to-watch-for-2012/

http://www.tnooz.com/predictions2012?utm_source=Tnooz+Mailing+List&utm_medium=email&utm_campaign=6dbed648b2-RSS_EMAIL_CAMPAIGN

http://www.tnooz.com/2011/12/20/how-to/part-one-of-two-social-media-in-travel-2012-beyond-reviews/

http://www.tnooz.com/2011/12/21/how-to/part-two-of-two-social-media-in-travel-2012-beyond-reviews/?utm_source=Tnooz +Mailing+List&utm_medium =email&utm_campaign=e2f953ab29-RSS_ EMAIL_CAMPAIGN

http://blogs.hbr.org/cs/2011/12/six_social_media_trends_for_20.html

http://www.tnooz.com/2011/11/08/news/gamification-trend-to-take-hold-in-travel/

http://www.eyefortravel.com/distribution-strategies/forecasting-top-travel-trends-2012

http://www.emarketer.com/Article.aspx?R=1008702&ecid= a6506033675d47f881651943c21c5ed4

http://www.emarketer.com/Article.aspx?R=1008669

http://www.tnooz.com/2011/11/14/mobile/survey-business-travelers-go-mobile-and-do-travel-planning-at- destination/?utm_source=Tnooz+Mailing+List&utm_medium=email &utm_campaign=8409524ba8-RSS_EMAIL_CAMPAIGN

http://www.newmediatrendwatch.com/index.php?option=com_content&task=view&id=922&Itemid=2

http://www.emarketer.com/Article.aspx?R=1008707&ecid=a6506033675d47f881651943c21c5ed4

http://www.emarketer.com/Article.aspx?R=1008711&ecid=a6506033675d47f881651943c21c5ed4

http://www.phocuswright.com/research_updates/mobile-rising-german-adoption-trails-france-and-uk?mkt_tok=3RkMMJWWfF9wsRoku6zAZKXonjHpfsX56%2 BorXqSg38431UFwdcjKPmjr1YADTcp0dvycMRAVFZl5nRxQFe OAb5dS8%2FJVHw%3D%3D

http://jeffhurtblog.com/2011/10/26/ten-2012-strategic-technology-trends/

http://www.eyefortravel.com/distribution-strategies/top-5-issues-expected-influence-travel-industry-2012

http://www.hotel-industry.co.uk/2010/05/travel-industry-embraces-social-media/
http://www.hotel-industry.co.uk/2011/11/travel-trends-2012/
http://www.hotel-industry.co.uk/2011/02/social-media-marketing/
http://sgentrepreneurs.com/commentary/2011/12/12/five-trends-from-travel-startups-that-will-define-the-tourism-industry/
http://www.ced.travel/en/destinations-news/155-pata-reveals-tourism-forecast-for-2011-13.html
http://www.multivu.com/mnr/49249-tripadvisor-announces-2012-travel-trends-forecast
http://www.tnooz.com/2011/08/26/news/google-facebook-and-tripadvisor-on-what-is-next-for-travel/
http://www.tnooz.com/2012/05/18/mobile/google-throws-its-social-travel-planning-service-schemer-onto-mobile/
http://aboutourism.wordpress.com/2012/02/15/tourism-trends-tools-to-reach-destination-target-markets/
http://mashable.com/2012/05/16/gogobot-2/?WT.mc_id=en_my_stories& utm_campaign=My+Stories&a mp;utm_medium=email&utm_source=newsletter
http://ceoworld.biz/ceo/2012/05/14/apponomics-the-world-of-mobile-apps-infographic
http://www.tnooz.com/wp-content/uploads/2012/05/mobile-change-travel-FULL.jpg
http://www.mediabistro.com/alltwitter/tweetaflight-on-twitter_b22038
http://mashable.com/2012/05/01/frommer-travel-guides/
http://staceydahl.me/2012/global-travel-goes-trendy-with-social-media-mobile-phones-in-tow/
http://travel2dot0.com/2011/01/howdestinationsusetwitter/
http://mashable.com/2012/03/24/how-tech-is-changing-travel-infographic/?WT.mc_id=en_my_stories&utm_campaign=My+Stories&utm_medium=email&utm_source=newsletter
http://www.marketwatch.com/story/tripit-now-makes-travel-easier-on-any-android-tablet-2012-03-20

Buhalis, D. and Law, R. (2008). "Progress in information technology and tourism management: 20 years on and 10 years after the Internet—the state of eTourism research." *Tourism Management*, 29 (4): 609-623.

Mohamed, I and Moradi, L. (2011). "Trends in Service Innovation enhanced by mobile services in the field of tourism in rural and mountain areas." *Australian Journal of Basic and Applied Sciences,* 5(12): 877-883.

Hannes, L. (2010). "How can service innovations support sustainable tourism in rural regions?" *Aosta Seminar*, 21–23, 11.

8

Scope of Responsible Tourism

Best Practices in Urban Areas

Anitha, R. and *Ambeeshmon, S.*

Introduction

When responsible tourism was introduced at Kumarakom, its objectives were confined to limited areas such as community participation, poverty alleviation, women empowerment, organic farming, art and craft development and souvenir development etc. The hotels and resorts of Kumarakom played a vital role in the success of implementing RT practices at Kumarakom. Today it has a wider scope. Along with the government, the private sector can play a significant role. "Government have relatively few instruments to influence this sector, particularly in developing countries where fiscal and planning instruments for capturing non-commercial benefits are generally weak" (Ashley, 2000).[1] By public private participation, the downtrodden section of the urban areas or cities can be benefited from responsible tourism practices.

Review of Literature

The importance of responsible tourism was highlighted in the earth summit in Rio-de-Janerio in 1992 with Agenda 21 and the Rio declaration, which articulated the main principles for sustainable development in the 21st century (Cited by Merwe and Wocke, 2007).[2] "There is a need for a greater communication and sharing of best practices. It is necessary for the environmentally mature organisations to work with the small and medium organisations to assist in moving the agenda forward and to showcase practical how–to examples of how good practice can be achieved (Graci and Dodds, 2008).[3] Responsible tourism (RT) is not a tourism product or brand. It is a way of doing tourism[4] (Harrison and Husband, 2010). "Responsible tourism is about everyone involved taking responsibility for making tourism more sustainable" (Harold Goodwin, 2011).[5] Responsible tourism is a process, a way of developing tourism, and a considerate method of practicing tourism........... considerate of the environment, considerate of the locals not involved in the business of tourism, and, equally importantly, considerate of future generations of both humans and wildlife who will appreciate and depend upon the same natural resources. Responsible tourism needs a vision of the future, the input of the locals, and the guiding hand of a forward thinking government to ensure that the resources are protected and the benefits are shared equitably (Roy, A. Cook, 2012)".[6] As a term, RT may be generally attributed to the late 1980s, though certainly more explicitly to the 1990s. The developing environmental agenda of the 1960s/1970s had led to much attention to the impacts of tourism in the 1980s and to the emergence and/or development of terminology to describe various forms of tourism considered in some way(s) different from that which had gone before: for example, from Turner and Ash's (1975) Sunlust/Wanderlust tourists, to concepts such as 'hard' or 'soft' tourism, and to 'green', 'sustainable' or 'eco' tourism. These terms emerged within the context of established concerns arising over the impact of agricultural and industrial practices on the physical environment and the rapid growth of tourism, particularly in the 1970s, with the development of already popular resorts and the establishment of new destinations: in effect, what became known as "mass tourism."[7] He concluded the study as "Responsibility in tourism though is not just about the more obvious connections with local people and with their environment, not just about the environmental performance and policies of those involved in supply and demand, it is also about wider considerations which have been accentuated by climate change and sustainability" (David Leslie, 2012).[8] Late 20th century observers and scholars of tourism, as well as many visionary service providers, have realised the unsustainable imbalance of mass tourism and offered alternatives, that seems to provide more feasible, long-term options for destination communities. Responsible tourism is one such alternative; this is not itself a type of tourism, but rather than approach to a variety of type of tourism (e.g. heritage, sport, nature based, religion) development that is guided by principles of sustainability, such as equity, holism, balance, harmony, cultural and ecological integrity and the economic and social good of destination" (Timothy, 2012).[9] "The department of tourism of all States and Union Territories will adopt the sustainable tourism criteria for India, developed by the Ministry of Tourism for developing tourism in a sustainable manner" (*The Tourism India Magazine*, 2014).[10] In 1988 the UNWTO defined sustainable tourism as leading to management of all resources in such a way that economic, social, aesthetic needs can be fulfilled while maintaining cultural integrity, essential ecological process, biological diversity and life support systems. Later in 1992, the earth summit in Rio established the triple principles of environmental, economic and social sustainability. Since then the principles of sustainable tourism have been adopted by the tourism industry worldwide. (incredibleindia.org).[11] It can be summarised from reviewed literature that each and every person involved in tourism industry, whether he is a guest or a host or a stakeholder have equal responsibility to preserve and protect the destinations by responding the issues and the best practices in tourism are found to be a way of achieving sustainability.

Objectives of the Study

1. To analyse the best practices in tourism industry.
2. How best practices can be incorporated with responsible tourism?
3. To study how the best practices are useful to the city/urban people.
4. Ways and means of creating employments through responsible tourism and how it is useful to the society and community.

Significance of the Study

The implementation of RT initiatives at various destinations in the world are found to be successful. It get momentum after the Cape Town declaration in South Africa. The tourism stakeholders like travel agents, tour operators, airlines, hotels take this initiative as their responsibility also. Since the private sector is a key player in tourism industry, as a corporate social responsibility many come forward to form partnership with this innovative programme. In urban areas, there are immense potential for responsible tourism practices.

Research Methodology

The study is based on secondary data. The various sources of information are tourism websites, journals, and research reports. Online journals such as ephost, emerald insight, springer are referred intensively. The period of study was from April to August 2016.

Definition

Best Practices: According to Ministry of Tourism, 2005[12] "A tourism best practice is an innovative policy, strategy, programme, process or practice that is shown to produce superior results." Responsible Tourism: Responsible tourism is about "making better places for people to live in and better places for people to visit" (Goodwin, 2011).[13] Responsible tourism is one response to the challenge of sustainability for a particular area of consumption; it is about taking responsibility for making the consumption and production of tourism more sustainable (Goodwin 2011).[14] It was in 2007 that World Travel market launched World RT day.[15] Some of the best practices in tourism that can incorporate responsible tourism and can be practised in urban areas are described below:

- *Use of Public Transport*: Based on the demand of the destination and tourist population, non-polluting or battery powered vehicles can be used to minimise pollution as introduced in the cities and streets near the Taj Mahal. Thus, we could create employment opportunities, conserve the natural resources like petrol, diesel and minimise traffic jam, Pollution, resource consumption rate and cost of travel can hence be minimised.
- *Waste Management*: Waste collection can be promulgated and encouraged by residents associations. For a certain number of houses, a person should be appointed to ensure proper waste management. Dustbins should be kept in public areas and public transport. Separate bins must be provided to dispose biodegradable and non-biodegradable wastes. Training and employment in sustainable waste collection, disposal and treatment should be provided. Vermi-composting and biogas units can be encouraged. The waste generated is completely processed through these methods. The waste generated from restaurants, hotels etc. can be collectively processed through joint participation. As a corporate social responsibility initiative, hotels should also promote this kind of effective waste management. Some of the best practices are explained below:

(*a*) *Clean Technology*

The Beach-Tech-2000, first of its kind in India has been used in cleaning Marina Beach in Chennai. This machine is extensively used in Chile, Australia, USA, Spain etc. for cleaning beaches and removing seaweed and algae. Zero waste Kovalam project of Kearala is also prominent. Such waste disposal and waste treatment methods can be implemented in urban areas with beaches.

(*b*) *Effective Micro-organisms for Reduction of Wastes*

Effective micro-organisms (EM) and the processing of garbage through earthworms methods in Goa is a good practice. Organic wastes often contain traces of inorganic wastes. By using effective micro-organisms, the volume of organic matter and hence the wastes can be minimised.

(*c*) *Installation of Waste to Energy Plant*

In order to recover energy from solid waste, an innovative step by establishing a waste to energy plant for meat and fish market. This plant can process up to 250 kg of meat and fish wastes per day. This plant was started in Pathanapuram, at Kollam district in the year 2003. It started function by receiving subsidy of Ministry of Non-conventional Energy.

(*d*) *Nirmala Nagaram Nirmala Bhavanam*

This project of Aleppey district of Kerala Government the award of Central Ministry. A family can set up a plant with a cost of Rs. 14,500. From that they can treat the waste and produce cooking gas. People can approach the ward councillors for setting up the plant. In the municipal area of Aleppey around 40 wards, this project is implemented. The Kudumbasree arranged interest free loans for these aerobic plants.

- *Energy Management (EM)*: In special occasions, festive seasons, exhibitions etc., the light and sound production and energy usage is very high. The usage of LED bulbs should be promoted. Solar powered lighting systems can be encouraged at these destinations and also among Tourist stakeholders like hotels, travel agencies, tour operators, restaurants, home stays, etc. World's first airport completely powered by solar energy is in our own "God's own country". The initiatives of Energy management centre, Government of Kerala is remarkable. For conducting light and sound shows ITDC has a separate division and hundreds of such shows are organised annually. Hence, EM methods can be adopted in these light and sound shows.

- *Water usage:* Rainwater harvesting should be promoted and encouraged in hotels, resorts, houses, flats etc. In western countries in flats they practice the use of laundry services. For an entire flat the laundry services are common. Separate areas are there. Instead of using washing machines by all the occupants three or four washing machines are common and laundries are employed. This minimise the use of energy, water in addition to minimise the e-waste. People can save the cost of washing machine also. Water audit is also useful. In the current situation of climate change and drought it is a priority area of responsible tourism initiative at Kumarakom.
- *Conventions/Conferences:* In western societies, such events are carried out by Convention bureaus. Each city has a Convention Visitor Bureau (CVB). Event Management companies and resident associations are prominent in many cities. These associations make use of both skilled and unskilled labour and hence employ many people. Such initiatives can be linked and associated with Tourism Department. Since Wedding tourism is an emerging segment in the MICE tourism industry and hotels are the partners of it most of the best practices can successfully implemented in these centres.
- *Minimise Pollution:* Encourage environment friendly products instead of plastic items. In states like Himachal Pradesh and Sikkim, plastic is banned and people hardly use plastic items. Awareness campaigns can be conducted in schools and colleges. Most of our schools and colleges are plastic free. Some clubs conduct awareness campaigns and impart training to women to produce cloth bags, paper bags etc. There are many such units in Kochi.
- *Craft Units/Souvenir Units:* Each tourist destination has its own identity. For example at Kumarakom, many people are employed in making miniatures of houseboats, country boats etc. People employed in indigenous crafts should be identified and their products should be made available for buying and selling in the cities. Responsible tourists are high end tourists and are often

interested in ethical and fair trade. During their travel, they prefer to stay in responsible tourism hotels. Most of the hotels at Kumarakom encourage such practices and predominantly exhibit local products. Handicraft items, clothing items, jewellery, ornaments, utensils, wooden craft items etc. can be promoted in such manner. The state of Odisha is famous for craft works and RT practices are prominent in these destinations.

- *Imposing Fine for Littering:* Spitting and peeing in public places should be prevented by imposing fines or punishment. The state of Goa has enacted stringent laws to maintain cleanliness and prevent peeing and spitting in public places.
- *Greening initiatives:* Celebration of Environment day, earth day, water day etc. are very relevant and are useful in creating awareness among people. As part of the corporate social responsibility today NGOs and many firms come forward to organise and promote such practices. The tourists are also engaged in such programmes.
- *Adopt a Monument Scheme:* This scheme was first implemented in the state of Rajasthan in 2006. The SBT of Bikaner and Jaipur adopted the "Hawa Mahal" and Vedanta group adopted "Sahelio-ki-Bari" in Udaipur. In Maharashtra, the State Archaeological Department have selected 50 monuments across the state to private companies. The basic infrastructure, conservation, cleanliness, landscaping, gardening, security, tourism etc. are ensured by the respective firms for a certain period of time for an agreed price. (Now, it is fixed for ten years.)
- *Culture/Yoga/Ayurveda:* In the contemporary society, tourists have a great demand for traditional medicine and Ayurveda. It should be ascertained that such centres are authentic and certified. In the background of the introduction of International Yoga Day these segments are the image boosting areas and responsible services must be ensured there.

Results

1. In a fast growing population of the world with fastest urbanisation and fast growing tourism movement, to address the climate change and carbon offsetting the triple bottom line approach of RT is found to be very significant.
2. From research reports of many of the travel/tour companies, the

tourists are aware of the negative impacts of tourism. While choosing a holiday the foreign tourists are more concern about responsible tourism.

3. In India today people have an "eating out" habit than the past especially in the urban areas. The rise of the middle class with a high disposable income have a greater capacity to spend more on food.
4. To promote the best practices, many international certification and awards schemes are implemented by various international agencies. The prominent one are the UNWTO, UNEP, PATA etc. It is found that these schemes are useful in minimising impacts and maximising the benefits. It also promote peace and harmony among countries.
5. The trends that are favourable for the domestic tourism segment of India are found to be MICE, wedding, pilgrimage, weekend trips and short trips. An affluent family in a small town of India spend 1 to 3 crores for wedding. The best practices described above are very relevant and it can be incorporated with the urban tourism. There is huge employment potential in these areas in future.
6. Most of the stakeholders are aware of giving awareness about RT. An online survey by Thomson and first choice holidays (2010) suggested that" more than 80 per cent of holiday makers always turn off lights when they leave the room, and do not keep the room unnecessarily cool." Over 70 per cent say they always take shower rather than a bath, even though they are more likely to take a bath at home (Goodwin, 2011).[16]
7. The accommodation sectors are contributing more to the growth and prosperity of our nation. The growth of tourist arrivals to India mostly depends on accommodation. So, Investment is encouraged on Public private participation. (In India the travel tourism sector is estimated to create 78 jobs per million rupees of investment, compared to 45 jobs in the manufacturing segment for similar investment.[17] (www.incredibleindia.org) In future more investments are likely to arise in the urban areas.
8. In Kerala, there are 2329 hotels in Panchayata,1283 hotels in municipality,1150 hotels in corporation put together a total of 4762 hotels constituting 77,973 rooms. There is enough scope for the best RT practices.

9. Out of 4762 hotels eco-friendly measures such as rainwater harvesting is practiced by 541 hotels, waste management by 777 hotels and solar energy by 1004 hotels and have facility for sewage and water treatment plant by 950 hotels. At present 1117 (23%) of the hotels are depending Kudumbasree's assistance in waste disposal. If a responsible tourism policy is adopted to minimise the impacts of tourism, there is a huge potential for the best RT practices.

Recommendations

- Resource persons should be appointed for educating, empowering and training human resources under separate RT cells as well as to control and monitor the activities appropriately.
- Code of conduct is inevitable for RT practices.
- Policies and guidelines should be introduced and practices should be monitored.
- Encourage public-private participation in planning and implementing best practices and promoting destinations.
- The best practices should be promoted by IT tools.
- Adequate wages should be provided to the employees to sustain their interest and ensure commitment.
- Appoint employees with minimum wage rules and regulations.
- Best projects in the cities should be certified under RT.
- RT Cells can function as a separate division under Tourism department.
- Green audit, water audit, energy audit etc. are recommended in hotels.
- A fee can be collected from tourists for the best practice initiative.

Conclusion

Any policy which is successfully implemented in the initial stage is often not monitored properly at regular intervals and becomes futile after some time. An efficient institutional mechanism should be adopted to ensure the success and proper functioning of these initiatives. Stuart Levy (2010)[18] in his study pointed that "while local job creation was often cited among the most promising initiatives focused on workforce development, allowing workers the opportunity to secure management and even ownership positions, rather than settle for entry level opportunities with little upward career mobility. In addition, local business or labour sourcing of significant elements of the visitor experience (e.g. lodging, transport, food, souvenirs) were considered major factors in reducing economic leakage". Any destination either in city or in rural area, the aesthetic appeal is important in visitor satisfaction. Definitely through such responsible tourism initiatives in urban areas, we could make our destinations the best choice for a stay in future. Best practices can be introduced appropriately according to the nature of the destination.

NOTES

1. Caroline Ashley, Charlott Boyd and Harold Goodwin (2000). " Pro poor Tourism: Putting poverty at the heart of the tourism agenda" published by ODI Series, DFID Number 51, March.
2. M.V.D. Merwe and A. Wocke, (2006) An investigation into Responsible Tourism practices in the South African Hotel Industry, *South African Journal of Business Management*, 38(2): 1–13.
3. Sonya Graci and Rachel Dodds (2008) "Why go green? The business commitment in the Canadian Hotel Industry". *Anatolia: An International Journal of Tourism and Hospitality Research*, pp. 250-270.
4. Harrison & Husband, (2010) *Practicing Responsible Tourism: International Case Studies in Tourism, Planning, Policy and development*, John Wiley & Inc. Sons, p. 2.
5. Roy a Cook, Bonnie Berg Maclaird, (2012). "West Marin : A Case Study of RT", Dorling Kindersley (India Private Ltd.). Licensees of Pearson. p. 434.
6. Harold Goodwin, (2011). *Taking Responsibility for Tourism*, Woodeaton, Oxford.
7. David Leslie (2012). *Responsible Tourism: Concept, Theory and Practice*, CAB Publishers, UK, p. 1.
8. *Ibid.,* p. 165.
9. *Ibid.,* Timothy (2012). *Destination Communities and Responsible Tourism: Concept, Theory and Practice*, CAB Publishers, UK, p. 72.
10. *The Tourism India Magazine* (2014). September Volume 17, No. 5.
11. Sustainable Tourism for India: Criteria and Indicators, www.incredibleindia.org: Accessed on 20/8/2016, p. 5
12. Ministry of Tourism, MR Division (2005). "Documentation of Best Practices adopted by the State Government for the Development of Tourism", Vol. II, Intercontinental Consultants and Technocrats Pvt. Ltd., New Delhi, India. www.incredibleindia.org.
13. Harold Goodwin (2015). info/blog accessed on April 6, 2015.
14. Harold Goodwin (2011). *Taking Responsibility for Tourism*, Good Fellow Publishers Ltd., Oxford, UK, p. 1.

15. *Ibid.*, p. 69.
16. *Ibid.*, p. 66.
17. Sustainable tourism for India: Criteria and Indicators—www.incredibleindia.org accessed on August 24, 2016, p. 5.
18. Stuart E. Levy, Donald E. Haukins (2010), "Peace Through Tourism Commerce Based Principles and Practices", *Journal of Business Ethics*, Springer, 89: 569-585.

REFERENCES

Survey Design Division (2016), Directorate of Economics and Statistics, Report on Hotels and Restaurants in Kerala: 2014-2015.

FHRAI, (2004) "Research Report by HVS International", Himalaya House, New Delhi, p. 12.

www.dnaindia.com, 6th July, 2016.

www.biotech-india.org, accessed on 6th July, 2016.

www.beach-tech.com, accessed on 6th July, 2016.

Trends in Travel and Tourism (2013) TravelBiZmonitor.com.

9

Potentials to Stimulate Radical Changes at Destinations

A Study on Event Tourism in Odisha

Preji, M.P.

Introduction

Special Interest Tourism (SIT) of Odisha has got significant importance as it has inherited typical resources for many SIT segments, which distinguish Odisha from other states of India. Those resources cover natural, cultural and societal elements which have got immense potential as far as SIT is concerned. Even though the state has not explored the chances of building a strong SIT base to take tourism out of the routine destinations visits that it is famous for—mainly around the "Golden triangle of Odisha". The strong base of SIT of Odisha lies mainly with Event Tourism, Aribada Tourism, Spalio Tourism where no other state of India is having such potential avenues in contemporary tourism scenario. The study intends to unveil the prospects of event tourism in Odisha by calling for an integrated planning with forward and backward integration.

Odisha has got many events to its credit like dance and music festival, tourism fairs, trade fairs, folk and tribal dances, sand and art festival etc. Most of these festivals fall in the touristic season itself but despite that only less number of tourists are specifically coming to Odisha and becoming spectators of such events. To name a few, Konark Festival, Dhauli-Kalinga Mahotsav, Mukteswar dance festival, Raja Rani Music festival, Thosali festivals are coming in this line.

Need and Significance of the Study

Events are the reflection of cultural and societal life of a place. The question of making the event tourism viable, but at the same time taking guard of the sensitivity of the destination and people are the biggest challenge in the promotion of event tourism. In Odisha, the scenario is that it has got many events both traditional and institutional to its credit. Many of such events are having the potential of showcasing the tradition and lifestyle of a destination. But majority of the tourists who have become a part of the events made their trip unknowingly. This is interpreted in the sense that tourists were becoming a part of these events as part of a package they have opted or as free individual travellers. During the course of their travel, they got dragged into these events. The study is initiated in this scenario to build pull factors for event tourism as such and how a campaign can be coined to build the push factors in the generating markets.

Objectives

- To identify the potential events which mainly fall in the touristic season of Odisha.
- To study the role of destination attributes in promoting event tourism.
- To suggest a framework for analysing the destination attributes in relation to event tourism.
- To validate the framework by analysing a selected event(s) at Konark and its reflections in the social life.

Methodology

The study unearths the information by primary and secondary data analysis. Structured interview and field observation method were employed to collect primary data. The analytical output of such data is used to present the inferences and implications of the study. Secondary data involves data published by OTDC, newspaper article, information provided in the websites etc.

Profile of the Study Area

Tourism in Odisha, India has grown considerably in recent years due to the various attractions of Odisha, ranging from wildlife reserves, beaches, temples, monuments, arts and festivals. Many of the events of Odisha are closely linked with cultural and societal life of Odisha. Odisha has got many events to its credit which are mainly in the form of Fairs and festivals. These have the capacity to sensitize tourist's inflow especially if such events fall in touristic seasons.

Now-a-days, the tourism planners are trying to connect with the government and other NGO groups for making arrangements at important tourism destinations to organise ethnic shows, cultural evenings, light and sound shows, craft *melas*, food plazas, tribal *melas*, fairs, dance festivals, sand festivals etc. Such events can be an ideal platform for showcasing the culture and social life of many destinations in Odisha. Thus events can be a better and effective tool in promoting the typicality of each destination. Such events will bestow a better ambience to the tourists and will take them to the vast and diverse cultural traditions of Odisha. In addition to that it creates more employment options, economic exchanges and will lend a hand in the socio-economic development of the destination.

The study discusses the potential of such events in attracting more number of tourists and as a potential lucrative segment. It has the capacity to drive more tourists if organised, managed and promoted appropriately. A standardised and highly coordinated promotion has the capacity to etch a niche image for Event tourism in Odisha.

Analysis and Interpretations

(a) Potential Events of Odisha which Fall in the Touristic Season

Tourism Department of Odisha has been organising many events, which mainly falls in the tourist season. The one which is lacking is the proper coordination to promote these events to the tourism limelight. The tourism campaigns of Odisha hardly project such events. The authorities have not reckoned its capacity to attract more tourists. Many events are unique in their own respect and are derived out of the cultural and societal life of Odisha is still to be explored in promoting tourism of the state (See Table 9.1)

(b) Role of Destination-Attributes in Promoting Event Tourism

Parameters like upward trend in foreign and domestic tourist arrivals, infrastructure development, identification of new tourism circuits and

Table 9.1: Potential Events which Fall in the Touristic Season of Odisha

Sl. No.	Time	Events	Venues
1.	November	Gotipua Dance Festival	Rabindra Mandap, Bhubaneswar
2.	November	Puri Beach Festival	Puri
3.	November	Parab (Annual Tribal Festival)	Koraput
4.	December	Konark Festival	Open Air Auditorium, Konark
5.	December	International Sand Art Festival	Chandrabhaga Beach, Konark
6.	December	Dhauli Kalinga Mahotsav	Dhauli
7.	December	Toshali National Crafts Mela	Janta Maidan, Bhubaneswar
8.	December	International Odissi Dance Festival	Rabindra Mandap, Bhubaneswar
9.	January	Odissi Music Festival	Rabindra Mandap, Bhubaneswar
10.	January	Gopalpur Beach Festival	Gopalpur
11.	January	Chandipur Beach Festival	Chandipur
12.	January	Kharavela Mahotsav	Bhubaneswar
13.	January	Mukteswar Dance Festival	Mukteswar Temple Complex, Bhubaneswar
14.	January	Rajarani Music Festival	Rajarani Temple Complex, Bhubaneswar
15.	February	Konark dance and Music festival	Konark

Source: Department of Tourism, Government of Odisha.

vibrant marketing can help tourism to be on the upward scale. Odisha tourism also marked significant growth overall by drawing national and international attention by blending tourism with culture. Odisha has improved its stand in relative tourist arrival to 0.06 (in million) against Indian share of 6.29 (million) during the year 2012.

Table 9.2: Category-wise Tourist Arrival in Odisha (2013)

Season	Domestic	Foreign
Peak Season	49,27,337	37,354
Lean season	33,43,920	23,368
Total	**82,71,257**	**60722**

Source: Department of Tourism, Government of Odisha.

By analysing the above statistics, it clearly throws light on the touristic arrival of Odisha in relation to the national share. It identifies the need of building destination attributes in major touristic centres in tune with the industry requirements. It reveals the need of building a unique value with each destination. For identifying the values associated with each destination, it is proposed to highlight the speciality of each destination within which events can be a better medium in building values to the destination.

Need for hand in hand promotion of events and destination to build destination image

For holistic development of tourism at place, events have to be promoted hand in hand with the destination attributes. The success *mantra* of such development lies with how travel value has been set for the tourists by coining the leisure options at the destinations. Events are seen as an important motivator in tourism (Getz, 2008), and as an effective enhancer of destination image (Hall, 1992; Ritchie, 1984). (Hallmark, 2008) events, for example, usually held in prime destinations have been labelled "our new image-builders" (Burns and Mules, 1986) and a whole new discourse, including a new set of definitions and terminology, has been developed to examine the phenomenon.

The promotion of events to build the destination image and to attach a unique value lies with the setting of an array of pull factors at the destination. Festivals and events of destinations are staged so as to yield economic benefits by raising the profile of places, their products and institutions by attracting flows of tourists, capital and inward investment. A key motivation in developing festival and event strategies has been to recover from long-term economic decline. Festivals and events have been part of a wider range of new "cultural strategies".

(c) Proposed Framework to Analyse the Destination Attributes and its Social impacts in relation to Event Tourism

The study proposes a framework for building better destination experience by attaching pull factors for the events at each destination. The touristic experience of events in each destination can be augmented with a view of improving the service quality by properly coordinated marketing efforts. This cannot be materialised without guiding the reach of economic assistance to the community and audience (tourist) analysis. This highlights the need of matching the push factors by fine-tuning the deliverables at the destination for specified tourists (pull factors) by shaping the destination attributes.

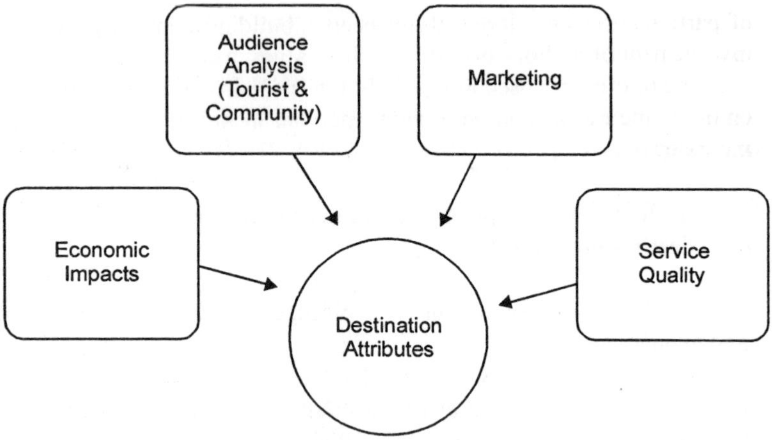

Fig. 9.1: Contextual Framework for Building Pull Factors.

(d) Validating the Framework by Analysing the Dance and Sand Festivals of Konark

The audience analysis and service qualities are precised based on field observation of the selected destination—Konark. The marketing and economic analyses are advisory in nature.

(i) Audience analysis

Konark, the coastal destination of Odisha is home to Konark dance festival, Sand festival and many people congregate on the occasion of big festival *Magha Saptami* Day. During the festive evenings, the atmosphere is surcharged with rhythmic dancing beats and melodious tunes accompanied by the waves of the coastal destination.

Table 9.3: Touristic Arrivals for Sand and Dance Festival at Konark

Events	*Foreign*	*Domestic*
Sand Festival	450	8,127
Konark Dance Festival	422	12,278

Source: Department of Tourism, Government of Odisha.

Field observation method was used to make a note of the touristic movements on the occasion of Dance and Sand festivals of Konark. The audience analyses are being made by outlining the nature and discipline of participation of tourists, purpose of visit of tourists and nature of involvement of community.

The figure shows the touristic arrivals to the events at Konark. Based on the framework it has been found that potential tourist arrivals can be increased if developed holistically with forward and backward integration.

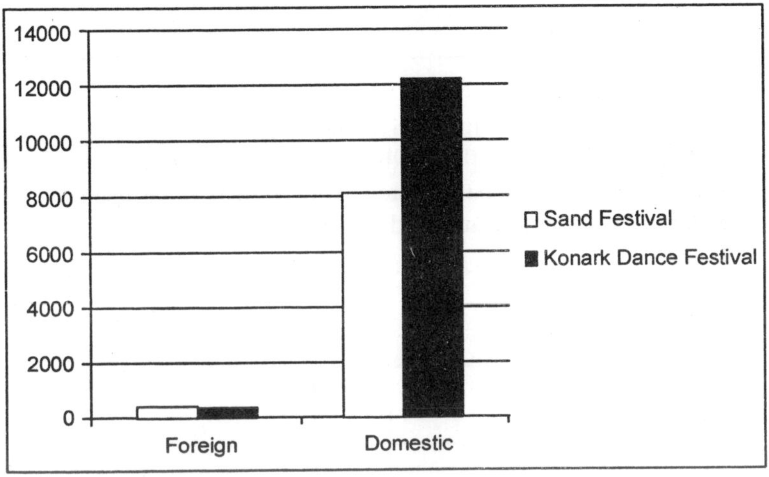

Fig. 9.2: Touristic Arrivals in Dance and Sand Festival of Konark.

Source: Department of Tourism, Government of Odisha.

(ii) Service Quality

Amenities including sanitation, potable drinking water points and other public conveniences as well as wayside cafeterias are suggested for Konark. It has been decided to organise both the dance and sand festival as ticketed shows to check disruptive crowd.

Profile of Artists of Sand and Dance festival

The quality of deliverables will also be determined by the rank and file of the participants and performers which are indispensible for giving quality experience to the tourists. In the year 2013, ten (10) national and another ten (10) internationally acclaimed artistes and groups have confirmed their participation for Konark dance festival. They include Kathakali maestro Sadanam Balakrishnan, Odissi danseuse Aloka Kanungo, Kuchipudi dancer

Alekhya Punjala, Bharatnatyam dancer Anitha Guha, Kathak exponent Rani Karnaa and Odissi dancer Ileana Citaristi.

Table 9.4: Foreign and Domestic Groups for Sand and Dance Festival at Konark

	Foreign Artists and Groups	Domestic Artist and Groups
Sand festival	5	20
Dance festival	10	10

Source: Ibid.

In the year 2013, The International Sand Art Festival had as many as 30 sand artists, including five from abroad. In 2013, four women sand artists from Odisha have participated in the festival. It has been decided to organise a competition among the participants.

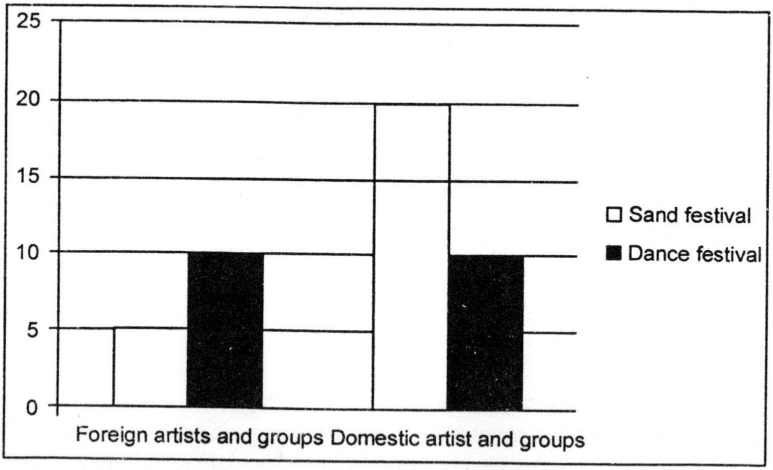

Fig. 9.3: Foreign and Domestic Groups for Sand and Dance Festival at Konark.
Source: Ibid.

The field observation analysis found that the quality of the deliverables offered at the sand and dance festival are on par with the international standards.

(iii) Marketing

Printing of brochures in different Indian languages as well as foreign languages is been called for taking events to next level of growth. Tourism Promotion Campaign has to be extended to other parts of India and across the world to get more tourists to this lucrative segment in tourism. Being the chief promoter of Odisha tourism, the State Government has to participate in tourist festivals like TTF, IITM, TAAO, IATO, SATTE, PATA, TAI etc. and international fairs like WTM, London & ITB, Berlin.

The structured interview conducted among the tourists paved light to the need of rigorous marketing of the events of Odisha. Among the tourists who have attended the dance and sand festival at Konark in 2013, only 40 per cent of tourists know about the Konark dance and sand festival prior to their visit. The main source of such tourists was websites. Nearby 8 per cent of tourists came to know about the events of Konark by other sources like word of mouth of fellow tourists, articles, travel magazines and travel fairs. Majority of the tourists (52%) who visited the Konark have made it by chance but not by choice. Most of them have come as part of tour package. The study was an eye opener towards the need of more meticulous targeted marketing for popularising the event tourism of Konark.

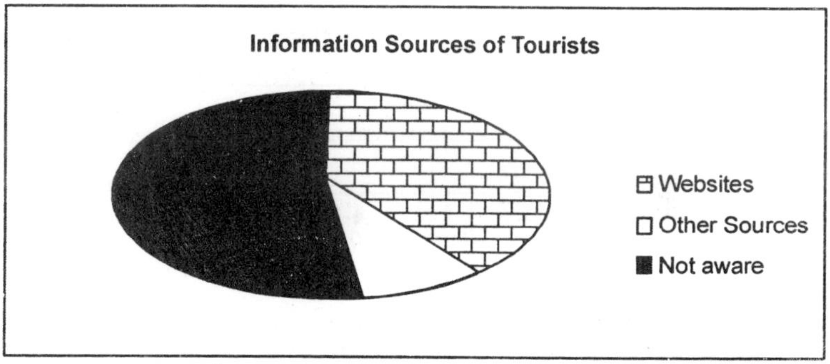

Fig. 9.4: Information Sources of Tourists Who Attended the Sand and Dance Festival at Konark.

Source: Ibid.

Presence in the cyber world will be a great mileage in the promotion of events. Event specific CD-ROMs, advertisement and publicity in media and national paper, linkages with hospitality to travel writers, Tour Operators at different capacity, Celebration of many more Tourism Festivals and Organisation of Weekly Cultural Programme in places like Bhubaneswar, Puri and Konark will do a long way in promoting the events of respective destinations.

(iv) Economic Impacts

The tourist always wants value for money while on their course of travel. This varies from tourist to tourist and destination to destination. Besides this it also varies for domestic and international tourists since they have different needs as well as motivations to seek an experience.

As per the structured interview conducted, the foreign tourists are more interested in Leisure activities along with attending dance and festivals at the destinations. On the other hand, domestic or day visitors are interested in visiting religious places, amusement facilities and also interested in attending Dance and festivals at destinations. This is comprehended in Fig. 9.5.

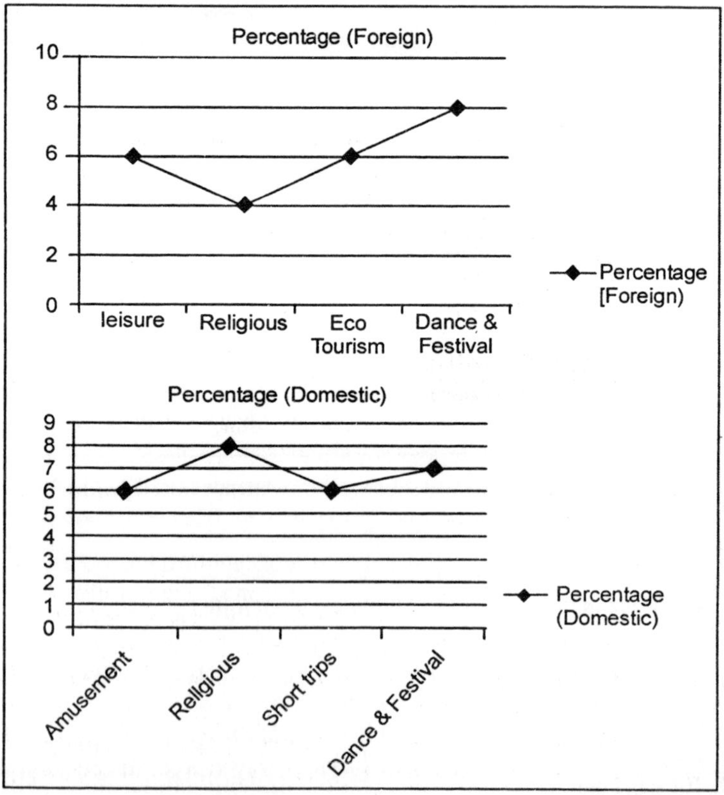

Fig. 9.5: Percentage Analysis of Preference and Choices of Foreign and Domestic Tourists.

Source: Ibid.

The analysis revealed that the foreign and domestic tourists both have high priority and preference towards attending events at destinations they visit. The study has explored the economic as well as social impacts as a result of the development of tourism at destinations.

Findings of the Study

After analysing the potential (pull factors) of Konark dance and sand festival in building destination attributes based on the proposed framework, the following findings have been made:

- After activating the framework, the instant impact will be on average spending and duration of stay of the tourists, to enjoy the improved amenities at spots
- Return on investment can be planned through imposing charges on various services offered for tourist.
- Preservation of heritage cannot be implemented without participation of local community. This will be an additional employment opportunity for them.
- The improved infrastructure facilities and demand created by increase in traffic would further accelerate the economic development of the area.

The proposed framework is to build destination attributes and the same is outlined to strike a balance among marketing, economic impacts, audience analysis and by enhancing the service qualities. Correct positioning of the destination is targeted by carving a niche on deliverables (pull factors) designed for the tourists at the destination.

Conclusion

The events of Odisha can be instrumental in promoting the state as the most sought after destination globally. Events can be a better medium of cultural appraisals and social understanding of the places that tourists visit during the course of tour. The uniqueness of Konark and events at such destinations of Odisha can catapult tourism to a different level of augmentation. By building the destination attributes and by enhancing public and private participation, event tourism can be better promoted with forward and backward integration. Inventiveness along with commitment in the segmentation of special interest tourism can bring a paradigm shift in the future development of tourism in Odisha.

REFERENCES

Bowdin *et al.*, (2006). *Special Events Great Britain Management.* Butterworth-Heinemann Amsterdam; Oxford.

Clare, G.A. (2002). *Tourism Planning* (Fourth Edition). Routledge, New York.

Formica, S., and Uysal, M. (1998). "Market segmentation of an international cultural-historical event in Italy." *Journal of Travel Research*, 36 (4): 16-24.

Getz, D. (2007). *Event Studies: Theory, Research and Policy for Planned Events.* Cognizant Communication Corporation, New York.

Jago, L.; Chalip, L.; Brown, G.; Mules, T.; and Shameem, A. (2003). "Building events into destination branding: Insights from experts." *Event Management,* 8 (1): 3-14.

McIntosh, R.W. (1977). *Tourism Principles, Practices and Philosophies.* Ohio, Grid.

Mehmetoglu, M., and Ellingsen, K. (2005). "Do small-scale festivals adopt "market orientation" as management philosophy?" *Event Management*, 9(3): 119-132.

Mitchell, C. and Wall, G. (1986). *Impacts of Cultural Festivals on Ontario Communities.*

Ritchie, B., Beliveau, D. (1974). "Hallmark events: An evaluation of a strategic response to seasonality in the travel market." *Journal of Travel Research,* 14(2): 14-20.

Ritchie, J. and Geoffery, C. (2003). *The Competitive Destination.* CABI, Wallingford, UK.

Ross, G.F. (1994). *The Psychology of Tourism.* Hospitality Press, Melbourne. Tomlijenovic.

R., and Weber, S. (2004). "Funding cultural events in Croatia: Tourism-related policy issues." *Event Management*, 9 (1/2): 51-59.

Event calendar of Odisha retrieved on 27 December, 2014 from: http://orissatourism.gov.in/Portal/

Recent initiatives on event tourism retrieved on 25th September, 2014 from: http://www.tourism.gov.in/

10

Regional Competitiveness and Disparity in Foreign Tourists Arrivals in Kerala

A.D. Rajeev Kumar and *S.V. Sudheer*

Introduction

Justifying the claims made by its proponents as the biggest industry of the world, tourism has been registering enormous and inexorable rate of growth for the last few decades. Supporting this, WTO (2010:2) reports that, despite occasional shocks, international tourist arrivals have shown virtually uninterrupted growth like 25 million in 1950, 277 million in 1980, 438 million in 1990, 681 million in 2000, and 880 million in 2009.

It is obvious that, irrespective of the development status, now almost all countries of the world are tapping their tourism resources for the overall well-being of their people. India also is not an exception in this regard. Tourism in India has been showing tremendous growth over the years, especially after the 80s. Despite showing slow growth in few years mainly due to some global issues, the foreign tourist arrivals to India has grown continuously from 1.28 million in 1981 to 1.71 million in 1990, to 2.65 million in 2000 and to 5.11 million in 2009.

Kerala, the most idyllic state in India which enjoys a unique blend of varied tourism products, is attracting a large number of foreign tourists every year. Diverse natural resources, rich cultural heritage, home for holistic medicine of Ayurveda together with the favourable location and moderate climate make Kerala a tourist paradise. In short, Kerala is amazingly gifted with wide variety of tourism products which provide multitude of experience to the tourists.

Kerala is the pioneer state in India to identify the economic potential of tourism and develop it in consonance with the overall socio-economic development of the state (Vijayakumar, 2007:11). As stated above, acknowledging its economic potential, government declared tourism as an industry in 1986, the first state in India to do so. Thereafter, the government came up with several plans, policies and programmes to ensure the sustainable development of this industry. Department of Tourism under the Ministry of Tourism functions as the nodal agency for the development of tourism in the state. As part of effective marketing, Kerala branded itself with a catchy phrase, *"God's own country"*, a brand which captured the global attention and acceptance within a very short span of time. Likewise, Kerala tourism has been acknowledged with number of meritorious awards and citations by many reputed agencies at national and international level. Among these, the 'Partner State' status by the WTTC, number of PATA gold awards, and the citation by National Geographic Traveller after two years of research as *one of the 50 must see destinations of a lifetime* and *one of the 10 paradises of the world* are few which deserve special mention.

International inbound tourism in Kerala has been showing an increasing trend over the years. Table 10.1 shows the FTAs and the Foreign Exchange Earnings (FEEs) from tourism for the period from 2000 to 2009. WTTC (2003:11) reports that Kerala is one of the fastest growing regions of the world with a growth rate well above the national and international average. Similarly, various research studies show that international tourism in Kerala has a better future prospect and will keep on its upward growth trajectory. Table 10.1 shows the FTAs and FEEs from tourism in Kerala for a ten year period from 2000-2009.

Regarding earnings from tourism, Table 10.1 shows that the foreign exchange earnings increased or decreased directly in association with an increase or decrease in the number of foreign tourist arrivals except for the year 2001. For the year 2001, there was an increase in earnings despite a decrease in tourists arrivals. It could also be seen that except for the year 2009, the change in earnings were more than proportionate to the change in arrivals.

For a region-wise analysis, the state of Kerala has been divided into three regions namely southern, central, and northern. As the name indicates, southern region covers the districts of southern part of the state like Thiruvananthapuram, Kollam, Alappuzha and Pathanamthitta. Central region covers the districts of central part of Kerala, like Eranakulam, Kottayam, Idukky and Thrissur. Northern region is the largest region in

Table 10.1: Foreign Tourists Arrivals and Foreign Exchange Earning from Tourism in Kerala for a Ten Year Period from 2000-2009

Years	*No. of FTA*	*Percentage of Variation Over Previous Year*	*FEEs (Rs. in Crores)*	*Percentage of Variation Over Previous Year*
2000	209933	3.84	525.30	26.25
2001	208830	–0.53	535.00	1.85
2002	232564	11.37	705.67	31.90
2003	294621	26.68	983.37	39.35
2004	345546	17.28	1266.77	28.82
2005	346499	0.28	1552.31	22.54
2006	428534	23.70	1988.40	28.09
2007	515808	20.37	2640.94	32.82
2008	598929	16.11	3066.52	16.11
2009	557258	–6.96	2853.16	–6.96

Source: Compiled from Kerala Tourism Statistics, Department of Tourism.

area and it covers six northern districts of Kerala like Palakkad, Malappuram, Kozhikkode, Wayanad, Kannur and Kasargode.

From Table 10.2, it is evident that there is uneven distribution of FTAs over different regions in Kerala. That is, widespread disparity among regions in the number of FTAs, especially when comparing the north with the rest. Spatially, the internatioanal tourism sector of Kerala is dominated by south and central regions together with a mighty share ranging from 94 to 97 per cent of the total FTAs. A comparison of south with central shows that the latter is having a better share with a clear edge

Table 10.2: Region-wise Percentage Share of FTA in Kerala for a Ten Year Period from 2000-2009

Years	*Percentage Share of FTA to Total*			
	Southern Region	*Central Region*	*Northern Region*	*Total*
2000	49.55	45.54	4.91	100.00
2001	41.27	55.09	3.64	100.00
2002	39.20	57.84	2.96	100.00
2003	44.09	53.08	2.83	100.00
2004	43.45	52.54	4.01	100.00
2005	45.42	49.23	5.35	100.00
2006	45.80	48.31	5.89	100.00
2007	47.26	47.23	5.51	100.00
2008	49.04	45.86	5.10	100.00
2009	39.24	54.84	5.92	100.00

Source: Compiled from Kerala Tourism Statistics, Department of Tourism.

over the former except in few years. Though largest in area, the share of northern region is very little and ranged from only 3 to 6 per cent of the total. A proper understanding and management of the factors causing this disparity is necessary to ensure balanced regional growth of tourism. In this context, the present study analyses the competitiveness of regions in attracting foreign tourists by examining their preferences.

Study Method

Hall and Page (2006: 1) state that "tourism, tourists and their impacts are clearly not evenly distributed". They further stated that there is substantial differentiation which takes place at a variety of international, regional and local scales. It is empirically evident that there is positive relation between the number of tourists arrivals and impact on tourism. This chapter analyses the regional disparity in foreign tourists arrivals in Kerala by examining the preferences of foreign tourists in attractions and facilities and also the competitiveness of different regions in their supply. In this study, attractions refers to both natural and man-made resources which can attract tourists like forest, hill stations, beaches, backwaters, historic monuments, pilgrim centres, souvenirs, ayurvedic centres, festivals, traditional art forms etc. The term facilities refers to "all man-made facilitations that complement tourists" (Sudheer, S.V, 1993:34) and it mainly include food, accommodation, transportation, entertainment, information/communication, healthcare and others. For this study, as stated earlier, the state of Kerala has been divided geographically into three regions as southern, central, and northern and this was done in line with the way followed by the State's department of tourism for preparing the tourists statistics for the year 2009. The study used both primary and secondary data. Primary data has been collected from foreign tourists through a questionnaire. From each region, a sample of 50 were selected and the total sample size was 150.

Tourist Preferences

Tourists seek attractions and certain facilities in making a trip to destination. Tourists normally have varied preferences over these attractions and facilities mainly based on their personal interest. Tables 10.3 and 10.4 show the ranking done by foreign tourists to show their preferences in attractions and facilities. Ranks are converted into points by assigning point values in reverse order, i.e. for rank 1 point value 10 and for rank 10 point value is 1. Tables 10.5 and 10.6 show the cumulative point values of different variables.

Table 10.3: Ranking by Tourists in the Category of 'Attractions'

Sl. No.	Category of attractions	Ranks assigned										
		I	II	III	IV	V	VI	VII	VIII	IX	X	Total
1.	Forest and wildlife	15	18	18	24	30	21	10	9	2	3	150
2.	Hill stations	10	18	8	15	23	9	16	18	24	9	150
3.	Traditional art forms	7	13	11	9	14	24	22	18	12	20	150
4.	Beaches with tourist facilities	31	29	25	27	12	13	4	3	6	—	150
5.	Backwaters with houseboat facilities	37	34	33	22	12	3	7	2	—	—	150
6.	Historic monuments	23	18	21	26	16	24	5	6	11	—	150
7.	Pilgrim centres	5	4	2	3	6	12	15	25	36	42	150
8.	Souvenir shopping (e.g. handicrafts)	—	2	3	5	24	15	30	24	23	24	150
9.	Ayurvedic treatment	13	11	22	17	6	11	23	18	6	23	150
10.	Festivals and events	9	3	7	2	7	18	18	27	30	29	150
	Total	**150**	**150**	**150**	**150**	**150**	**150**	**150**	**150**	**150**	**150**	

Source: Primary Data.

Table 10.4: Ranking by Tourists in the Category of 'Facilities'

Sl. No.	Category of facilities	Ranks assigned							
		I	II	III	IV	V	VI	VII	Total
1.	Accommodation	61	39	45	5	–	–	–	150
2.	Access	53	29	27	35	6	–	–	150
3.	Food & beverages	18	33	32	47	20	–	–	150
4.	Information/Communication	–	–	–	18	78	36	18	150
5.	Entertainment	18	47	46	29	10	–	–	150
6.	Health care	–	2	–	16	36	84	12	150
7.	Other	–	–	–	–	–	30	120	150
	Total	**150**	**150**	**150**	**150**	**150**	**150**	**150**	

Source: Primary Data.

Table 10.5: Ranking by Tourists in the Category of 'Attractions'

Sl. No.	*Category of attractions*	*Point values*											*Rank*
		I (10)	*II (9)*	*III (8)*	*IV (7)*	*V (6)*	*VI (5)*	*VII (4)*	*VIII (3)*	*IX (2)*	*X (1)*	*Cumulative point values*	
1.	Forest and wildlife	150	162	144	168	180	105	40	27	4	3	983	4
2.	Hill stations	100	162	64	105	138	45	64	54	48	9	789	6
3.	Traditional art forms	70	117	88	63	84	120	88	54	24	20	728	7
4.	Beaches with tourist facilities	310	261	200	189	72	65	16	9	12	–	1134	2
5.	Backwaters with houseboat facilities	370	306	264	154	72	15	28	6	–	–	1215	1
6.	Historic monuments	230	162	168	182	96	120	20	18	22	–	1018	3
7.	Pilgrim centres	50	36	16	21	36	60	60	75	72	42	468	10
8.	Souvenir/shopping (e.g. handicrafts)	–	18	24	35	144	75	120	72	46	24	558	9
9.	Ayurvedic treatment	130	99	176	119	36	55	92	54	12	23	796	5
10.	Festivals and events	90	27	56	14	42	90	72	81	60	29	561	8
	Total	**1500**	**1350**	**1200**	**1050**	**900**	**750**	**600**	**450**	**300**	**150**	**8250**	

Source: Primary Data.

Table 10.6: Ranking by Tourists in the Category of 'Facilities'

Sl. No.	*Category of facilities*	*Ranks assigned*							*Total*	*Rank*
		I (7)	*II (6)*	*III (5)*	*IV (4)*	*V (3)*	*VI (2)*	*VII (1)*		
1.	Accommodation	427	234	225	20	–	–	–	906	1
2.	Access	371	174	135	140	18	–	–	838	2
3.	Food and beverages	126	198	160	188	60	–	–	732	4
4.	Information/Communication	–	–	–	72	234	72	18	396	5
5.	Entertainment	126	282	230	116	30	–	–	784	3
6.	Health care	–	12	–	64	108	168	12	364	6
7.	Others	–	–	–	–	–	60	120	180	7
	Total	**1050**	**900**	**750**	**600**	**450**	**300**	**150**	**4200**	

Source: Primary Data.

Regional Competitiveness

Southern Region

This region is blessed with some of the outstanding tourism spots in the state like Kovalam, Varkala and Alappuzha. Thiruvananthapuram International Airport, the second busiest airport in Kerala is located in this region. All the districts of this region are well connected each other and with other regions and states through roads and rail. This region is also connected through many inland waterways. A region-wise analysis of accommodation facilities shows, the share of this region in classified hotels category is 24 per cent, 35 per cent in home stays and 33 per cent in *grihasthali* category. This region is immensely rich in the supply of state's unique tourism products like Ayurveda and house boats. For instance, state's tourism statistics shows that this region has 34 per cent of total classified Ayurvedic Health Centres and 85 per cent of classified house boats in the state.

Central Region

This region showcases some of the major tourist destinations of the state like Fort Kochi, Kumarakam, Thekkady and Munnar. Cochin International Airport, the largest and major tourist transit point of Kerala is located in this region. All the districts of this region are well connected each other and with other regions and states through roads. Railways connecting all the districts except Idukky give direct access to the region from other regions and states. The proposed Kochi Metro Railway Project will further enhance the accessibility. Kochi, the only major port in Kerala, though it is used by few as their entry points, gives the region a competitive advantage of access through water. This region also has well connected inland waterways. In accommodation facilities, this region is far ahead of other regions in all categories like classified hotels, home stays and *grihasthali* with respective share of 51 per cent, 54 per cent and 55 per cent. More than half of classified Ayurveda centres of the state are located in this region, this in turn give them competitive edge in the supply of Ayurveda/health tourism products.

Northern Region

Kappad beach, Muzhuppilangad beach, Wayanad, Bekal fort etc. are the major tourist spots of this region. Calicut International Airport (also known as Karipur Airport), the third busiest airport in Kerala is located in this region and the proposed Kannur International Airport also belongs to this region. All the districts of this region are well connected each other and with other regions and states through roads. With the opening of Konkan Railway, the region is now having a better rail connectivity with other regions/states than in the past. Though not fully utilised, the region is having greater scope for inland water connectivity. The region has a comparable share of 25 per cent in classified hotel category and lag behind in other forms like *home stays* and *grihasthali,* which are more tourism specific form of accommodation. Table 10.7 gives the region-wise share in different categories of accommodation.

Table 10.7: Region-wise Distribution of Classified Hotels, Home Stays, *Grihasthali*, in Kerala

Regions	*No. of Hotels*	*No. of Home Stay Units*	*No. of* Grihasthali *Units*
Southern Region	34 (24)	209 (35)	13 (33)
Central Region	73 (51)	323 (54)	22 (55)
Northern Region	35 (25)	68 (11)	5 (12)
Total	**142(100)**	**600(100)**	**40(100)**

Note: Figures in brackets are percentage to column total.

Sources:

1. Number of classified hotels–Compiled from Tourism Statistics, 2003.
2. Number of *Grihasthali* Units–Compiled from Statistics for Planning 2009, Department of Economics and Statistics.
3. Number of home stay units–Compiled from www.keralatourism.org (accessed on 21.08.2011).

Analysis

FTAs

Analysis of data on FTAs to Kerala for a ten year period from 2000 to 2009 reveal that there is uneven distribution of FTAs over different regions in Kerala. Widespread disparity among regions in the number of FTAs, especially when comparing the north with the rest can be noted. From Table 10.2, it is evident that both south and central regions together enjoy the major share of FTAs with a total ranging from 94 to 97 per cent, leaving the northern region for a meager share of 3 to 6 per cent. A comparison of south with central shows that the latter is having a better share with a clear edge over the former except in few years. Over the years, after many ups and downs, the share of southern region has fallen from 49.55 per cent in 2000 to 39. 24 in 2009, whereas, for the period, the share of central region has gone up from 45.54 per cent to 54.84 per cent. The share of northern region has never crossed the 6 per cent mark in any year during the period.

Tourist Preferences

Analysis of overall ranking of foreign tourists preferences reveal that, in attractions, backwaters with houseboat facilities ranked first with 1215 points, beaches with tourist facilities ranked second with 1134 points, historic monuments ranked third with 1018 points and so on. In facilities, accommodation ranked first with 906 points, access ranked second with 838 points, entertainment ranked third with 784 points followed by food and beverages, information/communication, healthcare and others in 4th, 5th, 6th and 7th ranks respectively. In short, based on rankings by tourists, the order of preferences in attractions is 1. backwaters, 2. beaches, 3. Historic monuments, 4. forest and wildlife, 5. Ayurveda, 6. hill stations, 7. traditional art forms, 8. festivals and events, 9. souvenir/shopping, and 10. pilgrim centres. In facilities, it is accommodation, access, entertainment, food and beverages, information/communication, healthcare and others.

Regional Competitiveness

Assessment of competitiveness of regions based on tourists preferences of attractions show that, southern region leads in the supply of backwater tourism with its houseboat facilities mainly at Alappuzha and also at Kollam. Central region also not far behind with its houseboat operations at the backwaters of Kumarakam and Kochi. Though northern region has backwaters like Valiyaparamba in Kasargode, the houseboat operations are comparatively less. Again, southern region has a clear advantage in the supply of beach tourism, with two beaches with international reputation at Kovalam and Varkala. Central region has Kerala's one and only International Marina at Kochi. Northern region has a number of good beaches like, Muzhuppilangad, the only drive-in beach in Kerala, Kappad etc. but all these clearly lack facilities. Historic monuments at Fort Kochi and Mattanchery give the central region an upper hand in this category, however, northern region also has many like Bakel fort (the biggest fort in Kerala), Edakal caves etc. Idukky of central region and Wayanad and Palakkad of northern region compete each other in the category of forest and wildlife. Munnar, the most favoured hill station in Kerala gives the central region a competitive edge over others. Southern region has another major hill station in Kerala at Ponmudy.

Facilities

Accommodation

Assessment of competitiveness of regions based on tourists preferences of facilities show that, in accommodation facilities, central region is far ahead of other regions in all categories of accommodation like classified hotels, home stays and *grihasthali* with a share of 51 per cent, 54 per cent and 55 per cent respectively. The share of southern region in classified hotels category is 24 per cent, 35 per cent in home stays and 33 per cent in *grihasthali* category. Northern region has a comparable share of 25 per cent in classified hotel category and lag behind in other forms like home stays and *grihasthali,* which are more tourism specific form of accommodation. Table 10.7 gives the region-wise share in different categories of accommodation.

Accessibility

In accessibility, all the regions are well connected with rest of India and World through roads, rails, air and water. A regional analysis shows that, all the districts of this southern region are well connected with each other and with other regions and states through roads and rail. Thiruvananthapuram International Airport, the second busiest airport in Kerala is located in this region and it is also connected through many inland waterways. Likewise, all the districts of this region are well connected with each other and with other regions and states through roads. Cochin International Airport, the largest and major tourist transit point of Kerala is located in this region and it also has well connected inland waterways. Railways connecting all the districts except Idukky give direct access to the region from other regions and states. The proposed Kochi Metro Railway Project will further enhance and speed up the accessibility. Kochi, the only major port in Kerala, though it is used by few as their entry points, gives the region a competitive advantage of access through water. All the districts of northern region are also well connected with each other and with other regions and states through roads. With the opening of Konkan Railway, the region is now having a better rail connectivity with other regions/states than in the past. Calicut International Airport (also known as Karipur Airport), the third busiest airport in Kerala is located in this region and the proposed Kannur International Airport also belongs to this region. Though not fully utilised, the region also is having greater scope for inland water connectivity.

Conclusion

From the above analysis, it can be seen that the international tourism and its impact in northern region is highly insignificant in comparison with southern and central regions. It is clear that central region receives the major share of FTAs to Kerala. The attractions like historic monuments at Fort Kochi and Mattanchery, wildlife at Thekkady, Munnar hill station along with better accommodation and access facilities are the contributing factors for this increased share. As far as southern region is concerned, internationally renowned beaches with various facilities at Kovalam and Varkala, backwaters with houseboat facilities at Alappuzha with a comparable accommodation and access contribute favourably for a good share of foreign tourists. It can be seen that the northern region of the state is completely isolated and poorly benefited from international tourism. Though further improvement is needed, this region is not short of attractions, but in comparison with other regions, it clearly lacks facilities, especially accommodation and access. For instance, in air connectivity, comparing to Calicut airport, both Kochi and Thiruvananthapuram airports are having upper hand in number of flights and their international services. Lack of awareness of the region, absence of long term tourism policy, lack of professional tour operators, highly limited infrastructure and facilities, lack of circuit developments, tough completion from within the state and from neighbouring states etc. are the major reported reasons for this dismal performance of this region (Mammootty and Raveendran, 2008).

For the overall development of the state, there should be more evenly distribution of tourists and benefits in all regions. Moreover, to manage the envisaged growth in tourism in a sustainable manner without disturbing the carrying capacity of major transit points and the major destinations of southern and central regions, it is imperative for the state to ensure the judicious dispersal of tourists to other transit points and destinations of the northern districts. This can be made possible through bringing the development of tourism in northern region in par with that of southern and central regions. Development of infrastructure and superstructure facilities, undertaking more promotional programmes, development of tourism circuits connecting various spots in the northern region and with those of other regions, formulating effective tourism marketing strategies, particularly, product positioning strategy etc. can be the recommended actions for the balanced regional growth of international tourism in Kerala. Realising this, government has already initiated some proactive efforts to give a facelift to the major destinations of northern region and the study concludes hoping that this region will improve its performance in international tourism by hosting for a better share of foreign tourists.

REFERENCES

Hall, Michael C., and Page, Stephen, J. (2006). *The Geography of Tourism and Recreation: Environment, Place and Space*, Routledge, London.

Mammootty, T.P., and Raveendran, P.T. (2008). "Promoting Malabar as a Tourism Destination: Perceptions of Tourists Visiting the Region", (Paper presented in a Conference on *Tourism in India: Challenges Ahead*, IIMK, May).

Sudheer, S.V. (1993). *Tourism: Problems and Prospects*, CBH Publications, Trivandrum, p. 146. UNWTO, *Tourism Highlights*, 2010 edition.

Vijayakumar, B. (2007). *The Trendsetter—Kerala*, Kerala Calling, April.

WTTC (2003). Kerala—The Impact of Travel and Tourism on Jobs and the Economy.

Part 2: Facets of Ecotourism

11

Socio-economic Profile and Standard of Living Aspects of the Ecotourism Communities of Kerala

Bijith, G.A. and *Rajasenan*, D.

Introduction

Ecotourism in Kerala is a source of income and livelihood to the outliers of the society who are dwelling in difficult terrains and forest. Community based ecotourism has always advocated the involvement of the local communities in the development initiatives as they are the most affected group during the conservation process. The ecotourism development of Kerala and the simultaneous increase in the flow of tourists to these destinations would help in providing livelihood opportunities to the local communities and the betterment of their lives. This pattern of tourism plays a pivotal role for the sustainable inclusive development option for the poor people. Therefore, the participation of the community in ecotourism ensures their inclusion in the development process along with the development of ecotourism. The local communities involved in ecotourism have a major role in decision-making and implementation. In this respect, analysing their socio-economic condition of the community is pertinent in designing and deriving strategies and action plans for the development of the ecotourism projects. This indeed helps to fine tune the ecotourism project in a way to optimise the benefits of the project both to the environment as well as to the local communities. Communities are part of local ecosystem and decision-makers should put in their time in understanding the communities involved. It also tries to situate the demographic and financial position of these communities. A general outlook in a socio-economic fabric of the community based on standard of living framework is analysed in this chapter.

Theoretical Framework and Methodology

The theoretical aspect of the study is based on the standard of living index framework, which in a way is connected to their socio-economics. The community participation in ecotourism creates livelihood security to the local communities without compromising the ecological balance of the destinations. The community development is pivotal in capacity building and developing the social capital of the local communities by using the skills, knowledge and practice (Gilchrist, 2004; Kuponiyi, 2008). Community development has been interpreted in terms of "participation, empowerment and community capacity" when linked to tourism (Singh, Timothy and Dowling, 2003; Talbot and Verrinder, 2005). Rajasenan and Abraham (2012) discuss the livelihood security and socio-economics of Community Based Ecotourism in Kerala.

Data pertaining to 600 community members from three zones–175 from South zone (Thiruvananthapuram, Kollam and Pathanamthitta), 250 respondents from Central zone (Kottayam, Idukki, Ernakulam and Thrissur) and 175 from North zone (Palakkad, Kozhikode and Wayanad) involved in various fields of CBET in Kerala are collected. The allocation to each zone was based on active community participation in the area and population proportion. The Standard of Living Index (SLI) with respect to zone, income and education of the ecotourism communities has been analysed using correspondence analysis.

Results and Discussions

Socio-economic Profile of the Community

The socio-economic and demographic matrix of the community members involved in eco-tourism activities brings out region specific differences. The employment in eco-tourism is male-centric, which is mainly determined by the kind of activity they work in. Males outnumber females in all the three zones as 75.70 per cent of the participating community members are males and the rest are females. Males mainly work as trekking guides, watchers, drivers etc., whereas females work in less risky activities like sweeper/cleaner, guides at visitor arrivals points, eco-shops, cooking, office jobs etc.

Most of the respondents (about 60%) are in the age group of 20 to 40 years. The average age of respondents in the three zones is between 35 and 37 years. Average family size is 4-5 members and differences are identified among zones. Majority has an education of 10th class and below i.e. about 60 per cent of the samples respondents have only basic school education like primary, secondary and high school (i.e. up to SSLC but not passed) level. Mere are SSLC passed, undergraduates and graduation and above. The same is depicted in Fig. 11.1.

Income and Employment

Activity-wise employment in eco-tourism activities are, guides (40%), followed by watchers (21%), Sweeper/cleaner (10.3%), eco-shops (8.8%), office related jobs including jobs as ticket collector, peon, clerical jobs etc. (7.8%), drivers and others (6.5% and 6%, respectively).

Average work days per month for the respondents are 15-25 days. A zone-wise variation in the average work days is identified with central zone with the highest average work days per month of 22 days, followed by south zone (21 days) and north zone has lowest with 19-20 days. Most of (about 75%) of the respondents are in the income category of Rs. 3001-5000 and a few have income more than Rs. 5000. A zone wise evaluation shows that the majority in the central-zone is in the income category of Rs. 4001-5000; the community members in the south-zone are mainly in the income category of Rs. 3001-5000; and respondents in north zone cover in the income category of Rs. 2001-4000. Zone-wise variation in income levels is also identified as central zone has comparatively higher average income (Rs. 4013) than the south-zone (Rs. 3819) and north zone (Rs. 3588). This is shown in Fig. 11.2.

Quality of Life

The factors determining the quality of living of the community members are mainly place of living, type of houses, area of houses, source of drinking water, sanitation facility, source of light, fuel for cooking, information source etc. Hence, it is analysed with respect to these attributes in the three zones.

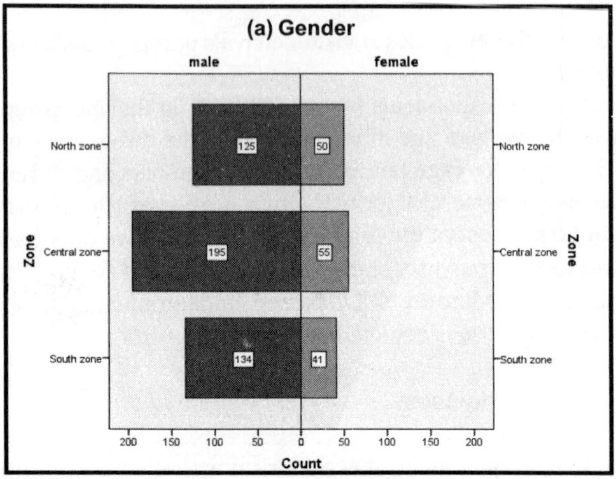
(a) Gender
male
female
North zone
Central zone
South zone
Zone
125
50
195
55
134
41
200 150 100 50 0 50 100 150 200
Count

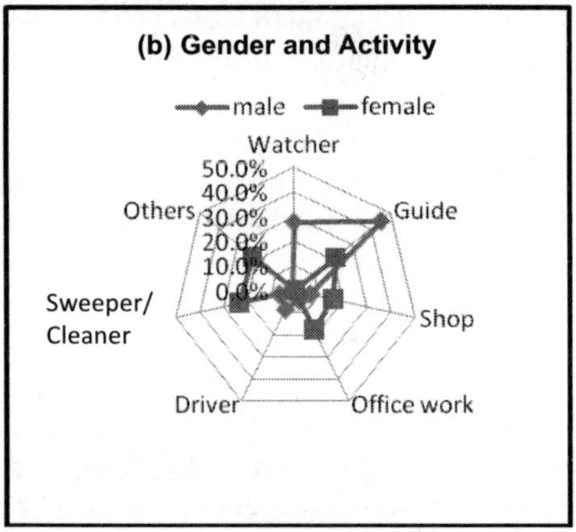
(b) Gender and Activity
male
female
Watcher
50.0%
40.0%
30.0%
20.0%
10.0%
0.0%
Guide
Others
Shop
Sweeper/
Cleaner
Driver
Office work

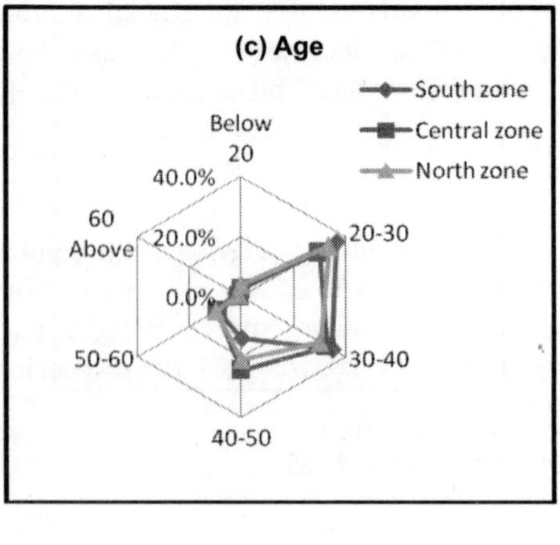
(c) Age
South zone
Central zone
North zone
Below
20
40.0%
60
Above
20.0%
0.0%
20-30
30-40
50-60
40-50

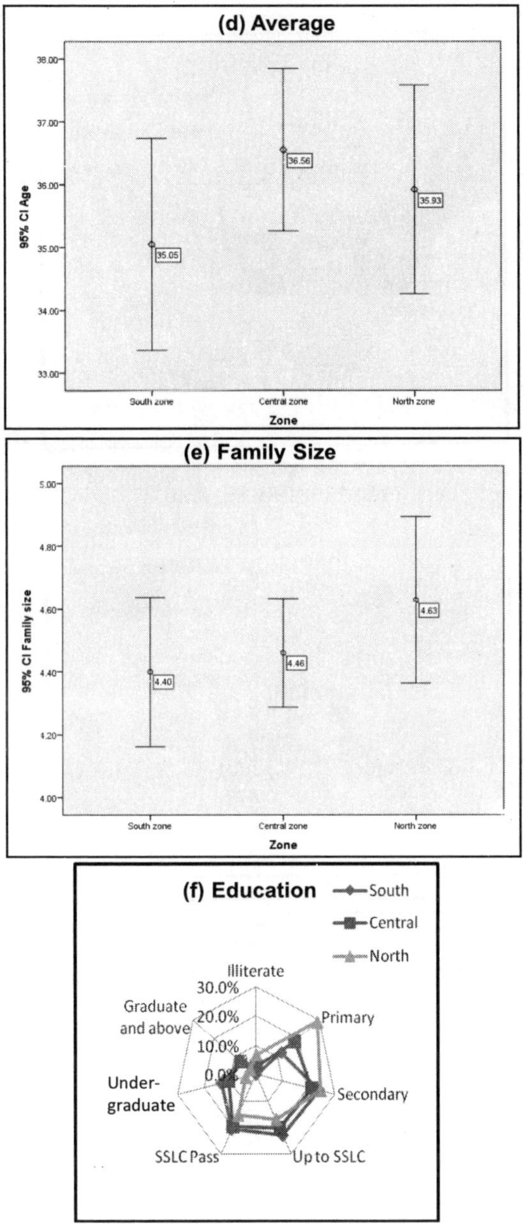

Fig. 11.1: Socio-Economic Profile.
Source: Worked out from survey data.

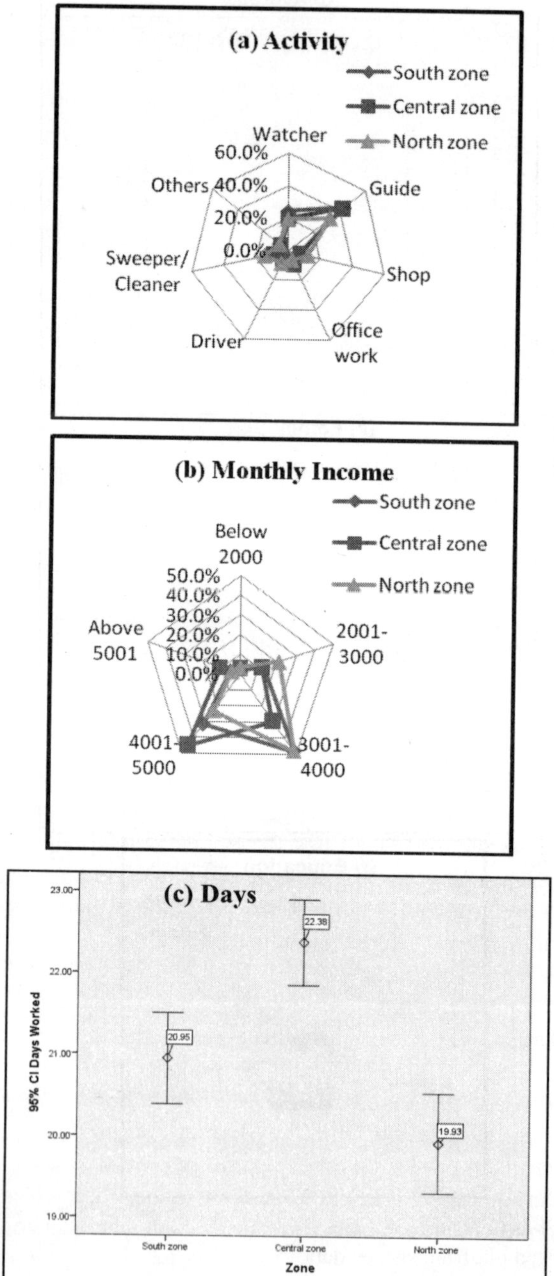
(a) Activity
South zone
Central zone
North zone
Watcher
Guide
Shop
Office work
Driver
Sweeper/ Cleaner
Others
60.0%
40.0%
20.0%
0.0%
(b) Monthly Income
South zone
Central zone
North zone
Below 2000
2001-3000
3001-4000
4001-5000
Above 5001
50.0%
40.0%
30.0%
20.0%
10.0%
0.0%
(c) Days
95% CI Days Worked
23.00
22.00
21.00
20.00
19.00
22.38
20.95
19.93
South zone
Central zone
North zone
Zone

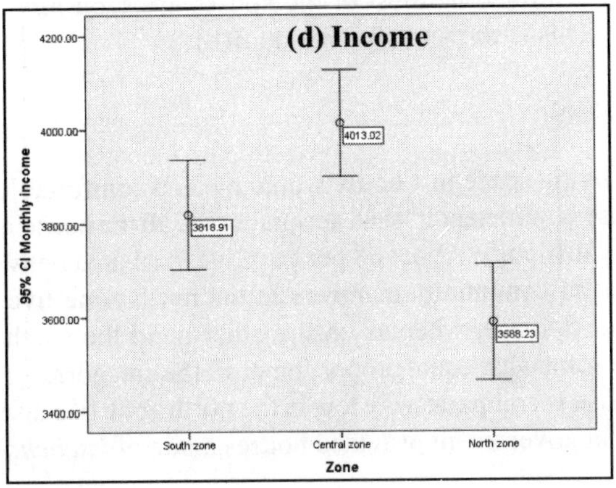

Fig. 11.2: Employment and Income.
Source: Worked out from Survey data.

Place of Living

Analysis about the place of living brings to light that 37 per cent of respondents live in their own houses followed by 25.7 per cent in government funded/provided houses and 21 per cent in their parent's houses and 3.5 per cent in rented houses. About 12 per cent of the respondents have other kinds of accommodation facilities such as staff quarters etc. The same is depicted in Fig. 11.3(a). This implies that more than 55 per cent of the respondents are self-sufficient with regard to accommodation/housing facilities. Zone-wise analysis also gives similar outcomes. But in the case of north-zone majority i.e., 52 per cent primarily depend on the government funded house. This means that government programmes for providing house construction has been effective in this region.

Type of House

The house type is categorized into *pukka*, semi-*pukka* and *kuchcha* levels. Most of them have replied that they live in houses which are built of *kuchcha* and semi-*pukka* materials. There are zone-wise differences with respect to the quality of housing. Compared to the other two zones, north-zone has reported more *kuchcha* and serviceable *kuchcha* houses. But in the case of central zone most of the houses are semi-*pukka* and *pukka* conditions. This is shown in the Fig. 11.3(b).

Area of House

Sufficient living space in a house would mean a comfortable living. The area of house is sufficient if it can accommodate all the household members without any difficulty. About 68 per cent live in an area between 201-500 sq. ft. Most of community members in the north zone live in less than 301-400 sq. ft space, whereas on the other hand the south and central zones have somewhat equal proportion in all the categories [Fig. 11.3(c)]. Area of house is comparatively low in the north zone because majority of them lives in government provided houses made of *kuchcha* materials.

Source of Drinking Water

Source of drinking water is one of the major determinants of the quality of life of the households. It can be identified that that the majority, i.e. above 50 per cent depends on public and open source of water (public tap, public well and canal/river/pond). Only 26.7 per cent have their own well, 15.5 per cent share water from others and 7 per cent their own house connection. As depicted in Fig. 11.3(d) except the north zone, the source of drinking water is same in the other two zones. The majority (31%) of the community members in the north zone depends on others, 29.1 per cent on public well/tap, 28.6 per cent depend on river, stream and canal. However, the respondents in the central and north zones mainly depend on own well followed by public source etc.

Sanitation Facility

Sanitation facility is another aspect important for quality living. Most of them have claimed that they do not posses *pukka* latrine facilities. About 42 per cent have latrine facility with door wall but no roof, 37.7 per cent have serviceable latrines. South zone outnumbers central zone having latrine facility with only door and wall [Fig. 11.3(e)]. However, north zone shows a dismal picture of households with regard to the latrine facilities.

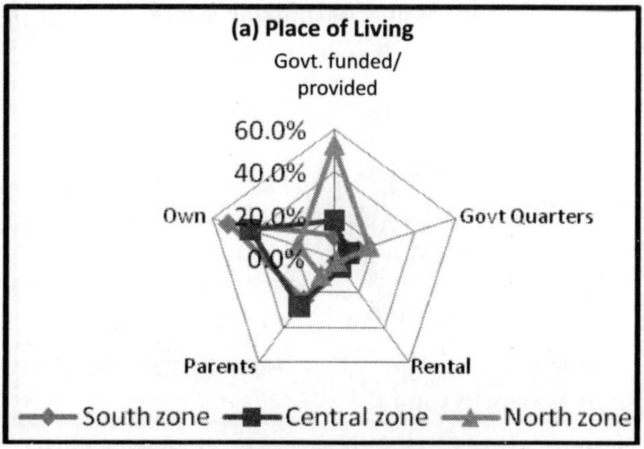
(a) Place of Living
Govt. funded/ provided
60.0%
40.0%
20.0%
0.0%
Govt Quarters
Rental
Parents
Own
South zone
Central zone
North zone

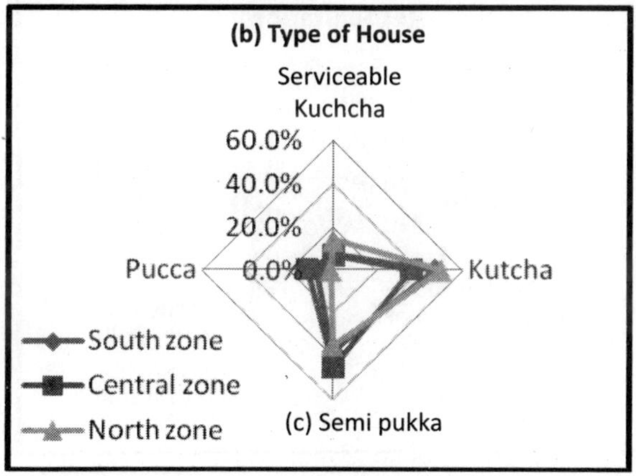
(b) Type of House
Serviceable Kuchcha
60.0%
40.0%
20.0%
0.0%
Kutcha
(c) Semi pukka
Pucca
South zone
Central zone
North zone

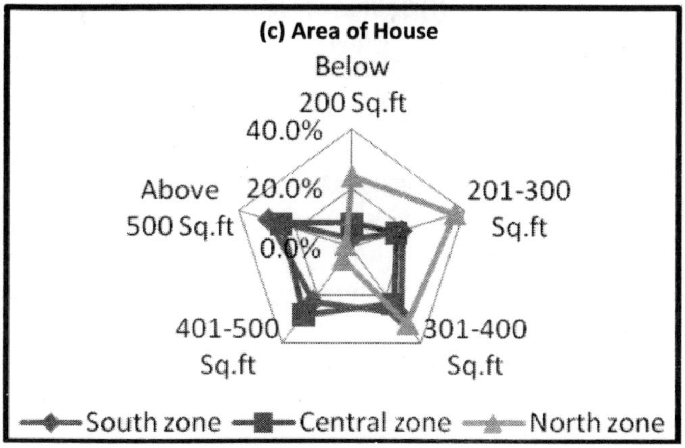
(c) Area of House
Below 200 Sq.ft
40.0%
20.0%
0.0%
201-300 Sq.ft
301-400 Sq.ft
401-500 Sq.ft
Above 500 Sq.ft
South zone
Central zone
North zone

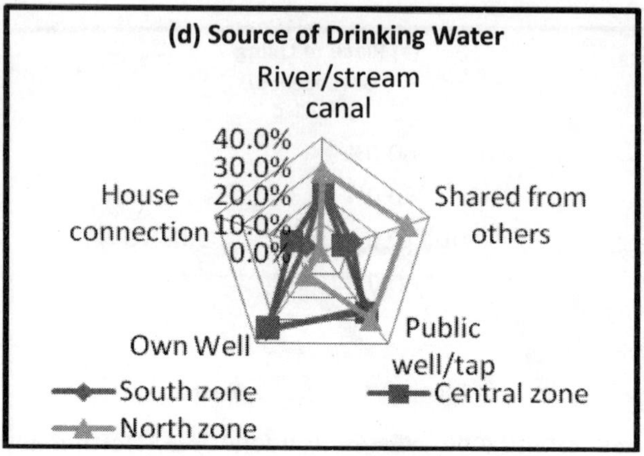
(d) Source of Drinking Water
River/stream canal
40.0%
30.0%
20.0%
10.0%
0.0%
House connection
Shared from others
Public well/tap
Own Well
South zone
Central zone
North zone

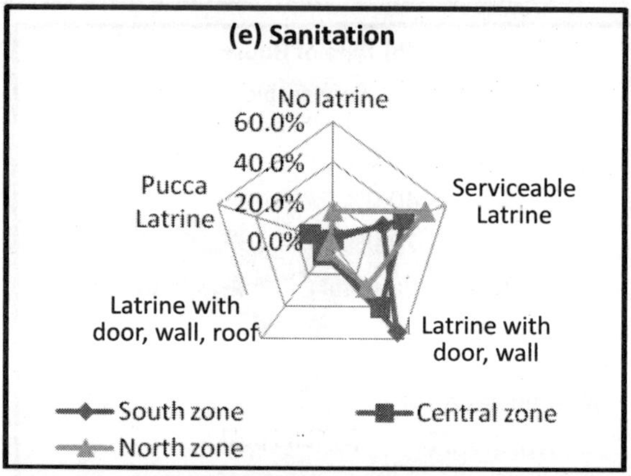
(e) Sanitation
No latrine
60.0%
40.0%
20.0%
0.0%
Pucca Latrine
Serviceable Latrine
Latrine with door, wall
Latrine with door, wall, roof
South zone
Central zone
North zone

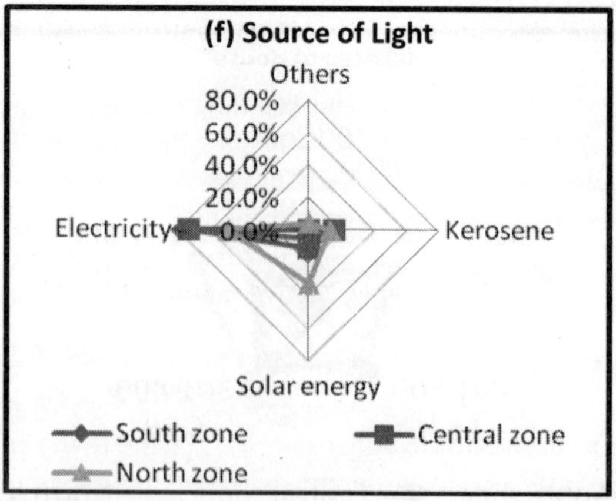
(f) Source of Light
Others
80.0%
60.0%
40.0%
20.0%
0.0%
Electricity
Kerosene
Solar energy
South zone
Central zone
North zone

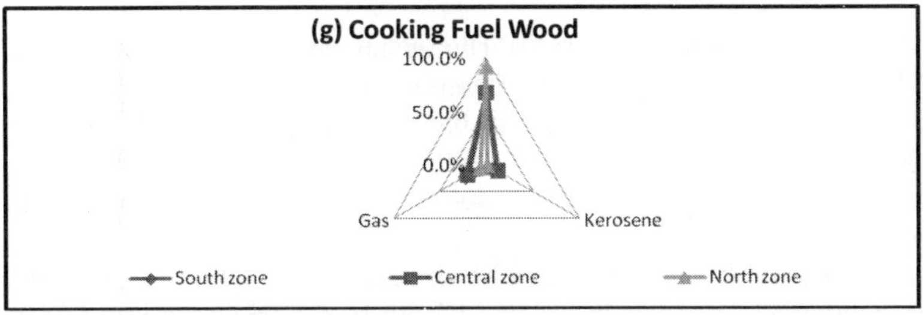

Fig. 11.3: Quality of Life
Source: Worked out from survey data.

Source of Light

For majority of the respondents (67.8%), electricity is the main source of light in their homes, which is followed by solar energy (15.7%) and kerosene (14.5%). Zone-wise analysis also gives similar results with most of the respondents having electricity connection. But in the case of central and north zones, the usage of solar energy is reported due to the difficulty in getting electric connections as they live in difficult terrains. However, in the houses with electricity connection, there are frequent power disruptions especially during the rainy seasons. Fig. 11.3(f) shows zone-wise source of lighting. The south and central zones show a similar pattern, whereas in the north zone those using solar energy as main source of light in their houses are 32 per cent.

Fuel for Cooking

Majority of the respondents (74%) depended on wood for cooking. Depending on their financial condition, they go for gas connection. The respondents have stated that even though they have gas connection their main source of cooking fuel is wood. This is because of the high and fluctuated price of the gas connection. The inter-zone difference is marked in this case where 92 per cent of the respondents from the north-zone prefer wood to other fuels. About 20 per cent each from south and central zones have gas connection. This is shown in Fig. 11.3(g).

Standard of Living

SLI is an index constructed to understand the general living conditions of people taking into account different indicators of lifestyle and living standards (Rajasenan *et al.*, 2013). This include socio-economic conditions like ownership of house, type of house, area of house, drinking water, sanitation facility, source of light, fuel for cooking etc. Each indicator was given scores in the band of one to three, where 1 is given for minimum value, i.e. low SLI, 2 for medium value or medium SLI and 3 for maximum value or high SLI.

Majority of the respondents have medium SLI values (42.3%); the remaining 47.7 per cent have low SLI and 10 per cent have high SLI. It can be inferred from the zone-wise analysis (Fig. 11.4) as well as through the Chi-Square results (Table 11.1) that there is a significant difference in the proportion of low, medium and high SLI values between the three zones. While comparing the SLI and zones it shows clearly that south zone and central zone have 52 per cent in Medium SLI, and the North Zone contains 79 per cent in the Low SLI. It can be derived that the south and central zones occupy the medium SLI region whereas north zone lies in the low SLI region.

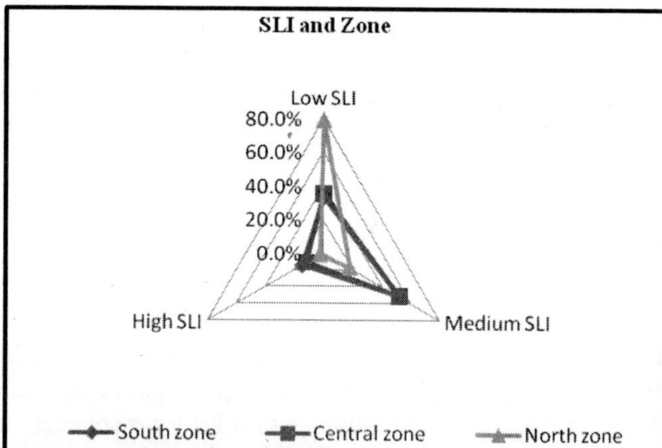

Fig. 11.4: SLI and Zone.
Source: Worked out from the Survey data.

The correspondence summary (Table 11.2) shows that two dimensions were derived. It shows a significant difference in the SLI between zones with a Chi-Square p-value <0.001. The model explains 17 per cent of the variance in the original correspondence table. The dimension 1 accounts for 16.8 per cent of the total 17 per cent of the inertia. The proportion of inertia for the dimension 1 accounts for 99.4 per cent of the total inertia.

The correspondence map shows (Fig. 11.5) that the low SLI lies in the north zone whereas the medium SLI is near to the Central zone and south zone and south zone have shorter distance from the High SLI.

Table 11.1: Chi-Square Tests SLI and Zone

	Value	*df*	*Asymp. Sig. (2-sided)*
Pearson Chi-Square	101.714	4	.000
Likelihood Ratio	107.161	4	.000
Linear-by-Linear Association	69.599	1	.000
No. of Valid Cases	600		

Source: Worked out from survey data.

Table 11.2: Correspondence Summary SLI and Zone

Dimension	*Singular Value*	*Inertia*	*Chi Square*	*Sig.*	*Proportion of Inertia*		*Confidence Singular Value*	
					Accounted for	*Cumulative*	*Standard Deviation*	*Correlation*
								2
1	.410	.168			.994	.994	.035	.023
2	.033	.001			.006	1.000	.047	
Total		**.170**	**101.714**	**.000**	**1.000**	**1.000**		

Source: Worked out from survey data.

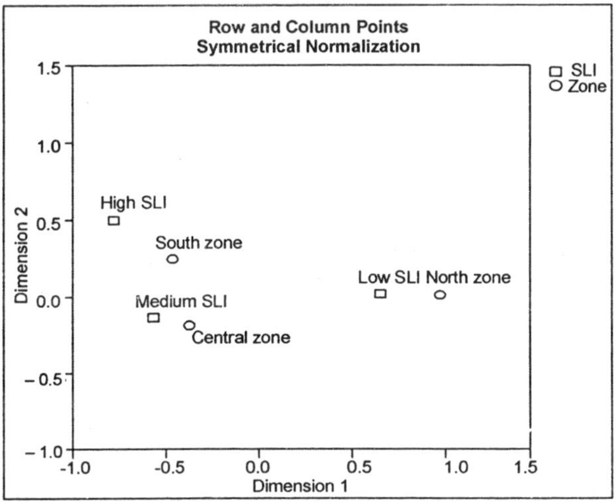

Fig. 11.5: Correspondence Map-SLI and Zone.
Source: Worked out from survey data.

Income and SLI

In the income groups below Rs. 4000, majority of the community members are from low SLI. Majority in the income groups above Rs. 4000 has medium SLI. It can be inferred that the majority in the high SLI is from the income category Rs. 5000 above. The same n:is portrayed Fig. 11.6. The Chi-Square shows that (Table 11.3) there is significant difference between the standard of living parameters and income level of the community members.

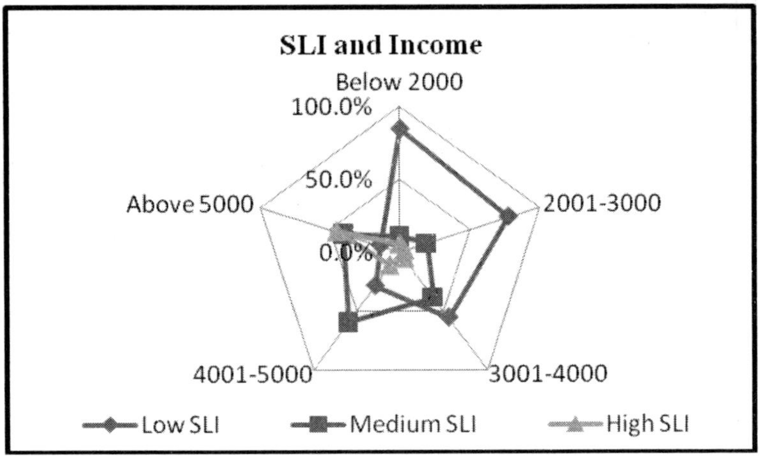

Fig. 11.6: SLI and Income.
Source: Worked out from survey data.

Table 11.3: Chi-Square Tests SLI and Income

	Value	*df*	*Asymp. Sig. (2-sided)*
Pearson Chi-Square	144.934	8	.000
Likelihood Ratio	128.768	8	.000
Linear-by-Linear Association	102.108	1	.000
No. of Valid Cases	600		

Source: Worked out from survey data.

The correspondence summary (Table 11.4) shows that two dimensions were derived. It shows a significant difference in the SLI between zones with a Chi-Square p-value <0.001. The model explains 24.2 per cent of the variance in the original correspondence Table 11.4. The dimension 1 accounts for 18.3 per cent of the total 24.2 per cent of the inertia. The

Table 11.4: Correspondence Summary SLI and Income

Dimension	*Singular Value*	*Inertia*	*Chi Square*	*Sig.*	*Proportion of Inertia*		*Confidence Singular Value*	
					Accounted for	*Cumulative*	*Standard Deviation*	*Correlation*
								2
1	.427	.183			.757	.757	.037	.407
2	.242	.059			.243	1.000	.051	
Total		**.242**	**144.934**	**.000**	**1.000**	**1.000**		

Source: Worked out from survey data.

proportion of inertia for the dimension 1 accounts for 75.7 per cent of the total inertia and dimension 2 accounts 24.3 per cent. The correspondence map shows (Fig. 11.7) that the income category above Rs. 5001 lies in the high SLI whereas the low SLI constitutes the income categories below 3000 and medium SLIs have income categories between 3001-5000.

This indicates that the income of an individual plays a pivotal role in determining their household living standards. Here, it is heartening to note that more than 90 per cent of the respondents derive their earnings from eco-tourism and related activities. It points out towards the prominence of eco-tourism employment in bettering the income and livelihood situation of the locals, majority of who belongs to the marginalized sections of the society. The earnings coupled with various development programmes targeting these localities have enabled some of the households to attain enviable position in terms of household amenities and assets. This has had a positive impact on their standard of living.

Educational Qualification and SLI

It can be drawn from the analysis that there is variation in the SLI value

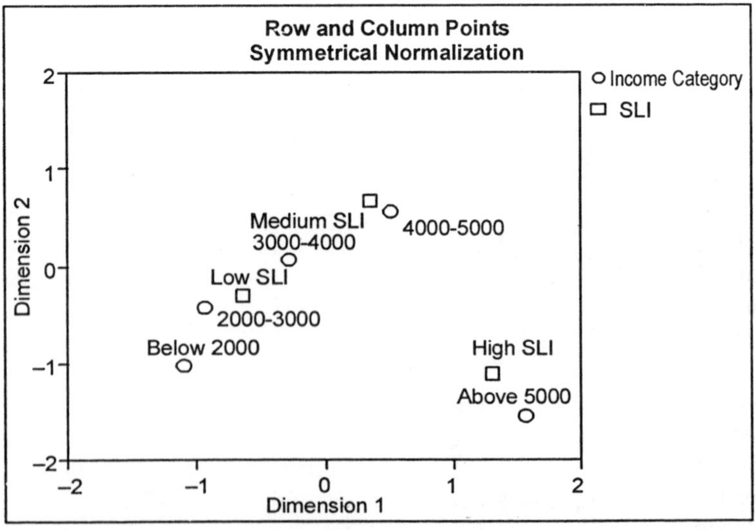

Fig. 11.7: Correspondence Map—SLI and Income.
Source: Worked out from survey data.

based on the educational qualification attained by the individual. The results are shown in Fig. 11.8. It can be seen that most of the respondents have low SLIs with educational qualifications secondary schooling and below. In the medium SLI category the majority has educational qualification from high school and above. In high SLI group, most of them are graduates, followed by under graduates and SSLC pass.

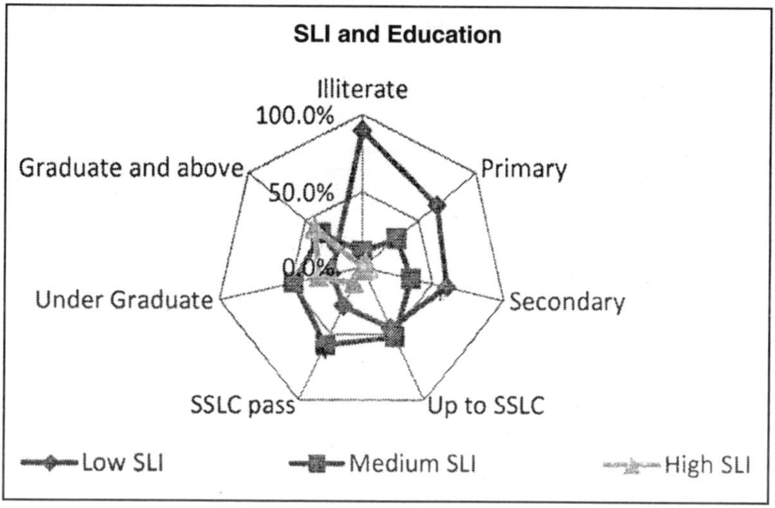

Fig. 11.8: SLI and Education
Source: Worked out from survey data.

Thus, the respondents who are having high educational qualifications showed elevated tendency to be in the high SLI category and *vice-versa*. The Chi-square test (Table 11.5) also shows that there is significant difference in the SLI value of the respondents based on the educational qualification attained by them. A positive relation between education and the income level of the respondents was identified earlier with better educated groups with high earnings.

The correspondence summary (Table 11.6) shows that two dimensions were derived. It shows a significant difference in the SLIs between zones with a Chi-Square p-value <0.001. The model explains 23.1 per cent of the variance in the original correspondence table. The dimension 1 accounts for 18.2 per cent of the total 23.1 per cent of the inertia. The proportion of inertia for the dimension 1 accounts for 79 per cent of the total inertia

Table 11.5: Chi-Square Tests—SLI and Education

	Value	*df*	*Asymp. Sig. (2-sided)*
Pearson Chi-Square	138.347	12	.000
Likelihood Ratio	124.899	12	.000
Linear-by-Linear Association	100.498	1	.000
N of Valid Cases	600		

Source: Worked out from survey data.

Table 11.6: Correspondence Summary—SLI and Education

Dimension	*Singular Value*	*Inertia*	*Chi Square*	*Sig.*	*Proportion of Inertia*		*Confidence Singular Value*	
					Accounted for	*Cumul-ative*	*Standard Deviation*	*Correla-tion*
								2
1.	.427	.182			.790	.790	.041	.318
2.	.220	.048			.210	1.000	.040	
Total		**.231**	**138.347**	**.000**	**1.000**	**1.000**		

Source: Worked out from survey data.

and dimension 2 accounts 21 per cent. The correspondence map shows (Fig. 11.9) that the graduate and above category and undergraduates

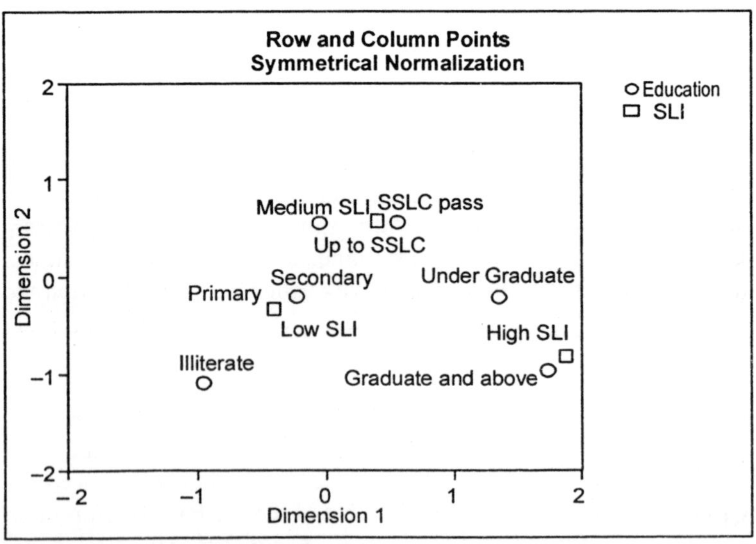

Fig. 11.9: Correspondence Map-SLI and Education.
Source: Worked out from survey data.

categories lie near to the high SLI whereas the low SLI constitutes the educational category below secondary schooling. Medium SLI occupies with the high school (i.e. up to SSLC but not passed) and the SSLC pass groups.

Education plays a key role in determining the income of the local communities as they need frequently to interact with the national and international tourists. Only through better interactive skills, they can communicate effectively with the tourists, which will have a positive impact on their income. Income, in turn assists them to attain better living standards.

The analysis regarding the socio-economic profiles of the community members provide clear-cut information about their present living situation. Community participation in ecotourism, by and large, ensures the income and livelihood security to the local communities to a great extent. This kind of community involvement, in a sense, is a form of inclusive development which will in turn help for the development of sustainable ecotourism along with sustainable livelihood.

Conclusion

There are zone-wise differences with respect to the socio-economic profiles of the community and hence it reflects in the basic indicators like quality of housing, source of drinking water, use of energy sources and latrine facilities. Standard of living measured in SLI frameworks shows that majority of the respondents have medium SLI values. A zone-wise difference in living standards of community members has also been identified. Majority in the south zone and the central zone are in the Medium SLI categories. The result obtained from the study shows that standard of living mainly depended on income and education of the community members. There exists significant difference between the Standard of Living and income level of the community members as those with impressive living standards are in the high income category. Also, a variation in the SLI value based on the educational qualification attained by the individual can be identified as it shows positive relationship between SLI and the level of educational qualification, which shows that low SLI groups are in the low educational groups.

REFERENCES

Gilchrist, A. (2004), "The well-connected Community: A Networking Approach to Community Development", Community Development Foundation (Great Britain), The Policy Press, UK.

Kuponiyi, F.A. (2008). "Community Power Structure: The Role of Local Leaders in Community Development Decision Making in Ajaawa, Oyo State, Nigeria", *The Anthropologist*, 10(4): 239-243.

Rajasenan, D. and Abraham, Bijith George (2012). "Livelihood Security and Socio-economics of Community Based Ecotourism (CBET) in Kerala", *South Asian Journal of Socio-Political Studies*, January-June, Vol. XII, No. 2.

Rajasenan, D., Abraham, Bijith George, and Rajeev, B. (2013). "Health, Education and Employment in a Forward-Backward Dichotomy Based on Standard of Living Index for the Tribes in Kerala." *Journal of Economics and Sustainable Development*, *4*(7): 100-107.

Singh, S.; Timothy, D.J., and Dowling, R.K. (eds.). (2003), *Tourism in Destination Communities*, Cambridge, USA: CABI Publishing.

Talbot, L. and Verrinder, G. (2005). *Promoting Health: The Primary Health Care Approach*, (3rd ed.): Elsevier, Churchill Livingstone, Australia.

12

Segmentation Strategy for Promotion of Ecotourism Products

Evidence from Thenmala Ecotourism Destination in Kollam District of Kerala

Manoj, P.K.

Introduction

It is widely recognised that tourism is an industry with immense potential for employment generation and economic development. Hence, tourism is promoted aggressively particularly by the developing nations like India. Globally, tourism is ranked second highest in terms of income generation, next to the oil industry. Tourism is one of the world0's largest and most rapidly growing industries. Increased leisure and higher purchasing power have combined to enable more people take into tourism. Every country has a decisive role to play in tourism and tourism industry is projected as very valuable particularly for the development of international transport and communication. Of late, tourism industry is receiving good attention as a foreign exchange earner and in most parts of the world it is promoted primarily for the purpose of earning of foreign exchange. The disbursal of tourist expenditure on accommodation, food, transport, recreation and so on has a linkage effect leading to the overall development of a country. After independence the focus of attention of the Government of India was on development of sectors like agriculture, industry, infrastructure etc. Hence, tourism was never seen as a sector with high growth potential and it was growing at its own pace. Only since the last two decades or more, tourism is being seriously promoted by the Government of India.

So, Indian tourism could not exploit the vast tourism potential of the country. Analogous to the poor tourism performance of India among comparable world nations, the relative tourism performance of Kerala state in the Indian Union has been very poor *vis-à-vis* other Indian states. Despite its enviable tourism resources, Kerala is lagging far behind most other Indian states often with much lower level of tourism endowments.

Ecotourism has got an excellent growth potential in India, particularly in states like Kerala, because of the huge demand for ecotourism from foreign tourists. Yet, ecotourism is yet to pick up momentum in Kerala. The author has made a few studies on Indian tourism, including a few empirical studies on Kerala tourism. In particular, in a very recent paper, the impact of ecotourism on the environment has been analysed based on an empirical study at Thenmala–the first planned ecotourism destination in India (Manoj, 2017).[22] Despite the notable ecosystem management at Thenmala and high satisfaction levels of the tourists, the need to limit the tourists to a level which ensures that the natural environment can withstand the pressures has been specifically noted by the author. As a continuation of this paper *viz.* Manoj (2017)[22] and a few earlier ones, this chapter seeks to identify the design considerations for ecotourism products based on an analysis of the linkages between the nature of tour and various other relevant factors (like, socio-economic and demographic variables) and accordingly to suggest strategies for more effective promotion of ecotourism.

Relevance and Significance

The vast development potential of tourism is well acknowledged in the available literature. This is particularly true in respect of ecotourism as it gives added thrust for preserving and conserving the natural environment and ecological balance. Similar is the case of allied types of tourism like responsible tourism, rural tourism, farm tourism etc. Earlier studies by the present author on the prospects of tourism in India, particularly those on sustainable and environment-friendly tourism models, Manoj (2008)[15] & Manoj (2009)[16] have pointed out the vast growth potential of tourism in India. The growth prospects of tourism in Kerala state in particular has been dealt with a focus on ecotourism in Manoj (2010)[17]. An empirical study on the prospects of ecotourism with reference to Kumarakam tourism destination in Kottayam district of Kerala by the author (Manoj, 2015)[18] has revealed its vast growth prospects. Similar positive findings are noted in another empirical study by the author with reference to

Kumbalangi–a major rural tourism destination in Ernakulam district of Kerala and the first model tourism village in India—on the prospects of rural tourism, in Manoj (2015)[19]; this study being delved further, in Manoj P.K. (a)[20] and, in Manoj (2016) (b)[21] to assess the impact of tourism and the determinants of sustainable tourism etc. A recent study by the author (Manoj, 2017)[22] about the impact of ecotourism with reference to Thenmala ecotourism destination has noted high satisfaction levels by the tourists and appreciable ecosystem management, but cautioned about the need to restrict the number of tourists to a level which the natural environment can withstand. The present paper is an extension of the said paper *viz*. Manoj, 2017)[22] and a few earlier papers of the author, especially an empirical study on ecotourism, Manoj (2015).[18] This chapter too focuses on Thenmala ecotourism destination in Kollam district of Kerala—the first planned ecotourism destination in India—as in the case of the earlier paper of the author *viz*. Manoj (2017).[22] The chapter seeks to study the significance of the socio-economic and demographic variables of the tourists and the nature of their tours, on their selection with ecotourism products (like, tour packages). As there is enough scope for prudent policy decisions based on the study findings, this chapter is relevant from the policy perspective also.

Objectives

(1) To study the extent of relationship between the socio-economic and demographic variables of tourists at Thenmala ecotourism destination on the one hand and the nature of their tours on the other, and hence to identify the relevant design considerations.

(2) To suggest Segmentation, Targeting and Positioning strategy for ecotourism promotion.

Hypotheses of the Study

H_o: There is no significant relationship between socio-economic and demographic variables of the tourists and the nature of tour undertaken by them (Null Hypothesis–Main).

H_a: There is significant relationship between socio-economic and demographic variables of the tourists and the nature of tour undertaken by them (Alternate Hypothesis–Main).

Methodology of the Study

This study is descriptive—analytical and exploratory in nature. Both primary and secondary data are used for this study. Primary data are collected using a sample survey with the help of an Interview Schedule from *Thenmala*—a major ecotourism destination in Kollam district in Kerala and the first planned ecotourism project in India—from four groups of respondents *viz.* 120 domestic tourists, 120 foreign tourists, 60 local residents and 23 tourism officials. Secondary data are collected from the publications of United Nations World Tourism Organization (UNWTO), World Travel and Tourism Council (WTTC), World Economic Forum (WEF), Kerala Tourism Development Corporation (KTDC), Kerala State Planning Board, the tourism statistics (reports) of the Government of Kerala and Government of India, industry reports published by reputed agencies like FICCI, IBEF etc. Popular statistical tools are used for data analysis. The four groups of respondents are shown in Table 12.1.

Table 12.1: Profile of Respondents

Group I	Officials in Thenmala Ecotourism Project	23
Group II	Local Residents in Thenmala	60
Group III	Domestic Tourists Arrived in Thenmala	120
Group IV	Foreign Tourists Arrived in Thenmala	120

Source: Based on the Sampling frame set for the study.

This study has been structured with the objective of studying the significance of the relationship between socio-economic and demographic variables of tourists and the nature of tours preferred by them. For this purpose, information has been collected through a structured interview schedule from four categories of respondents. The respondents were selected purely on random sampling technique without considering their age, sex, class, country, religion and income. Questions asked to Groups I and II were relating to ecotourism administration, management, planning, impacts—social, economic, environmental and ecological, problems and prospects of ecotourism in Thenmala ecotourism project; while, that of Groups III and IV were concerned with hospitality services, travel problems, attractions and personal experiences in Thenmala ecotourism project.

Literature Review and Research Gap

From the review of the existing literature on tourism it is noted that globally there has been an increasing focus on the adverse impact of tourism on the ecology and environment. Worldwide, the Governments have initiated tourism for developmental needs, with greater attention on preserving the environment. This trend is very clear since the mid-1980s. The implications of tourism initiatives on the society at large is often studied from a socio-ecological perspective and the conceptual model suggested by Brundtland (1987)[22] called "Ecologically Sustainable Development Framework" is employed for the above purpose. This framework is being used globally for managing various crucial tourism-related development issues. 'Ecotourism' (ecologically sustainable tourism) and its variants like rural tourism and responsible tourism are fast gaining popularity worldwide. Norton (1987)[23] opined that many people who travel to natural areas do so specifically to indulge in experience with nature, regardless of what activities they choose to do. Lane (1991)[12] has noted that ecotourism projects should strive to provide satisfying jobs to the local community without adversely affecting the environment. McNeely *et al.* (1992)[14] and Brandon (1996)[7] hope that tourism would instil a sense of local pride to villagers and would promote or strengthen cultural heritage. Bhatia (1993)[3], has noted that the underdeveloped region of a country can greatly be benefited from tourism development. Many regions of the world have areas of excellent scenic beauty and are highly culturally attractive too, though such regions are economically backward. These areas if developed for the use by tourists can bring in prosperity to the local people. This tourism development process reduces regional imbalances by creating more income and employment in the less developed and depressed areas. Healy, Robert G. (1994)[9] has noted that most constituents of the tourism commons are subject to tourists and locals as 'free riders'; the most vulnerable being BTEs (Basic Tourism Elements), the natural environment and infrastructure. But, everything depends on the power of government to restrict "free riding" incidents through various mechanisms such as resources use regulation and pricing. The lack of rules and/or their inadequate implementation in several countries victimize many components of the tourism commons. Lindberg and Enriquez (1994)[13] has cited many examples of local earnings from tourism related employment surrounding protected areas in Belize, Nepal, Costa Rica and Australia. In Nepal, for instance, two thirds of the residents' families at Sagarmatha national parks earn livelihood from guiding tourists, sale of local goods and cloths as well as arranging accommodation to them. Besides economic benefits, tourism contributes towards improving inter-cultural appreciation and understanding for both host communities and tourists.

Coccossis, Harry & Nijkamp, Peter (1995)[6] have noted that extension of tourism affects many tourism spots and numerous activities ranging from transporting to nourishing of people. The social, economic and environmental impact of tourism are numerous and diverse. Clark (1991)[5] discerns a shift in the understanding of ecotourism. He argues that there has been a paradigm shift from the original understanding of ecotourism as being small scale, educative and minority interests towards an understanding of sustainable tourism that requires best practice by tourism operations of all sizes in terms of minimizing their impacts on environment. Ajith Kumar (1998)[1] has studied the psycho-graphic, demographic and lifestyle features of tourists to Kerala. It is noted that spending pattern is a part of the lifestyle features of tourists since spending is determined by demographic factors, income level and psycho-graphic factors like the purpose of visit, especially the motivation to visit Kerala.

Ferhan (2006)[8] has observed that the rapid development as well as high concentration of tourism activities result in adverse effects on the natural and cultural environment, and when investment of locals is minimal or lacking, the outcomes would be especially unacceptable to the host community. Singh, Ratandeep (2008)[28] in his book on *Tourism Marketing* has discussed the various dimensions of tourism marketing. It is pointed out that as tourism industry is mainly services-oriented and labour intensive, it is a major source of employment. It generates wide range of economic activities and provides direct socio-economic benefits through higher employment opportunities. Manoj (2008)[15] in his research paper, "Sustainable Tourism in India: A Study from a Global Perspective with Focus on Tourism Prospects of Kerala" has made a macro level study of the prospects of sustainable tourism in Kerala from an international perspective and offered some strategies for the faster growth of sustainable tourism initiatives in Kerala.

Oommen (2008)[25] has pointed out the danger of overlooking the environmental sustainability in development initiatives in the context of Kerala state in India. The author while referring to the growing environmental problems in Kerala from the broader perspective of the development of the state (*viz.* Kerala model of development) has pointed out the environmental and ecological issues that the state faces leading to a situation of "Ecological Overkill". Four major dangers emanating from this situation have been pointed out as (i) serious damage of the hydrological cycle; (ii) high distortion of the vast coastal system of the state of 580 km; (iii) high destruction of the unique, extremely distinguished, rich and diverse natural resources as well as bio-diversity which together constitute a beautiful agro-eco-system; and (iv) highly consumerist society that throws out heavy solid, liquid and medical wastes.

Manoj (2009)[16] in his research paper "Environment Friendly Tourism for Sustainable Economic Development in India" has studied the vital significance of tourism for faster economic development of India and has suggested strategies for environment-friendly and sustainable tourism development in India. In another research paper by this author *viz.* Manoj (2010)[17] entitled "Tourism in Kerala: A Study of the Imperatives and Impediments with Focus on Ecotourism", the case of tourism sector in Kerala state in India is studied with Strengths, Weaknesses, Opportunities and Threats (SWOT) analysis of the tourism sector. Strategies for faster and sustainable growth of tourism in Kerala are suggested by the author. In another study by the author Manoj (2015)(a)[18], entitled "Prospects of Ecotourism in Kerala: Evidence from Kumarakam in Kottayam District" an empirical study of ecotourism gives made a few suggestions for sustainable development of ecotourism based on the study findings. Another study by the author Manoj (2015)(b)[19], entitled 'Employment Generation from Rural Tourism: A Field Study of the Local Community at Kumbalangi, Kerala" has made an empirical analysis of the response of the local community regarding the employment prospects arising from rural tourism, expectations of the tourists about the required Governmental interventions etc. The high prospects of employment generation and economic development and the need for enhancing the tourism infrastructure, primarily through Governmental initiatives have been highlighted in the paper.

World Economic Forum (WEF) (2015)[33] in its report "The Travel and Tourism Competitiveness Report" makes a detailed study of the competiveness of individual countries in the travel and tourism front at the regional and global levels in respect of various parameters. According to WEF report, the global competiveness of Indian tourism is only 52 while that of China is 17, thus showing a wide gap between these two neighbouring developing nations. At the regional level (*viz.* Asia Pacific region) too, there is large difference in competitiveness, because India is ranked in the 12th position while China is in the sixth position. In spite of the vast natural resources (17th rank), cultural resources (10th), unique intangible heritage (8th) etc. India's overall position 52nd is very low because of poor rankings in respect of tourism-specific infrastructure (109th), health and hygiene (106th), ICT readiness (114th), safety and security (97th), desperately low level of environmental sustainability (139th) and so on. WTO (2015)[34] in its report, "UNWTO Tourism Highlights 2015 Edition', has pointed out that China has been the fastest growing source market for tourism in the recent years. China has been ranked first in international tourism expenditure, third in international tourism receipts, fourth in international tourism arrivals. The four major players in global tourism have been United States, Spain, China and France. The growth of tourism in India has been 11 per cent as against 20 per cent for Sri Lanka. India has been one among the source markets that showed double digit growth in expenditure, though it is not one among the best 10 markets in terms of growth in expenditure. WTTC (2015)[35] in its latest report, "Economic Impact of Travel & Tourism 2015–Annual Update" has made an elabourate account of the relative performance of various countries of the world in the tourism front, including region-wise performance and future projections. WTTC has reported that South Asia, led by India and the Middle East, are globally the fastest growing regions in terms of the total contribution of Travel and Tourism to GDP. So, India is one among the bigger, fast growth markets along with China, Indonesia, South Korea and Turkey.

In a recent empirical study by the present author, Manoj (2016) (a)[20], "Impact of Rural Tourism on the Environment and Society: Evidence from Kumbalangi in Kerala, India", which in turn is a continuation of Manoj (2015) (b)[19], it has been observed that from the perspective of the local community members there are obvious benefits to the local community because of rural tourism, and further that the behaviour of tourists to the local people has been encouraging. But, it has also been pointed out that there are adverse effects of rural tourism on the society and environment which in turn may adversely affect its sustainability in the long run. As high as 61.67 per cent of the local community members have felt that rural tourism would definitely degrade the natural environment. In another paper by the author, Manoj (2016) (b)[21] entitled as "Determinants of Sustainability of Rural Tourism: A Study of Tourists at Kumbalangi in Kerala, India" in *International Journal of Advance Research* in *Computer Science and Management Studies,* which in turn is a continuation of Manoj (2016) (a)[20] noted above, the author has identified the major factors influencing the sustainability of rural tourism at Kumbalangi and has suggested strategies for its sustainable development. The very recent paper, Manoj (2017)[22], by the author entitled,

"Impact of Ecotourism: Evidence from Thenmala Ecotourism Destination in Kollam District, Kerala" in *Asian Academic Research Journal of Multidisciplinary* has studied the impact of ecotourism on the environment and local community. The positive response from the stakeholders and appreciable ecosystem management at the destination have been noted, but the urgent need to restrict the tourists to the level which the natural environment can withstand has been pointed out in order to ensure its long term sustainability.

From the foregoing discussions, it is noted that there are many studies on Indian tourism and a few on Kerala tourism, including some studies by the present author himself, *viz.* Manoj 2008[15], 2009[16], 2010[17], 2015 (a)[18], 2015 (b)[19], 2016 (a)[20], 2016 (b)[21] and 2017.[22] It is noticed, however, that empirical studies that focus on the identification of design considerations for effective promotion of ecotourism products are virtually nil in the Kerala context. This is the research gap identified for this study. As a continuation of the earlier ecotourism studies, particularly three studies *viz.* (i) study on the prospects of tourism in Kerala with a focus on ecotourismin Manoj (2010)[17]; (ii) empirical study on the prospects of ecotourism with reference to Kumarakam tourism destination in Kottayam District of Kerala in Manoj (2015)(a)[18]; and (iii) empirical study on the impact of ecotourism with reference to Thenmala ecotourism spot in Kollam District of Kerala in Manoj (2017)[22], this paper seeks to bridge the above research gap.

Analysis and Discussion

Regarding the Age-Sex classification of the respondents under Group II, 63 per cent of them are female residents while the rest 37 per cent are male residents. Under Group III, the percentage share of female domestic tourists is 48 per cent while it is 52 per cent for the male domestic tourists. Out of 120 domestic tourists 38 are in the age group 25-40, the lowest share, i.e. 21 are in the age group of 56 and above. In Group IV, the percentage share of male foreign tourists is 51 per cent and that of female foreign tourists is 49 per cent. Out of 120 foreign tourists, 34 are in the age group 41-55, the lowest share, i.e. 23 are in the age group below 25. Thus, among the total 300 respondents, 145 (48%) are male tourists and the rest 155 (52%) are female tourists. Among the total 300 respondents 90 are from the age group 41-55 and the least share 58 are from the age group 56 and above (Table 12.2).

Table 12.2: Age-Sex Classification

Group / Age Group	Group II		Group III		Group IV		Total		
	M	*F*	*M*	*F*	*M*	*F*	*M*	*F*	*Total*
Below 25	5	9	13	14	11	12	29	35	64
Between 25-40	6	11	22	16	17	16	45	43	88
Between 41-55	7	15	19	15	18	16	44	46	90
56 and above	4	3	8	13	15	15	27	31	58
Total	**22 (37)**	**38 (63)**	**62 (52)**	**58 (48)**	**61 (51)**	**59 (49)**	**145 (48)**	**155 (52)**	**300 (100)**

Note: Figures in brackets are percentage to column total.
Source: Field survey.

In fact, educational background of the local people, domestic tourists and foreign tourists is a major factor that influences the economic development of an area, especially with regard to ecotourism-related activities. Since people from different countries and from different states with different languages are involved in ecotourism, the educational status of the domestic and foreign tourists arriving at Thenmala and that of local residents in Thenmala is a significant factor. Table 12.3 shows that in Group II, out of the total 60 (100%) respondents 6 (10%) have primary education, 21 (35%) have higher secondary background, 24 (40%) are graduates (or equivalent Professional Diplomas), 9 (15%) are post-graduates or those having equivalent Professional degrees (like, Technical degree etc.). In Group III, primary, higher secondary, graduate, post-graduate or professional degrees is in the ratio of 8: 40: 48: 24 or 6.67 per cent 33.33 per cent, 40 per cent, 20 per cent respectively. Group IV is in the ratio of 16: 18: 42: 44 or 13.33 per cent, 15 per cent, 35 per cent, 36.67 per cent respectively. Thus, among the 300 total respondents–belonging to the three groups *viz.* Groups II, III and IV—the largest share is 114 (38%) with graduation, the lowest share is 30 (10%) has only primary education (Table 12.3).

Table 12.4 shows the average monthly income of male and female in Groups II, III and IV. In Group II, out of the 60 respondents 26 are in the middle income group, i.e. 15000-30000 whereas only 3 are in the income class of 30000-50000. In Group III, out of the 120 respondents, 44 are in the income class of 30000-50000 whereas only 12 are in the class of 'Below 15000'. In Group IV, out of the 120 respondents 46 are in the income class of 'Above 50000' whereas nobody has been there in the income class of 'Below 15000'. Thus out of the total 300 respondents in the three broad groups *viz.* Groups II, III and IV, as high as 96 respondents are in the middle income group of 15000-30000 whereas there are only 23 respondents who were in the income class 'Below 15000'.

Table 12.3: Educational Status

Level of Education \ Group	Group II		Group III		Group IV		Total	
	No	%	No	%	No	%	No	%
Primary	06	10.00	08	06.67	16	13.33	30	10.00
Higher Secondary	21	35.00	40	33.33	18	15.00	79	26.33
Graduate or equivalent	24	40.00	48	40.00	42	35.00	114	38.00
P.G. or equivalent	09	15.00	24	20.00	44	36.67	77	25.67
Total	**60**	**100.00**	**120**	**100.00**	**120**	**100.00**	**300**	**100.00**

Source: Field survey.

Table 12.4: Monthly Income

Income \ Group	Group II			Group III			Group IV			Total		
	M	F	Total	M	F	Total	M	F	Total	M	F	Total
Below 15000	3	8	11	5	7	12	0	0	0	8	15	23
15000-30000	16	10	26	21	16	37	16	17	33	45	51	96
30000-50000	0	3	3	28	16	44	29	12	41	54	34	88
Above 50000	3	17	20	8	19	27	16	30	46	28	65	93
Total	**22**	**38**	**60**	**62**	**58**	**120**	**61**	**59**	**120**	**135**	**165**	**300**

Source: Field survey.

Nature of tour means whether the tour is organised by the tourists themselves or arranged by tour operators for a single payment. It is found from the Table 12.5 that majority of the domestic tourists (56.67%) have organised their travel themselves. But majority of the foreign tourists (54.17%) have selected package tour.

Table 12.5: Nature of Tours

Nature of Tour	*Domestic Tourists*		*Foreign Tourists*	
	No. of tourists	*Percentage*	*No. of tourists*	*Percentage*
Self-Organised	68	56.67	55	45.83
Package	52	43.33	65	54.17
Total	**120**	**100.00**	**120**	**100.00**

Source: Field survey.

Testing of Hypotheses

The Chi-squire test is used to test the significance of the association between the socio-economic status of the tourists and their opinions and preferences. Ch-Square is calculated as:

$$\chi^2 = \frac{\Sigma(Oij - Eij)^2}{Eij}$$

E = (Row Total × Column Total) ÷ Grand Total
χ^2 = Chi-square
O = Observed Frequency
E = Expected Freqɪency

Table 12.8 shows that majority of the domestic tourists, in general, have preferred Self-organised tours. But, two age groups have differed from the above general norm; the '25-40' and 'Above 56' groups have more inclination to Package tours, as against the other groups.

The relevant sub-hypotheses (Null and Alternate) about the relationship between age of domestic tourists and the nature of tour undertaken by them can be specified as follows:

H_o: There is no significant association between the age of the domestic tourists and the nature of the tour undertaken by them.
H_a: Age of the domestic tourists significantly influences the nature of their tours.

The computed value of Chi-squire (χ^2) *viz.* 20.867 is higher than the Table (Critical) value of 11.345 at 1 per cent level of significance (LOS) and the value of 7.815 at 5 per level of significance (LOS). So, the Null Hypothesis is not accepted and the Alternate hypothesis is accepted. It is proved that there is significant association between the age of the domestic tourists and the nature of their tours, both at 5 per cent LOS and 1 per cent LOS (Table 12.6).

Table 12.6: Nature of Tour and the Age of Domestic Tourists

Age	*Nature of Tour*		*Total*
	Package	*Self-organised*	
Below 25	08 (29.63)	19 (70.37)	27 (100)
25-40	28 (73.68)	10 (26.32)	38 (100)
41-55	10 (29.41)	24 (70.59)	34 (100)
56 & above	06 (28.57)	15 (71.43)	21 (100)
Total	**52 (43.33)**	**68 (56.67)**	**120 (100)**

Note: Figures in bracket represent percentage. Here, p-value =0.000111, i.e. Significant].
Chi-Square (χ^2)=20.867, df=3, Table Value = 11.345 (1%) and 7.815 (5%).

Source: Field survey.

Majority of the foreign tourists have preferred package tours, generally; but 'Below 25' and '41-50' groups are inclined towards Self-organised tours (Table 12.7). Sub-hypotheses relating to the relation between age of foreign tourists and their nature of tour are follows:

H_o: There is no significant association between the age of the foreign tourists and the nature of the tour undertaken by them.

H_a: Age of the foreign tourists significantly influences the nature of tour preferred by them.

The computed Chi-squire (χ^2) value 13.628 is higher than the Table (Critical) value at 11.345 (at 1% LOS) or 7.815 (at 5% LOS). So, the Null Hypothesis is not accepted. Instead the Alternate hypothesis is accepted. It is statistically proved that there is significant association between the age of the domestic tourists and the nature of their tours, both at 5 per cent LOS and 1 per cent LOS (Table 12.7).

Majority of the domestic tourists with primary education (62.50%) have chosen package tours. Most of the highly educated tourists too *viz.* post-graduates or professional graduates (70.83%) have preferred package tours. These two groups (32 tourists) constitute over one-fourth (26.33%) of the total tourists. But, among the rest of the tourists (88 tourists or 73.33% of the total) majority have opted self-organised tours. Thus, 70

Table 12.7: Nature of Tour and the Age of Foreign Tourists

Age	*Nature of Tour*		*Total*
	Package	*Self-organised*	
Below 25	06 (26.09)	17 (73.91)	27 (100)
25-40	21 (63.64)	12 (36.36)	25 (100)
41-55	16 (47.06)	18 (52.94)	49 (100)
56 & Above	22 (73.33)	08 (26.67)	19 (100)
Total	**65 (54.17)**	**55 (45.83)**	**120 (100)**

Note: Figures in bracket represent percentage. Here, p-value = 0.00346, i.e. Significant.
Chi-Square (χ^2) = 13.628, d.f=3, Table Value = 11.345 (1%) and 7.815 (5%).

Source: Field survey.

per cent of the tourists with Secondary/Higher Secondary level education and 62.50 per cent of those with Graduation or Professional Diplomas have opted self-organised tours. (Table 12.8). The relevant hypotheses in this case can be specified as follows:

H_o: There is no significant association between the educational level of the domestic tourists and the nature of the tour undertaken by them.

H_a: Educational level of the domestic tourists significantly influences nature of their tours.

Table 12.8: Nature of Tour and Educational Level of Domestic Tourists

Educational Status	*Nature of Tour*		*Total*
	Package	*Self-organised*	
Primary	05 (62.50)	03 (37.50)	08 (100)
Secondary/Higher Secondary	12 (30.00)	28 (70.00)	40 (100)
Graduate (Professional Diploma)	18 (37.50)	30 (62.50)	48 (100)
Post-Graduate (Professional Degree)	17 (70.83)	07 (29.17)	24 (100)
Total	**52 (43.33)**	**68 (56.67)**	**120 (100)**

Note: Figures in bracket represent percentage. Here, p-value = 0.00689, i.e. Significant.
Chi-Square (χ^2) = 12.149, d.f=3, Table Value = 11.345 (1%) and 7.815 (5%).

Source: Field survey.

The computed Chi-squire (χ^2) value of 12.149 is higher than the Table (Critical) values of at both 5 per cent LOS (7.815) and 1 per cent LOS (11.345). So, the Null Hypothesis is not accepted and the Alternate hypothesis is accepted. It is statistically proved that domestic tourists' perception towards nature of tour is statistically dependent on their educational level, both at 5 per cent LOS and 1 per cent LOS (Table 12.8).

In general, majority of the foreign tourists have preferred package tours; particularly by those with only Primary level education (68.75%) and also those with very high level of education like Post graduation or equivalent (68.18%). While foreign tourists with Secondary/Higher Secondary level of education have higher preference (55.56%) of Package tours, those with Graduation or equivalent have definite preference (66.67%) of Self-organised tours (Table 12.9). Here, the relevant hypotheses can be set as follows:

- H_o: There is no significant association between the educational level of the foreign tourists and the nature of the tour undertaken by them.
- H_a: Educational level of the foreign tourists significantly influences nature of their tours.

Table 12.9: Nature of Tour and Educational Level of Foreign Tourists

Educational Status	*Nature of Tour*		*Total*
	Packages	*Self-organised*	
Primary	11 (68.75)	05 (31.25)	16 (100)
Secondary/Higher Secondary	10 (55.56)	08 (44.44)	18 (100)
Graduate (Professional Diploma)	14 (33.33)	28 (66.67)	42 (100)
Post Graduate (Professional Degree)	30 (68.18)	14 (31.82)	44 (100)
Total	**65 (54.17)**	**55 (45.83)**	**120 (100)**

Note: Figures in bracket represent percentage. Here, p-value = 0.0067, i.e. Significant.
Chi-Square (χ^2) =12.209, d.f=3, Table Value = 11.345 (1%) and 7.815 (5%).

Source: Field survey.

The computed Chi-squire (χ^2) value is 12.209 and this is higher than Table (Critical) value at 1 per cent LOS (11.345) and also 5 per cent LOS (7.815). So, the Null Hypothesis is not accepted and the Alternate hypothesis is accepted. It is statistically proved that foreign tourists' perception towards nature of tour is statistically dependent on their educational level, both at 5 per cent LOS and 1 per cent LOS (Table 12.9).

From Table 12.10, it is seen that vast majority of the domestic tourists with income levels 'Upto 15000' have opted Self-organised tours. Similarly, rich tourists viz. 'Above 50000' group too have opted Self-organised tours. Majority of them in the '15000 to 30000' group (67.57%) have opted for Package tours whereas those in higher middle income group '30000 to 50000' prefer Self-organised tours. So, the two hypotheses can be set as follows:

H_o: There is no significant association between the income level of the domestic tourists and the nature of the tour undertaken by them.

H_a: Income level of the domestic tourists significantly influences the nature of their tours.

Table 12.10: Nature of Tour and Income of Domestic Tourists

Income	*Nature of Tour*		*Total*
	Package	*Self-organised*	
Upto 15000	04 (33.33)	08 (66.67)	12 (100)
15000-30000	25 (67.57)	12 (32.43)	37 (100)
30000-50000	18 (40.91)	26 (59.09)	44 (100)
Above 50000	05 (18.52)	22 (81.48)	27 (100)
Total	**52 (43.33)**	**68 (56.67)**	**120 (100)**

Note: Figures in bracket represent percentage. Here, p-value = 0.00102, i.e. Significant.
Chi-Square (χ^2) =16.214, d.f=3, Table Value = 11.345 (1%) and 7.815 (5%).

Source: Field survey.

The computed Chi-squire (χ^2) value *viz*. 16.214 is higher than Table (Critical) value at 1 per cent LOS (11.345) and also 5 per cent LOS (7.815). So, the Null Hypothesis is not accepted. Instead the Alternate hypothesis is accepted. It is statistically proved that domestic tourists' perception towards nature of tour is statistically dependent on their income level, both at 1 per cent LOS and 5 per cent LOS.

From Table 12.11, it is noted that there has not been any foreign tourist with monthly income upto Rs.15000 (about USD 300 per month). Among the tourists in the '15000-30000' monthly income group, majority

(81.82%) have opted for Package tours. However, in the higher income group of '30000-50000' more than a half (51.22%) have preferred tour packages. Among the rich foreign tourists, i.e. those in the 'Above 50000' monthly income group majority (63.04%) have preferred Self-organised tours (Table 12.11). The Hypotheses (Null and Alternate) can be set as follows:

H_o: There is no significant association between the income level of the foreign tourists and the nature of the tour undertaken by them.

H_a: Income level of the foreign tourists significantly influences the nature of their tours.

Table 12.11: Nature of Tour and Income of Foreign Tourists

Income	*Nature of Tour*		*Total*
	Package	*Self-organised*	
Upto 15000	00 (00.00)	00 (00.00)	00 (00.00)
15000-30000	27 (81.82)	06 (18.18)	33 (100)
30000-50000	21 (51.22)	20 (48.78)	41 (100)
Above 50000	17 (36.96)	29 (63.04)	46 (100)
Total	**65 (54.17)**	**55 (45.83)**	**120 (100)**

Note: Figures in bracket represent percentage. Here, p-value = 0.00037, i.e. Significant.
Chi-Square (χ^2) =15.795, d.f= 3, Table Value = 11.345 (1%) and 7.815 (5%).

Source: Field survey.

The computed Chi-squire (χ^2) value is 15.795 and this is higher than Table (Critical) value at 1 per cent LOS (11.345) and also 5 per cent LOS (7.815). So, the Null Hypothesis is not accepted. Instead the Alternate hypothesis is accepted. It is statistically proved that foreign tourists' perception towards nature of tour is statistically dependent on their income level, both at 1 per cent LOS and 5 per cent LOS.

Major Findings and Suggestions

Major findings of the study are interpreted hereunder. Besides, a few strategies are suggested so as to promote ecotourism products and to position them more meaningfully, as follows:

- Socio-economic and demographic variables of the tourists are significantly influencing their selection of ecotourism products, like, tour packages. Hence, a proper STP (*viz.* Segmentation, Targeting, and Positioning) strategy for promoting ecotourism should be developed by the tourism providers, including the Central and State Governments, so as to optimally utilise the limited ecotourism resources and also to enhance the earnings from tourism, particularly the foreign exchange earnings. Factors like Age, Educational Level and Annual Income of the tourists, both domestic and foreign, have to be duly considered while framing the policy towards promotion of ecotourism. (It may be noted that all the six alternate hypotheses have been accepted in the present study). Focusing on specific customer segments ensures sustainability by preventing over exploitation.
- As enhancing the foreign exchange earnings from tourism is the broad policy objective of the State and Central Governments, segments among the foreign tourists that fetch higher earnings should be targeted by positioning products (like, tour packages) that they prefer. It may be pointed out that as majority of the foreign tourists (65%) prefer Package tours (as against 52% of domestic tourists) offering Package tours to foreign tourists is always meaningful (Table 12.5). While promoting such packages to foreign tourists, targeting the two higher income groups among them (which together account for 74% of the total foreign tourists) is more prudent as these two groups among them are more inclined towards Package tours than the rich segment (Table 12.11). Among the foreign tourists, targeting specific segments like those with lower level of education (up to Higher Secondary level) and those with very high level of education (Post-graduate level or equivalent) is meaningful (Table 12.9). Similarly, targeting foreign tourists in their latter youth-hood (25-40 years' group) and older age (above 56 years) is also good because of their inclination towards package tours (Table 12.7).
- Government agencies themselves, like, Kerala Tourism and KTDC of the Government of Kerala or India Tourism (Incredible India) of the Government of India should offer specialised packages to foreign tourists. Duly segmenting the tourists based on their socio-economic and demographic profile while positioning such products to the target segments would be meaningful. Besides, collaborating with other Governmental

agencies (like, Indian Railways) would make such tour packages more attractive to all the stakeholders involved.

- For domestic tourists, such Package tours are of only less demand, because by and large they prefer Self-organised tours (Table 12.5). But, there is sizeable number of domestic tourists in the latter youth-hood (25-40 years' age group) who prefer such Packages (Table 12.6). Similarly, targeting those with very high level of education (Post-graduates etc.) (Table 12.8) and those in the lower middle income group (15000-30000 class) (Table 12.10) is also meaningful. But, the earnings from domestic tourists would be less.
- Last, but not the least in importance is the need to limit the provision of ecotourism services to a level that is within the carrying capacity of the environment. This is required for ensuring the long-term sustainability of ecotourism, because allowing too many tourists would result in irrecoverable harm to the ecotourism sites like Thenmala. This in turn points to the need for focusing on specific customer segments for promoting tourism rather than using a blanket approach to all customers.

Concluding Remarks

In view of the foregoing discussions, it may be noted that promotion of ecotourism in Kerala would ensure rich dividend in the days to come, given the huge growth prospects of ecotourism in the state. Careful analysis of the exact tastes and preferences of the customers, considering their socio-economic, demographic and such other factors is very important. The design considerations of various products like Tour Packages and ingredients thereof, should duly take into account the tastes and preferences of various segments. So, a well thought out STP strategy should be used for product design, delivery and re-design on a constant basis.

NOTES

1. Ajith Kumar, M.K. (1998). *Psychographic and Demographic Profiles of Foreign Tourists Visiting Kerala with special reference to Spending Patterns*, Unpublished Ph.D. Thesis, Cochin University of Science and Technology (CUSAT), Kochi, Kerala.

2. Brundtland, G.H. (1987). *The Brundtland Report,* World Commission on Environment and Development, Oxford University Press.
3. Bhatia, A.K. (1996). *Tourism Development: Principles and Practices,* Sterling Publishers Private Ltd., New Delhi.
4. Chatak, G.R. (2007). *Sustainable Tourism Codes and Guidelines*, Cyber-Tech Publications, Daryaganj, New Delhi, First Edition.
5. Clark, J.R. (ed.) (1991). *Carrying Capacity: A Status Report on Marine and Coastal Parks and Reserves,* University of Miami/US National Park Service, Washington, DC.
6. Coccossis, Harry. & Nijkamp, Peter. (1995). *Sustainable Tourism Development*, Ashgate Publishing, Union Road, Farnham–GU9 7PT (U.K.).
7. Brandon, K. (1996). *Ecotourism and Conservation: A Review of Key Issues.* Washington, DC: The World Bank.
8. Ferhan, G. (2006). "Components of Sustainability: Two Cases from Turkey", *Annals of Tourism Research*, Vol. 3, Issue 2: 442-455.
9. Healy, Robert G. (1994). "The 'Common Pool' Problem in Tourism Landscapes", *Annals of Tourism Research,* Vol. 21, No. 3: 596-611.
10. India Brand Equity Foundation (IBEF) (2017). *Tourism and Hospitality,* Industry Report, February (Available online at: www.ibef.org).
11. Kabia, Sunil K. (2005). *Tourism and Environment*, Mohit Publications, New Delhi, First Edition.
12. Lane, B. (1991). "Sustainable Tourism: A New Culture for the Interpreter", *Interpretation Journal*, Vol. 49.
13. Lindberg, K. and J. Enriquez (1994). *An Analysis of Ecotourism's Contribution to Conservation and Development in Belize*, Vol. 2. Washington: World Wildlife Fund.
14. McNeely, J.A.; J. Thorsell, and H. Ceballos-Lascurain (1992). *Guidelines: Development of National Parks and Protected Areas for Tourism*, WTO/UNEP/IUCN, Madrid.
15. Manoj, P.K. (2008). "Sustainable Tourism in India: A Study from a Global Perspective with Focus on Tourism Prospects of Kerala", *Proceedings of Second International Conference on Responsible Tourism in Destinations*, 21-24 March, 2008, p. 7. Available online in the website of Responsible Tourism Conferences:http://www.artyforum.info/documents/MicrosoftWord-MANOJ-Poster.pdf]
16. Manoj, P.K. (2009). "Environment Friendly Tourism for Sustainable Economic Development in India", *International Journal of Commerce and Business Management (IJCBM),* pp. 139-147.
17. Manoj, P.K. (2010). "Tourism in Kerala: A Study of the Imperatives and Impediments with Focus on Ecotourism", *Saaransh–RKG Journal of Management,* Vol. 1, No. 2, January 2010, pp. 78-82.
18. Manoj, P.K. (2015) (a), "Prospects of Eco-tourism in Kerala: Evidence from Kumarakam in Kottayam District, *International Journal of Research in Management and Social Science,* Vol. 3, Issue 1 (II), January–March 2015, pp. 54-59.

19. Manoj, P.K. (2015) (b), "Employment Generation from Rural Tourism: A Field Study of the Local Community at Kumbalangi, Kerala", *International Journal of Applied Services Marketing Perspectives (IJASMP),* Vol. 4, No. 4, October-December 2015, pp. 1880-1888.
20. Manoj, P.K. (2016) (a), "Impact of Rural Tourism on the Environment and Society: Evidence from Kumbalangi in Kerala, India", *International Journal of Advance Research in Computer Science and Management Studies (IJARCSMS)*, Vol. 4, Issue 2, February 2016, pp. 148-159.
21. Manoj, P.K. (2016) (b), "Determinants of Sustainability of Rural Tourism: A Study of Tourists at Kumbalangi in Kerala, India", *International Journal of Advance Research in Computer Science and Management Studies (IJARCSMS)*, Vol. 4, Issue 4, April 2016, pp. 17-30.
22. Manoj, P.K. (2017). "Impact of Ecotourism: Evidence from Thenmala Ecotourism Destination in Kollam District, Kerala", *Asian Academic Research Journal of Multidisciplinary (AARJMD)*, Asian Academic Research Associates, Vol. 4. Issue 1, January 2017, pp. 42-53. (Available online at: www.asianacademicresearch.org).
23. Norton, G. (1987). "Tourism and International Terrorism", *The World Today*, Vol. 43, Issue 2: 30-33.
24. Nigam, Satish C. (2006). *Ecotourism and Sustainable Development*, Rajat Publications, New Delhi, First Edition.
25. Oommen, M.A., (2008). "Reforms and the Kerala Model", *Economic & Political Weekly*, Vol. XLIII, No. 2, Jan. 12-18, 2008, pp. 22-25.
26. Rajan, J. (2005). "Eco-tourism Development: International Covenants", in Sarngadharan, M. & Raju, G. (Eds.) (2005). *Tourism and Sustainable Economic Development: Indian and Global Perspectives*, New Century Publications, New Delhi.
27. Sarngadharan, M. & Raju, G. (Eds.) (2005). *Tourism and Sustainable Economic Development: Indian and Global Perspectives*, New Century Publications, New Delhi.
28. Singh, Ratandeep (2008). *Tourism Marketing Principles, Policies and Strategies*, Kanishka Publishers & Distributors, New Delhi.
29. Sinha, P.C. (2006). *Global Tourism, Sustainable Tourism & Ecotourism: Code of Ethics, Charter, Guidelines, Resolutions*, SBS Publishers & Distributors Pvt. Ltd., New Delhi.
30. Sundaram, I.S., "Tourism: India Awakens to 'Incredible' Opportunities", *Business and Economic Facts for You*, December 2007, Vol. 28, No. 3: 7-10.
31. Verma, Jagdish (2007). *Dynamics of Indian Tourism: Issues and Challenges*, Cyber-Tech Publications, Daryaganj, New Delhi, First Edition.
32. ATREE (2006). *White Paper on Ecotourism Policy* (Draft), April, pp. 4-5.
33. World Economic Forum (WEF) (2015). *The Travel & Tourism Competitiveness Report 2015,* 91-93 route de la Capite, CH-1223 Cologny, Geneva, Switzerland.

34. United Nations World Tourism Organization (UNWTO) (2015). *UNWTO Tourism Highlights 2015 Edition*, CalleCapitánHaya, 42 28020 Madrid, Spain.
35. World Travel & Tourism Council (WTTC) (2015). *Economic Impact of Travel & Tourism 2015 Annual Update*, Harlequin Building, 65 Southwark Street, London, SE1 0HR, United Kingdom.
36. Government of Kerala (2016). *Kerala Tourism Statistics 2016*, Research & Statistics Division, Department of Tourism, Thiruvananthapuram.
37. Government of Kerala, *Economic Review,* Kerala State Planning Board, Thiruvananthapuram, Kerala–for the years 2008 to 2016.
38. Official website of World Tourism Organisation (WTO), www.unwto.org
39. Official website of World Travel and Tourism Council (WTTC), www.wttc.org
40. Official website of Kerala Tourism (Government of Kerala), www.kerala tourism.org

13

Rural Empowerment Through Ecotourism

A Case Study on Darap Village in Sikkim

T.G. Ramaiah

Introduction

Travel and tourism is the biggest industry in the world which makes up 11 per cent of the total GDP of the world and 8 per cent of total employed population in this world and has emerged as a powerful source of income and wealth creation and to some extent helps in fuelling tolerance in the world among different communities (Vikash Rikhye, 2008). In other words, it shows the importance of tourism as such in the economy of a country. India, with a vast stretch of land possessing different geographical conditions, communities and cultures has immense potential to explore in this regard. However, not much importance is provided to the sector in real terms. Since, most of the tourism attractions were still dominated by ancient structures and buildings that have historical importance. In this context, the very concept of rural tourism sweeping through most of the countries has made little impact in India.

Ministry of Tourism, Government of India has laid top importance to the concept of rural tourism. The Government document in this regard emphasizes the importance of rural tourism (Ministry of Tourism, 2010) in the following manner:

> "Tourism growth potential can be harnessed as a strategy for Rural Development. The development of a strong platform around the concept of Rural tourism is definitely useful for a country like India, where almost 74 per cent of the population resides in its 7 million villages. Across the world the trends of

> industrialization and development have had an urban centric approach. Alongside, the stresses of urban lifestyles have led to a "counter-urbanization" syndrome. This has led to growing interest in the rural areas. At the same time, this trend of urbanization has led to falling income levels, lesser job opportunities in the rural areas leading to an urbanization syndrome in the rural areas. Rural Tourism is one of the few activities which can provide a solution to these problems. Besides, there are other factors which are shifting the trend towards rural tourism like increasing levels of awareness, growing interest in heritage and culture and improved accessibility, and environmental consciousness. In the developed countries, this has resulted in a new style of tourism of visiting village settings to experience and live a relaxed and healthy lifestyle. This concept has taken the shape of a formal kind of Rural Tourism. Under this Scheme, thrust is to promote village tourism as the primary tourism product to spread tourism and its socio-economic benefits to rural and its new geographic regions. Key geographic regions are identified for development and promotion of Rural Tourism. The implementation is done through a Convergence Committee headed by the District Collector. Activities like improving the environment, hygiene, infrastructure etc. are covered for assistance. Apart from providing financial assistance, the focus is to tap the resources available under different schemes of Department of Rural Development, State Governments and other concerned Departments of the Government of India."

In fact, given the Indian context, the concept of rural tourism is defined (Ministry of Tourism and Culture, Government of India) in the following manner:

> "Any form of tourism that showcases the rural life, art, culture and heritage at rural locations, thereby benefiting the local community economically and socially as well as enabling interaction between the tourists and the locals for a more enriching tourism experience can be termed as rural tourism. Rural tourism is essentially an activity which takes place in the countryside. It is multi-faceted and may entail farm/agricultural tourism, cultural tourism, nature tourism, adventure tourism, and ecotourism. As against conventional tourism, rural tourism has certain typical characteristics like; it is experience oriented, the

> locations are sparsely populated, it is predominantly in natural environment, it meshes with seasonality and local events and is based on preservation of culture, heritage and traditions."

This in context, the Himalayan region is a big boon to promote rural tourism as an economic activity and at the same time promoting rural tourism. The Himalayan range possesses distinct geographical conditions and pattern of culture. The distinct nature of these two resulted in specific economic activities derived through geographical conditions, raw-material available, specific skills possessed by the people inhabiting in the vicinity etc. Thus, the Himalayan region has distinct place for promoting 'rural tourism.'

Though, the Himalayan region has been attracting tourism from all-over the world, the region's capacity to attract tourists on the basis of 'rural tourism' has not been widely practiced. Only a few such experiments were in vogue. One such experiment which has been considered as one of the successful 'rural tourism initiative' is observed in Darap village in Sikkim state.

Darap Experiment on Rural Tourism

Darap Village is situated 16 kilometre away from the West Sikkim district headquarter. Educated unemployed Youths of—Darap Village has initiated Rural/Village Tourism realizing the potential of the nearby situated villages like—Ipsing, Sidibung, Seingpheng, Lagey and Rimbi under Yangthang Assembly constituency, West Sikkim. As these villages are rich in natural resources, bio-diversity and particularly very rich in cultures and customs of local tribes called 'Limboo's' and is inhibited by 95 per cent of Limboo population with their fascinating village life style. Realizing the immense potential–natural beauty, rich bio-diversity and culture of various communities living in our state and to provide mechanism to boost up the village economy, the villagers, group of like minded people and the senior citizens constituted "Darap Eco-Tourism Committee" with Hon. Area M.L.A. Shri P.L. Subba as its Patron in Chief and Shri Sushil Tamang residence of Darap as president and organised ourselves into "Darap Eco-Tourism Committee" and had decided to promote and develop Rural/ Village Tourism believing that it could be one sustainable sources of livelihood for the villagers. The involvement of educated unemployed youths in Tourism sector at the very grassroots level are making serious attempts to pursue tourism business as a means of bringing about affective economic development for the community as a whole.

Darap Eco-Tourism Committee

"Darap Eco-Tourism Committee" is a full-fledged non-profit making, secular and Non-governmental Organization (NGO). From its initial establishment, the committee has been working towards providing livelihood especially to the villagers on sustainable basis by catering Tourist in the village. In order to support village tourism, construction of Tourism Centric Infrastructures or assets like: Ethnic Houses of three different communities of Sikkim i.e., Bhutia, Lepcha and Nepali, Traditional Limboo House is felt very necessary to attract Tourists. To demonstrate local culture to the Tourist, construction of combined Ampi-Theatre and Museum at the heart of the village is also felt very necessary. Darap Eco-Tourism Committee is the local community based organisation which is leading the village community for tourism development. It brings the village youth under one roof to sensitize them and other members towards the development of sustainable form of tourism in the village. It has its own tourism office at Darap. Its objectives are to build awareness about natural and cultural resources and to mobilize the villagers on tourism and conservation activities. Their vision is to develop Darap as vibrant village society that is self-reliant and empowered its tourism activities.

The Vision of Darap Rural Tourism is "to accomplish sustainable development the organisation has dedicated itself in nature conservation and promotional activities for the well-being of the people through sound eco-practice. Ultimately, the goal of the Committee is to strengthen the Village home-stays and establish links and promotion and cooperation between local communities and tourism stakeholders to benefit from tourism. As per the records available, the Mission statement of the Committee is as follows:

- To build capacity of Darap village community to cater tourist in home stay.
- To promote rural areas/village as eco-tourism and village tourist destination.
- To increase socio-economic status of rural areas/village through eco-tourism/village tourism.
- To raise the community participation level and to develop sense of ownership and belongingness.
- To conserve the environment this is main bio-diversity capital of our State.

- To conserve the culture and tradition of the communities living in the area.
- To make the development process of the village a sustainable one for the local people.

How does Darap Eco-Tourism Committee Work

Home Stay for the tourist is being organised by the "Darap Eco-Tourism Committee" at different houses of the members of the committee at Darap village. So far, the society has identified *thirty houses for Home stay, out of which 10 are the operators and one village resort and one village retreat under Darap Eco-Tourism Committee.* Beside this, the maintenance of other houses is also under way giving sanitation the topmost priority. Furthermore, in order to ensure the equitable benefits to the community, operational guidelines have been framed for equal opportunity for income and also the tourist gets good service.

Strategies for Promoting Rural Tourism

The rural tourism cluster has enough growth potential provided strategic intervention is made in certain "key areas".

The "key areas" in which the strategic interventions are as follows:

- Improvement in the interpretation of the site for better visitor satisfaction.
- Village beautification, waste management and hygiene issues.
- Skill Development Practical trainings for Diversification of product.
- Capacity building to sustain the product and provide better tourist satisfaction.
- Telecommunication facilities for the cluster for enhanced communication.
- Publishing promotional and publicity materials.
- Networking among tourism operators and other key stakeholders.
- Developing and strengthening the vertical and horizontal linkages.
- Awareness and tourism quality consciousness by conducting seminars, workshops and exposure visits.
- Orientation programmes for conservation and responsible practices.
- Product diversification and enhancement.

Darap Eco-tourism Project

The enterprenuring village youth, driven by the urge to conserve their culture and at the same time equipped with entrepreneurial skills, approached the government with a comprehensive project plan with an outlay of Rs. 34 lakhs, out of which Rs. 17 lakhs is the committee's investment. SABCOO Bank, Gangtok offered them a loan of Rs. 17 lakhs.

The broad activities of the project includes the following:

Budget

Table 13.1: Proposed Budget for Rural Tourism at Darap Nambu

Solano	*Activities*	*Cost*
1.	FEASIBILITY STUDY AND PLANNING FRAMEWORK	
1.1	Planning and Feasibility assessments	10,000
1.2	Initial sensitization of Stakeholder	10,000
2.	PRODUCT DEVELOPMENT AND SITE ENHANCEMENT	
2.1	Identification home stay operators	10,000
2.2	Village beautification–garbage/solid-waste management	15,000
2.3	Interpretation and signage in village and trails	20,000
3.	TRAINING CAPACITY BUILDING OF SERVICE PROVIDERS	
3.1	Spoken English	10,000
3.2	Organizational development training	12,000
3.3	Lodge and Home stay operator training	15,000
3.4	Guides training	16,000
3.5	Porters training & cooks training	12,000
3.6	Ecotourism Awareness Training	10,000
3.7	Computer operation and training	10,000
4.	MARKETING AND PROMOTION	
4.1	Market Survey	10,000
4.2	Development of promotional material	30,000
4.3	Exposure Visit	30,000
5.	MONITORING AND EVALUATION	
5.1	Mid-term evaluation	10,000
5.2	Final evaluation	20,000
6.	HUMAN RESOURCE COST	
6.1	Project Coordinator	5,000
6.2	Project Assistant	2,500

7.	**ADMINISTRATIVE COST**	
7.1	Stationery	2,000
7.2	Communication	1,000
8.	**LOCAL TRAVEL & CONVEYANCE**	
8.1	Travel cost	4,000
9.	**INFRASTRUCTURE COST**	
9.1	Village Marketing Centre	
10.	**EQUIPMENTS**	
10.1	Village Telecommunication Centre	

Source: Darap Eco-Tourism Committee.

Results from the Project

The systematic approach, attention on culture, care for environment and the strategy adopted resulted in successful implementation of the project. For instance, the project attracted 500 visitors in the initial year, i.e. 2005, and it rose to already 1070 visitors in the year 2010. Table 13.2 depicts the economy of the project from its inception year to till date.

Table 13.2: Investment on Eco-Tourism

Sl. No.	*Loan from the SABCOO Bank*	*Individual contribution*	*Total Investment*
1.	17,000,00 lakhs	17,000,00 lakhs	34,000,00 lakhs

Source: Darap Eco-Tourism Committee.

Table 13.3: Expenditure Particulars—Eco-Tourism Resorts

Sl. No.	*Year*	*Total no. of Visitors*	*Domestic*	*Foreigners*	*Income*	*Expenditure*	*Net Profit*
1.	2005	500	150	350	5,00,000	2,50,000	2,50,000
2.	2006	651	300	351	6,51,000	3,25,000	3,26,000
3.	2007	781	381	400	7,81,000	3,90,000	3,91,000
4.	2008	821	500	321	8,21,000	4,00,000	4,21,000
5	2009	930	600	330	9,30,000	4,50,000	4,80,000
6.	2010 till date	1070	686	384	10,00,000	5,00,000	5,00,000

Source: Darap Eco-Tourism Committee.

As observed from the information provided, the following important aspects can be derived:

- Dramatic progress in attracting domestic visitors.
- Consistency in attracting foreign visitors.
- Over 100 per cent increase in turn-over within a span of six years.
- Consistency in maintaining 100 per cent net profit against the expenditure incurred.

In other words, the novel idea of village/Rural/Ecotourism project in Darap village is increasing its strength and viability since its inception. Since the project is built on exposure on traditional culture, the tourist traffic is not disturbing their culture as well and this has been the bastion of the project.

Observations on Scope and Threats to the Project in Darap

The village has rich biodiversity and located adjacent to the Khangchendzonga National Park. Though the village has a mixed community, the social cohesion among the different ethnic groups is very strong. The villagers are very excited to have rural tourism development and the newly formed Darap Eco-Tourism Committee is spearheading the movement. The village is rich in agricultural produce with strong Animal husbandry practices. The site is accessible and had remarkable forests and waterfalls. However, due to lack of exposure and remoteness the villagers have been slightly marginalised. Though the village has many Government schools, they all are mostly primary and JHS with only one senior secondary school. Much of the state developmental packages have not reached the village due to its remote location. The young educated youth of the village feel deprived and have a great sense of economic backwardness. However, the village has an opportunity to become self-reliant and develop more employment opportunities for the youngsters. Farming and animal husbandry being the main occupation of the people can be incorporated in the tourism activities, by means of which people can earn the supplementary income. Developing tourism, would also give them a chance to develop their skills required for hospitality and conservation of their culture and environment. Improvement in sanitation facilities can benefit to improve overall standard of living in the village. Exposure with the outside world will give them a chance to improve their knowledge and awareness. With the presence of the Darap Eco-Tourism Committee, the organization can systematically monitor the tourism activities to empower the local people to be involved in innovative mechanisms. Being the tourism representative of the village cluster, infringement of outsiders in the village can be checked. The village has a strong potential to become a successful rural tourism destination, on working to their fullest strength and building upon their opportunities and addressing the threats.

Summary and Conclusion

Darap, a remote village in Sikkim, has shown the world the immense potential of rural tourism and its role in generating employment and economic development in the region. It has also excelled in how a enterprising and enlightened local people can turn the opportunities into great strength in terms of preservation of culture and at the same time utilizing the same for promoting economic development. The project as well earned enough attraction from the visiting tourism just by virtue of show-casing the local 'culture' and 'culture products' to the visiting tourists like pattern of agriculture, local artifacts etc. as an attractive element in promoting rural tourism.

The local Eco-tourism committee too displayed enough entrepreneurship skills by dovetailing its efforts with other business organizations. The novel feature of the project is it has been a successful rural tourism venture without disturbing the local culture and geographical terrain. This has been a rare success in the rural tourism sector which was backed by local wisdom, culture, entrepreneurial skills and the local leadership. If these issues are taken care of elsewhere, rural tourism ventures can be promoted in a quicker manner and provide immense employment opportunities to the local youth.

REFERENCES

Darap Eco-Tourism Committee

Ministry of Tourism and culture, Government of India, Website.http://tourism.gov.in/policy/schrural.htm

Vikas Rikhiye, (2008). http://www.vikasrikhye.com/2008/11/24/rural-tourism-in-india/

SITE PHOTOS

Traditional Cottage
Cherry Village Resort

Yuma Meditation Centre

Darap Cherry Village

Traditional Nepali Dance

Chabrung Dance

Farmer Ploughing the Field

Homestay

Tourists Enjoying Food at Cherry Village Resort

Mountain Scene from Upper Darap

14

Marketing of Ecotourism Destinations

Case of Tripura

Supriya Dam

Introduction

Ecotourism is a global phenomenon in recent years, especially during the early years of twenty-first century. The early definition of ecotourism was coined by the International Ecotourism Society (IES, 1991) which defines it as "responsible travel to natural areas that conserves the environment and sustains the well-being of local people". Ceballos-Lascurain (1996) has given a comprehensive definition on ecotourism which states "ecotourism is environmentally responsible travel to natural areas in order to enjoy and appreciate nature (and accompanying cultural features, both past and present) that promotes conservation, have low visitor impact and provide for beneficially active socio-economic involvement of local people". Similarly, UN World Tourism Organization (WTO) termed it as "travelling to relatively undisturbed natural areas with the specific object of satisfying, admiring and enjoying nature and its wild plants, animals as well as existing cultural aspects (both past and present) found in these areas". According to the data released by the World Tourism Organization (2006), eco-touristic journeys comprised up to 7 per cent (45 million of all journeys), while it is expected that the number will increase up to 70 million per year in 2010. Ceballos-Lascurain (1996) added that the share of ecotourism journeys reaches 20 to 60 per cent of all journeys.

The diversity in geography in India provides a wealth of natural areas that could support ecotourism activities. The natural reserved areas for the tourists include national parks, biosphere reserves, wetlands, mountain areas and forests, coral reefs and mangrove under ecotourism. In this way, the natural reserved areas have been opened for the tourists which include 13 biosphere reserves (to limited extent in outer buffer zone), 89 natural parks and 490 wildlife sanctuaries (MOIB, 2004).

The Government of India, through policy initiatives, has acknowledged the significance of ecotourism with policy measures. Both the Ministry of Tourism and the Ministry of Environment and Forests have responded to the development in the field of ecotourism. The Department of Tourism issued policy and guidelines on ecotourism in July, 1998 (Boora, 2005). In the midst of these developments, several State Governments have also taken policy measures to promote ecotourism. The Government of Himachal Pradesh has announced a "Policy on Development of Ecotourism" in May, 2001 with special focus on local people. The Government of Madhya Pradesh has announced an "Eco and Adventure Tourism Policy" for 2001-02 placing emphasis on the involvement of private sector. The Forest Departments of Kerala, Goa, Karnataka, Himachal Pradesh and Sikkim have designated officials to coordinate ecotourism activities. Several State Governments including Madhya Pradesh, Rajasthan, Karnataka and Andhra Pradesh have issued order for recycling of entry fees from protected areas for conservation and community development. The Forest Corporation of West Bengal and Uttarakhand has initiated ecotourism activities and Govt. of Kerala has launched the Thenmala Ecotourism Promotion Society to develop a model for ecotourism. The State has also taken pioneering step by creating separate directorate for ecotourism. The State of Tripura also joined the bandwagon of ecotourism development by bringing out ecotourism policy for State in 2004. However, it failed to touch upon the issues, which are considered essential for ecotourism development in Tripura.

Objectives

The basic objective of the study is to put forward an integrated marketing programme for tourism development in Tripura in general and ecotourism in particular. The objectives of the study are:

- To spell out tourism marketing-mix;
- To invigorate the issues relating to ecotourism marketing in Tripura; and
- To formulate measures for integrated ecotourism marketing network in the State.

Methodology

The nature of the study call for collection of both primary and secondary data. The secondary data have been collected from books, journals, published reports, and internet publications available for citation. Primary data for the study collected from the spot visits to destinations including observations, consultation with officials from Tripura Tourism Development Corporation (TTDC) Limited which are supplemented by the studies carried out to showcase the plight of ecotourism in the State. Collected data were processed and analysed by using suitable statistical tools as per the need of the study.

The framework of the chapter starts with present status of ecotourism resources in Tripura, including tourist inflows and revenue generation, followed by possible ecotourism marketing-mix for the State. This follows discussion and suggestion for integrated ecotourism marketing network for the State.

Review of Literature

Philip Kotler (1984) has linked marketing with tourism and related tourism products with services, persons, places, organizations and ideas. Tourism is a market driven economy. Marketing is an important function of special interest tourism like ecotourism (Weiler and Hall, 1992). Each of the four 'P's of traditional marketing mix (product, price, place and promotion) has an array of significant nuances when applied to ecotourism. Proper ecotourism marketing is critical to optimize its positive impacts on community, environment, society, culture as well as on the economic front (Magahey, 2012). He further added that "ecotourism marketing requires substantial planning and expertise to achieve its goals. Many of the principles and processes are still evolving as ecotourism continues to grow as an important subset of sustainable tourism and a popular form of special interest tourism".

The awareness and understanding of ecotourism must be created among the community that offers tourism. The greater involvement of the individual and community will attract tourists and benefit from tourism by receiving constant income continuously (Subbiah and Kannan, 2012). Gartner (1996) recognized the dynamic nature of image, investigated the structure and formation of a tourist destination image. In their view, perception of various attributes within a destination will interact to form a composite overall image. Tourists are individual actors that do not simply respond to physical stimuli or individual attributes; tourists define and interpret their world symbolically, assimilating and accommodating information into revised perception of place.

Bauld and Soriya (2006) divulge that, for capitalizing marketing efforts, ecotourism sites will need to be branded to ensure successful positioning in the minds of tourists. Product branding ensures that product is readily identifiable by its consumers. Brand name and brand mark are two elements of this process. A brand name should be way consumers refer to the product. There have been numerous cases where a brand name has become a term by which market refers to a type of product. Developing a brand name will catch the consumers attention and will be retained is key to developing brand loyalty. Within tourism industry, brand loyalty is particularly sought (Hawkins and Lamoureux, 2001). However, the grand scale of ecotourism products around the world, it is often difficult for small scale tourism ventures to be known. Promotion of package tour groups will require the services of inbound operators to promote the diversity of cultural attractions throughout the tourism sites (Bauld and Soriya, 2006).

The capacity building and training has got special attention amongst tourism researchers. Training on front office, house-keeping, tour guiding skills are essential to make tourists satisfied with the service quality of the park. Training should be focused on skill standards to make sure that the park staffs could perform their job upto the expected level of service quality of the job, then, provide tourist satisfaction across the different market segments. Therefore, training need to be on the job, practical and customized to the local conditions of the park (Cuong and Anh, 2010). DeCoursey's (1998) study revealed that training, education and institution building are major components of product development. The recommended activities include observation tour to established destinations; ecotourism working groups to carry-out ecotourism activities; porter union/cooperative; income generation and cultural preservation. Bauld and Soriya (2006) opined that many community based tourism ventures fail due to community's lack of understanding of the tourism distribution system and their ability to capture changing markets. Small scale marketing in the form of advertising in guidebooks and brochures will also assist in promoting community based ecotourism activities in tourism sites.

Ariane (2012) observed that "assessing market potential for ecotourism is not easy. Most available tourism statistics are very general and market surveys that are focused on ecotourism had difficulty in pinpointing market size, as what tourism or tour operators call ecotourism might actually not true to the definition of ecotourism'.

Integrated approach is a new paradigm in public policy and has become an intellectual sense for managing resources and environmental planning to achieve sustainable development of tourism (Hall, 2000). Ecotourism, being small entrepreneurship, impact is smallest but can be successful if integrated with other rural sectors horizontally creating supportive linkages reducing financial leakages. It can be coordinated with agriculture and horticulture in providing marketing for local produce (Hall, 2000; Stone and Wall, 2010). The management of ecotourism is generally carried out through either site management or visitor management. Site management actions rely on manipulating infrastructure, where visitors go and what they do. These include campsite and trail design and management. Visitors' management concentrates on managing visitors by regulating numbers, group size and length of stay. It also provides information and education as well as enforcement of regulations. Ecotourism management includes the incorporation of a number of voluntary strategies such as code of conduct, accreditation and best practices. The strategies employed by government organizations are regulatory in nature includes licensing and leases (Dowling and Fennell, 2003).

In the tourism industry, market segmentation has been applied to overcome the issues of tourist heterogeneity. It is identification of portions of the market that are different from one another. This is about channelizing resources towards potential customers who are not likely to be persuaded to visit the destination fit the profile of the 'type' of customer the destination wants to attract. Geographic, demographic, psychographic and behaviouristic criteria are used for the segments of consumer markets. By having market segmentation, proper marketing strategies can be established for the targeted segments (Penang National Park, Malaysia). Tourists' motivational research aims to identify various types and segments and their preferences for travel decisions of various tourist destinations (McKercher *et al.*, 2002; Jonsson and Devonish, 2008). The present piece of work attempts to spell out ecotourism marketing strategies for industrially starve Indian State like Tripura. The study is descriptive in nature to unleash issues pertaining to marketing of ecotourism products in Tripura.

Status of Ecotourism in Tripura

Having an area of 10491.69 sq. km, Tripura is a landlocked State surrounded by neighbouring country Bangladesh on its North, South and West side. The length of its international border with Bangladesh is 856 km (or 84 per cent of the total border); the rest 16 per cent of its border is shared with Indian States of Assam (i.e. 53 km) and Mizoram (i.e. 109 km). The State is connected with the rest of the country by National Highway No. 44, which passes through Tripura hills to the Karimganj District of South Assam. Apart from these, the State is also having three domestic airports out of which Singerbil Airport at State capital Agartala will be graduated to an international airport in near future.

The State has over 60 per cent of the geographical area under forest cover, out of which about 6 per cent of the area is protected in the form of four wildlife sanctuaries. The typical topography and demography of the State, with a sizeable tribal people from nineteen communities of varied traditions and culture, presents an opportunity for promotion of ecotourism in the State. Seven parallel hill ranges clothed with forests of varying density and a number of rivers dotting the valley with adjoining hill ranges and tribal helmets; provides a perfect landscape for tourists with different tastes and preferences. Innumerable low altitude trekking routes that marked the area can draw adventure loving tourists to venture out for trekking.

Major ecotourism attractions include Sipahijala Wildlife Sanctuary, Neermahal, Tepania Eco Park, Trishna Wildlife Sanctuary, Dumboor Lake, Jampui Hills, Baramura Eco Park, Kalapania Nature Park, Gumti Wildlife Sanctuary, Rowa Wildlife Sanctuary, Khumlung Eco Park etc. have harnessed entire State. State capital Agartala is boasting of the Ujjayanta Palace of Tripura Kings and a major heritage centre along with other historical monuments. Pilak in South Tripura is famous for its archaeological remains of Buddhism belonging to eighth/ninth century. There are a number of places known for Hindu pilgrimage centre like Tripureswari Kali Temple at Udaipur, Kali Temple at Kamalasagar, Shiva Temple at Unakoti etc. spread throughout the State. Glorious history and culture along with unique traditional craftsmanship might propel tourism enthusiasts to visit the State.

The Sipahijala Wildlife Sanctuary is the oldest wildlife sanctuary (WLS) in Tripura. Declared in 1987, the WLS has the prime objective of bio-diversity conservation through education, mass awareness and involvement. Covering an area of 18.53 sq. km, the WLS is safe heaven for seven different kinds of primates, leopard, clouded leopard, civets, binturong, barking deer, wild boar and 100 species of birds. The main attractions of the WLS include nature interpretation centre, eco-village

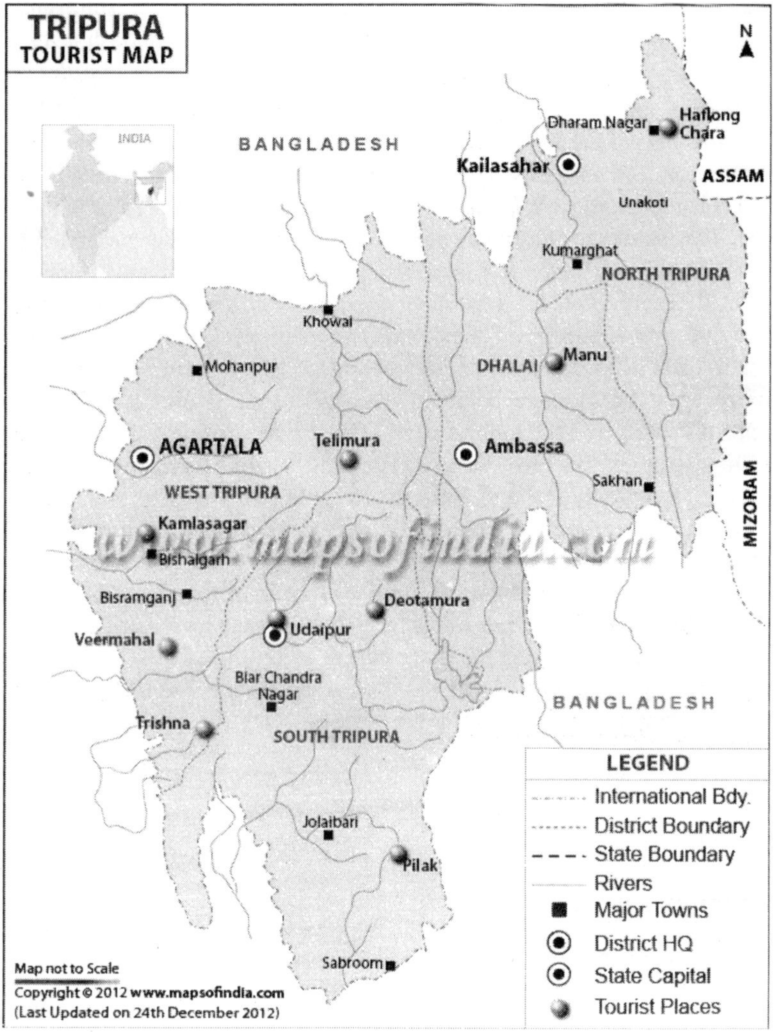

Fig. 14.1: Tourist map of Tripura.

with tree house accommodation, high rise watch tower, eco-park, children joy ride, zoo animals, picnic spots, botanical garden, lake view resort etc. Gomti WLS is the largest WLS in Tripura covering an area of 389.54 sq. km, famous for elephants, bison, samber, barking deer, wild goat, reptiles etc. It is also house of 72 species of trees, 40 species of shrubs,

25 species of grasses, 52 varieties of fauna etc. spread throughout WLS. Trishna WLS is the second largest WLS in the State covering an area of 194.70 sq. km. The sanctuary is well-known for bison locally recognized as 'Gaba' and several species of primates. The floral diversity of the sanctuary is unique and having medicinal value. There are 230 tree species, 400 herbs, 110 shrubs, and 150 climbers present in the sanctuary. Rowa WLS is the smallest WLS in the State overspreading an area of 0.86 sq. km. This sanctuary has some patches of large trees earlier protected by local community it shelters interesting bird life and is becoming popular as bird sanctuary. It is also house of a number of faunal varieties in the form of insects, reptiles, fishes, birds and mammals. Jampui hill range is the highest hill range in Tripura situated in the northern part bordering Mizoram. The average height of this hill range is about 900 metres approximately and the highest peak of the State is located at Betlingshib (992 metres) in this biosphere reserve. Animals like tiger, leopard, deer, gibbon, flying squirrel and endangered birds like pheasant found there. In every November, the Orange and Tourism Festivals are organized in this biosphere reserve.

Fig. 14.2 depicts domestic tourist arrivals in the State during the course of twenty years. The linear trend portrays the increasing inflow of domestic tourists visiting the State during 1992-93 to 2011-12; which is destined to go up in the years to come. On an average, 2,49,428 domestic tourists visited the State during the period.

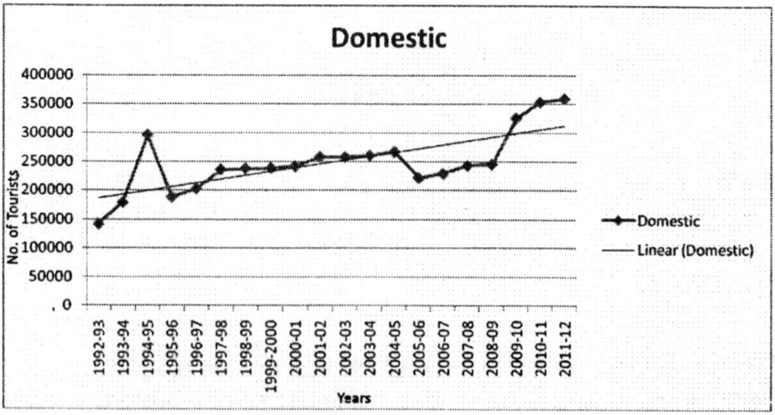

Fig. 14.2: Domestic Tourist Arrivals in Tripura during 1992-93 to 2011-12.
Source: Department of Tourism, Government of Tripura, 2013.

Eco-touristic survey reveals that of the total inflows, 51 per cent of the domestic tourist came from different parts of the state itself while 40 per cent from the rest belong to different regions of India. Amongst these 40 per cent, 17 per cent came from east India, 10 per cent each from north and west India while meager three per cent came from south India (Meena and Das Pan, 2012).

Fig. 14.3 portrays foreign tourist influx in the State during 1992-93 to 2011-12. The linear trend line illustrates that foreign tourist arrivals in the State are on the rise and destined to go up in coming years. The highest inflow is recorded in the year 2011-12 indicates that foreign tourists are gradually interested to visit the State as part of their itinerary. On an average, 2302 foreign tourists visited the state during the course of twenty years. Eco-touristic survey reveals that majority of foreign tourists came from neighbouring country Bangladesh and Himalayan country Nepal (Meena and Das Pan, 2012). The origins of foreign tourists visiting Tripura are not kept in order. However, officials from the Tripura Tourism Development Corporation (TTDC) divulge that foreign tourist arrivals (FTAs) comprise mainly from Bangladesh, Nepal, China, Canada, Germany, UK, USA, Netherland etc.

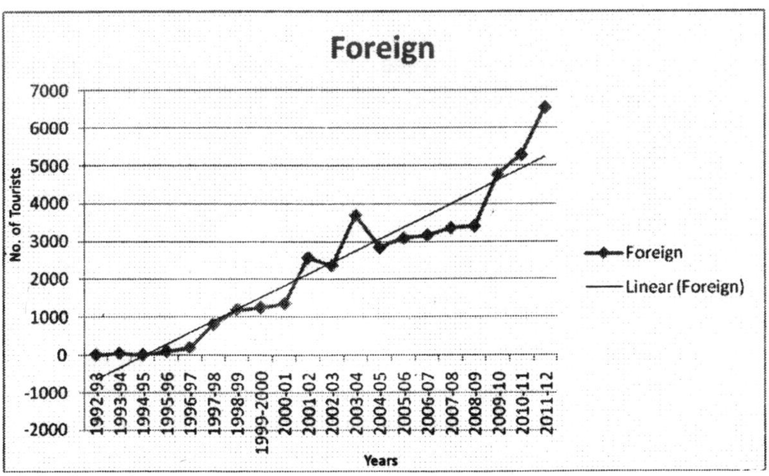

Fig. 14.3: Foreign Tourists visiting Tripura during 1992-93 to 2011-12.
Source: Ibid.

Fig. 14.4 divulges direct revenue generated from tourists during 1992-93 to 2011-12. This direct revenue comprised of room rent and food costs of eight tourist infrastructure maintained by TTDC. Thus, actual

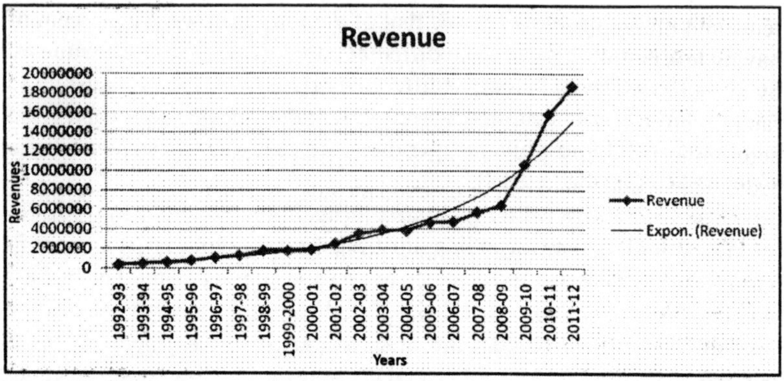

Fig. 14.4. Direct Revenue Generated from Tourists during 1992-93 to 2011-12.
Source: Ibid.

total direct revenue earned, including those from private sector, is much higher than whatever shown in Fig. 14.4. The exponential curve depicts that revenue realization is highest in 2011-12 which destined to go up in near future.

Tourism Marketing Mix

"Ecotourism products require a special environmental setting, one that features an area of pristine natural beauty and has the potential for related activities that appeal to certain type of tourists, known as eco-tourist or eco-traveller" (Wood, 2002). Product development requires discovery of those settings and the permission to operate tour there; either from local people or from local authorities. Whenever possible, ecotourism should highlight existing attractions and activities, and ecotourism facilities should be locally owned, locally operated at human scale. The only development normally required for ecotourism is reasonable access to the destination, provision of basic facilities or better yet, modifications to local ones and the training of local entrepreneurs and staffs in ecotourism principles and management (Magahey, 2012). "Depending on their content and conditions, ecotourism products provide that can be classified along a continuum, ranging from soft ecotourism in one end and to hard ecotourism on the other" (Zalaton and Gaston, 1996). As such, ecotourism has the potential to appeal a wide variety of travellers and add substantial value to a destinations product mix.

The pricing of ecotourism product varies from destination to destination depending on nature of the site. Eco-tourists, who stay in tents and home stays or walk along jungle trails or trek into mountains having less facilities should pay less than mass market tourists; who travel by air conditioned motor coaches, stay in deluxe hotels and visit world famous attractions. Ecotourism products are unable to benefit from economies of scale and which also suffer from seasonality. Some ecotourism experiences can be enjoyed by independent travellers, but most often these are sold in the form of package tours. These tours are all inclusive and thoroughly programmed with little opportunity for participants to deviate from the prepared itinerary. The main concern about pricing of ecotourism products are that these are priced so that operators attract enough customers for the destination to remain viable and stay in business (Magahey, 2012). With the increased interest in ecotourism products, more outbound companies are specializing in packaging, selling and operating ecotourism and adventure tourism products. Since these companies are located in source markets, they require services of local ecotourism companies to provide operational support for the destinations (Wood, 2002).

In case of promotion, only large ecotourism companies are able to print and distribute sales material, advertise in tourism publications or attend travel shows. The internet has become the most cost-effective promotion channel for providing ecotourism enthusiasts worldwide with basic information, contacts, and the means to reserve and pay for their arrangements (Special Report, 2006). Wary consumers who have learned to distrust the ecotourism level wholly rely on the internet to talk to other travellers (Special Report, 2006) and investigate ecotourism credentials (Ketchell, 2007). According to Roth (2011), peer reviewed travel sites have become the dominant influence on travel decisions and social media has become twice as important a source of information as advertising for eco-travellers. The activities of ecotourism associations and Government tourism promotion offices should also be utilized to reach distant market places. However, findings at the World Ecotourism Summit 2002 revealed a basic lack of knowledge of the market and how to reach them (WTO, 2002). The summit also stresses the need for additional public awareness of the concept of ecotourism in both the source markets and the host communities.

Most ecotourism companies are located in source markets and gateway cities, but they are the driving force for the destinations they serve in terms of market development and sales (Wood, 2002). They partner with local communities including authorities, facility managers, ecotourism professionals and staff to create and deliver ecotourism experiences that will satisfy their clients. These companies are external to the destination, but they are critical to its success and sustainability (Magahey, 2012).

Ecotourism certification has the potential to be a powerful marketing tool. For tourism companies, certification provides a seal of quality and authenticity of their products show their commitment for investigating environmental and social impacts; and enable them to market their products more effectively (WTO, 2003). For the distribution system, certification can distinguish which company among various operators a best travel agency, inbound tour operator or incentive planner should contact for services. For individual eco-tourist, it helps identify and select the company they will gain the most from their ecotourism experience (Magahey, 2012).

Site interpretation that translates available attractions into distinctive visitor experience are integral component of ecotourism (Mock and O'Neil, 2012). One of the primary motivation for eco-tourist is the desire to observe and appreciate the nature (Wood, 2002). Site interpretation activities of natural and cultural resources presented in person by trained local guides are among the most effective ways to create visitors' satisfaction (Magahey, 2012). Follows (1991) reported that "quality interpretation and quality tourism go hand in hand. Creating the experience is the key to successful marketing and promotion. The anticipation factor designed by tourism and marketing teams must match the integrity of the natural and cultural values being preserved".

Discussion

Ecotourism marketing hinges on the 'experience' eco-travellers want to enjoy. It does not require luxury facilities along the ecotourism sites. Rather, localized facilities with an aim to distribute earnings among the locals; who are voluntarily engaged in tourism activities. That experience can be natural by means of proper services or human made as in the case of Kerala. The State of Tripura is having a wealth of natural resources, beautiful landscape, historical monuments, palaces, enriched culture, archaeological sites, peace and tranquil atmosphere, devoid of terrorism problems; a perfect setting for growth of ecotourism. However, in the marketing front, the State has lagged behind most of the tourism practicing States" in India. The reason cited for this is geographical isolation coupled with lengthy modes of transportation. But is this the only reason for the State's improper growth of tourism?

Obviously, the State has its share of hindrances in the form of transportational bottleneck; in fact, State Government in general and Central Government in particular are unsuccessful in arranging 'transport corridor facility' for human mobility between Agartala to Kolkata (West Bengal) *via* Dhaka (Bangladesh) in reasonable timeframe. At present luxury buses (twice weekly) are plying between Agartala and Dhaka; such service can be extended to Kolkata to bring tourists (both domestic and foreign) from there. Further, the bus service itself can become a source of attraction for the tourists as it will slot in international experience. Eco-touristic survey (Meena and Das Pan, 2012) reveals that 62 per cent of them have expènditure pattern of around 600 Indian rupees per day per trip to ecotourism sites; a clear indication for budget minded tourists. Obviously, they will prefer cheapest mode of transportation to reach such destinations. To bring them back to Tripura requires cheap and time saving mode of transportation which is possible only if bus services are established between Agartala and Kolkata *via* Dhaka. Although, process is on to materialize such a possibility, but the sooner it is arranged, the better it will be for tourism prospect of Tripura. There is a proposal to extend railway facility between Agartala and Akhaura (Bangladesh); the latter is having rail connectivity with Sylhet and Dhaka. Such a facility will fetch more tourists not only from Bangladesh, but also from other parts of the world.

Survey (Meena and Das Pan, 2012) indicates concentration of tourists—both spot-wise and circuit-wise–overlooking other impoverished destinations. Sipahijala WLS alone accounts for more than 21 per cent of the eco-tourists interviewed followed by Trishna WLS (19%), Jampui (18%) and Tepania Eco-park (16%). Out of which, Sipahijala, Trishna and Tepania belong to South-West Tripura Circuit where State capital is situated. The circuit accounts for 56 per cent of the total tourist surveyed during the period. Amongst the rest, Jampui could attract 18 per cent of the tourist surveyed. The same trend is evinced by district-wise tourists influx during 2006-07 shown in Table 14.1.

Table 14.1 indicates that highest concentration of tourists (both domestic and foreign) in West District followed by South, North, Dhalai in descending order. It indicates tourist preferences for State capital and adjoining areas ignoring other prospective tourist destinations. Tourist inflow in the north district is large because of Jampui and Unakoti. It is heartening to note that 83 per cent of tourists reportedly impressed by ecotourism spots and facilities over there.

Seasonality is another area of concern for tourism stakeholders of

Table 14.1: District wise inflow of tourists in Tripura during 2006-07

Districts	*Foreign Tourists*	*Domestic Tourists*	*Total*
West	2851	168481	171322
South	184	31617	31801
North	142	28739	28881
Dhalai	—	784	784

Source: Department of Information, Cultural Affairs and Tourism, Government of Tripura.

the State. The maximum inflows were recorded in the month of October, followed by December, November, January, September etc. in descending order. Minimum inflows were recorded in the month of July, followed by August, April etc. in ascending order. Tourism seasonality badly affects tourism establishments, especially in ecotourism spots, which are situated in far flung areas. Locales, who are engaged in tourism, look for alternative avenues for earning may switch over to other profession for their sustenance; pave the way for scarcity of tourism service providers (TSPs).

Training need and exposure to established ecotourism spots is of paramount importance for TSPs. Although, Government of Tripura has decided to focus on hospitality management and instructed hotel owners to ensure training upgrades for their staffs at frequent intervals. There is also a proposal to set up Institute of Hotel Management in the State and necessary fund for infrastructure have been arranged. But the State lacks installed basic training facilities for TSPs, for especially those who are engaged in ecotourism. Interpretation is a vital component of ecotourism service providers. With the exception of Agartala, Sipahijala as well as adjoining areas, such services are almost non-existent in Tripura. Similarly, signages needs immediate attention and upgradation on the part of stakeholders in distant tourism destination.

Dissemination of right information is key to successful marketing of tourism products. It can influence decision of independent travellers on the one hand and package tour operators on the other. At present, tourist information centres at Agartala, Kolkata as well as Tripura house situated in New Delhi and North-East India catering to this service. There is also an internet site maintained by TTDC along with toll free tourist help line. Further, tourism brochures are also distributed on a limited scale destined for prospective tourism. However, most often than not, such information could not reach the needed ones. There is no interactive tourism site available as yet and the dissemination programmes unleashed by stakeholders are far from satisfactory.

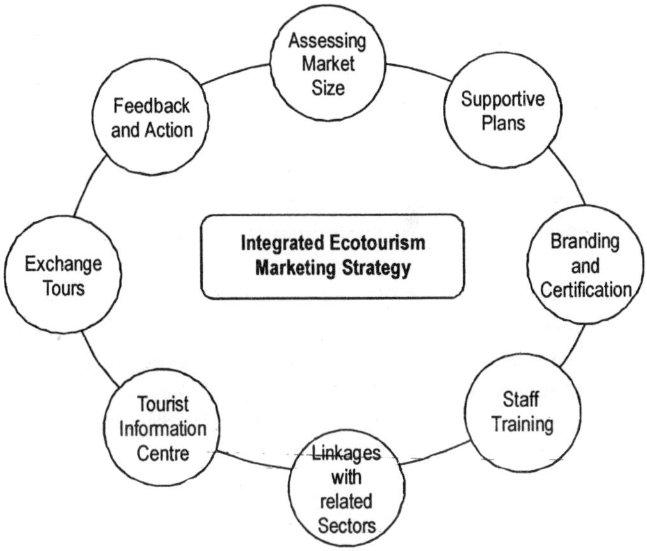

Fig. 14.4: Integrated Eco-tourism Marketing Strategy for Tripura
Source: Author's own.

Market segmentation is another tool to draw attention of tourism based on different stratum. It requires proper analysis of geographic, demographic, psychographic and behaviour of tourists' skims the market. Merely planning to bring foreign tourists from other North-East Indian States will serve no purpose. It requires a well thought out plans in the form of master plans and executing it with utmost sincerity. The existing perspective plan is out-dated which needs immediate revision. Conducted/ package tours are another aspect of tourism promotion, the State authorities has taken some steps to implement it. The TTDC has enlisted few local tour operators catering to this service. However, there is no international framework or tie ups visible among the tour operators; thus minimizing the chance of promoting package tours from abroad.

The above discussion points to an integrated marketing network for the State as a whole which will bring tourists in the one hand and promote other related sectors on the other.

Conclusion

Fig. 14.4 presents schematics of integrated ecotourism marketing strategy for Tripura. Initially, assessment of market size comes to the fore. It can be evaluated from minute appraisal of origin of tourist inflows (both domestic and foreign) for the last decade or so and proper evaluation of ecotourism resources. For example, domestic tourism market has not been fully prospered in the State so that it can compensate loss suffered from less number of inflows of foreign tourists. Survey (Meena and Das Pan, 2012) reveals that, out of 91 per cent of the domestic tourists' inflow, 51 per cent came from different region of the State itself; while rest came from other regions of India, is an indication which should be looked into. Availability of tourism resources points to the fact that Tripura has abundant ecotourism, heritage, and pilgrimage (both Buddhism and Hinduism) tourism resources to draw tourists from this segment. The State is yet to come out with a master plan for tourism development supportive each and every segment. The line of authority for performing a particular job should be clearly defined in the plans and policy guidelines.

Branding is a specialized job which requires professional expertise along the line in which protected areas are promoted. Site certification can also be arranged from the available professional bodies engaged in this field of activity. Staff training is a highly specialized job which requires expertise on the part of service providers. Capacity building programme should be arranged in the State itself so that it caters the service as and when need arises.

Tripura tourism has the potential to link it with fishery, agriculture and rubber plantation. Local handicraft industry can also be promoted by showcasing it in international tourism festivals and trade fairs, both in India and abroad. Tourist information centres (TICs) for Tripura tourism has been developed on a limited scale and not covered major airports and trade centres; so, such centres can be opened with the authority to arrange package from there.

Tour exchange programme by involving operators from national level and abroad is essential to bring 'high end' visitors from source countries. 'High end' visitors will spent more for realistic 'ecotourism experience' by extending overnight stays in the destination; which invariably will bring foreign exchange for the State. Lastly, feedback is regularly sought to take notice of developments and corrective actions whenever needed.

The State of Tripura is evenly poised to accept this challenge; however, further research should be carried out to pin-point the linkages and collaborative efforts, which are considered essential to realize such feat.

REFERENCES

Ariane, J. (2012). "Assessing the Market for Ecotourism in the Brazilian Amazon with focus on TEFE and Santarem", *UAKARI*, 8(2): 7-25, Special Issue: Sustainable Tourism.

Bauld, S. and Soriya, Y. (2006). *An Ecotourism Assessment of the Steung Treng Ramsar Site,* Steung Treng Province, Cambodia, Mekong Wetland Diversity.

Boora, S.S. (2005): "Ecotourism and Environmental Sustainability in India", *Bulletin of the National Institute of Ecology,* 15: 249-258.

Ceballos-Lascurain, H. (1996): *Tourism, Ecotourism and Protected Areas: The State of Nature Based Tourism around the World and Guidelines for its Development*, Gland, Switzerland: The World Conservation Union (IUCN), North Bennington, Vermount: The Ecotourism Society.

Cuong, N.D.H. and Anh, T.T. (2010). Market Survey for Developing Potential CBET Products and Services in Bidoup–Mui Ba, Prepared for WWF, Vietnam: Hanoi.

Dowling, R.K. and Fennell, D.A. (2003). "The Concept of Ecotourism Policy and Planning". In D.A. Fennell and R.K. Dowling (eds.) *Ecotourism Policy and Planning*, CAB International, pp. 1-20.

Follows, D. (1991). "The Role of Resource Interpretation in Alaska's Heritage Tourism Industry". In R. Tobata, J. Yamashiro and G. Cheron (eds.) *Proceedings of Heritage Interpretation, Intellectual Third Global Congress: Joining Hands for Quality Tourism,* Honolulu, H.A.: University of Hawaii Sea Grant Extension Service, pp. 117-120.

Gartner, W.C. (1996). *Tourism Development, Principles, Processes and Policies,* John Wiley & Sons, Inc.: New York.

Hall, C. (2000): "Rethinking Collaboration and Partnership: A Public Policy Perspective". In B. Bramwell and B. Lane (eds.) *Tourism Collaboration and Partnerships, Policies, Practice and Sustainability*, Channel View: Clevendon, pp. 143-159.

Hawkins, D.E. and Lamoureux, K. (2001). Development of Competitive Ecotourism Products for Rila and Central Balkan Pilot Sites—Manual for Entrepreneurs and Small Business Operators, ARD/BCEG Project funded by US AID and Government of Bulgaria.

Jonsson, C. and Devonish, D. (2008). "Does Nationality, Gender and Age affect Travel Motivation? A Case of Visitors to the Caribbean Island of Barbados", *Journal of Travel and Tourism Marketing*, 25(3): 398-408.

Katchel, M. (2007). "Rally Cry to Green Tourism". *The Courier Mail (Australia)*, Nationwide News Pvt. Ltd., 18.

Magahey, S. (2012). "Ethics, Obligations and Stakeholders of Ecotourism Marketing", *Intellectual Economics*, Vol. 6, No. 2, pp. 232-44.

Market Segmentation in Ecotourism, Penang National Park, Malaysia.

McKercher, B., Ho, P., du Cross, H., and So-Ming, B. (2002). "Activity Based Segmentation of Cultural Tourism Markets", *Journal of Travel and Tourism Marketing*, 12: 23-46.

Meena, B.L. and Das Pan, N. (2012): A Study of Ecotourism Potential in Tripura, North East India, *Indian Stream Research Journal*, Vol.1, Issue V, June, pp. 1-4.

Ministry of Information and Broadcasting (MOIB) (2004): India 2004—A Reference Annual Publication Division, MOIB, GOI, New Delhi.

Roth, T. (2011). *Second Annual Green Traveller Report*, San Francisco, C.A.: CMI Green/Community Marketing.

Special Report (2006). *Travel Marketing*. September, 1, Retrieved on 23rd May, 2013 from: http//www. bandt.com.au.

Stone, M.J. and Wall, G. (2010). "Ecotourism and Community Development: Case Studies from Hainan, China", *Environmental Management*, Faculty of Environmental Studies, University of Waterloo, Ontario, 78.

Subbiah, K. and Kanner, S. (2011). "The Management Strategies of Ecotourism Development in Papua New Guinea", *International Journal of Economics, Business and Management Studies,* 1(3): 114-120.

Weiler, B. and Hall, C. (1992). *Special Interest Tourism,* London: Belhaven Press.

Wood, M. (2002). *Ecotourism: Principles, Practices and Policies for Sustainability*, Paris: UNEP.

WTO (2002). *The World Ecotourism Summit Final Report*, Madrid: WTO.

WTO (2003). *Recommendation to Governments for Supporting and/or Establishing National Certification System Sustainable Tourism*, Madrid: Spain.

Zalaton, A. and Gaston, A. (1996). "Soft Tourism: The Substitution Effect", *Tourism Review*, 51(4): 42-48.

15

The HOLSAT Approach to Destination Satisfaction at Kumarakom Backwaters

Tejil Thomas and *M.A. Joseph*

Introduction

Kumarakom backwaters offers the tourist one of the most incredible tour destinations for pleasure and holiday enjoyments in Kerala. This backwater destination is made up of interconnected waterways, rivers, lakes and bays. It has a unique ecosystem that perfectly blends scenic beauty, soothing climate, traditional waterways travel on houseboats and delicious spicy foods for both foreign and inland tourists—a wonderful experience of an aquatic life. The village of Kumarakom is a cluster of little islands on the Vembanad Lake, and this small water world is part of the tranquil Kuttanad region with lots of coconut trees and shallow waterways. This enchanting backwater destination offers visitors many leisure options like boating, sightseeing and fishing facilities. Holiday packages on the Houseboats, traditional Kettuvallams provide a fabulous experience to tourists. Kumarakom is a beautiful place with a variety of flora and fauna where the natural bird sanctuary is offering a great experience for ornithologists. Many species of birds find shelter in the Bird Sanctuary. Moreover, Kumarakom backwater tourism hub is gaining a strategic place on the tourist map due to its natural charm and aesthetic beauty. The tropical specialities, natural beauty, days at houseboats, spicy foods, Ayurveda and soothing climatic conditions give an unforgettable journey to the tourists. In addition, the backwater destination is a dearest place for domestic tourists for holiday enjoyments and leisure irrespective of seasonable factors. They offer countless support for the tourism industry during the off season too. Therefore, it is advantageous to know about their expectation and experience on various destinations-attributes at Kumarakom to chalk out development strategies and remedial measures to provide them superior facilities and services.

Review of Literature

The HOLSAT Model (Tribe & Snaith, 1998) was used for assessing tourist satisfaction on various destination attributes. (Truong, T.H., & Foster, D., 2006)[7] reviewed the value of HOLSAT Model as a means of identifying tourists' satisfaction with a holiday destination. It proved to be easy to apply and a useful diagnostic tool that can be used in the future planning and management of the tourism industry, enabling wholesale and retail travel agents to improve levels of service and develop appropriate products to meet the expectations of the travel market. The tourist satisfaction is assessed from the results of a comparative process between experiences of holiday attributes in comparison with the expectations of those attributes. (V.J. Patil, 2009)[8] assessed the level of satisfaction of tourist and their views about various facilities provided to them at the destination and to identify the area requiring special attention. The tourist and residents of the destination can play a major role in this regard because mostly these two parties frequently come into contact, which will increase the popularity of the destination. It is found that there is a general dissatisfaction about accommodation and parking facilities. Recreational facilities needed to be expanded as the present places of recreation become overcrowded during peak season. (Aksu, A., İçigen, E.T., and Ehtiyar, R. 2010)[1] described that every satisfied tourist potentially will be revisiting the region and will be an ambassador of the region through "mouth to mouth publicity". Developing local means of transportation, improving cultural and artistic activities, increasing interaction between tourists and local population, increasing sports activities, conformity to hygienic rules, giving updated, detailed and correct information and developing the infrastructure of tourism destinations, are vital in tourism development. Today's world, feeling safe or having a perception of safety is very important and a key competitive advantage over rival destinations. (Ming fang, 2011)[4] evaluated inbound tourists' satisfaction using a comprehensive Tourist Satisfaction Index (TSI) system. High tourist satisfaction is likely to contribute benefit to not only tourism goods/service providers, but also local governments and residents. The overall satisfaction of the tourists was influenced by their experience with tourist related public sectors and retail shops most. (S. Sivesan, 2012)[6] found out the relationship between heritage attributes and satisfaction of tourist by evaluating heritage attributes through the variables of tourist package, style of historical building, cultural village, and entertainment. Strong positive correlations were available between tourist satisfaction and tour package and also other heritage attributes such as style of historical building, cultural village and entertainment. (Homsud & Samransart, 2012)[2] observe as that satisfaction was less than expected in historic places, people, architecture, religious place, cultural place, handicraft, activities, shopping place, souvenir, and toilet, while satisfaction was more than expected to travel to historic towns, travel in historic town, expense, drink, food, and local food. Moreover, satisfaction did not differ significantly from expectation in direction sign, monument, museum, information centre, art gallery, scenery, atmosphere, and climate. Another point, which should be considered, is shops and souvenir shops, which are the crucial factor to increase income to communities and help create the sustainable development. (Kuriakose, 2012)[3] analysed the satisfaction level of tourists relating to the backwater tourism in Alleppey and to get the perception, experience and expectations of tourists about the destination and the facilities. The success of backwater tourism depends on the level of facilities available in the houseboat. The tourists should take into account the various factors in terms of facilities; local attractions etc., before choosing their destination. The absence of any of these facilities may discourage them from travelling to enjoy the attractions of backwaters in Kerala. (Siby Zacharias, 2008)[5] studied the effect of backwater tourism on the environment and the use of Kettuvalloms of tourists arriving at the backwaters of Kerala. The inflow of tourist in backwaters of Kerala has generated social, cultural, economic and environmental problems. It is found that the local people are actually facing the problems of waste, plastic deposit, increase in the price of food items due to demand from the part of rich customers, decrease in the cultural and moral values as perceived by them. The available literatures on customer satisfaction pointed out that the gap score between experience and expectation depicts the level of tourist satisfaction. It is very hard to find such a study analysed the tourists' expectation and experience of the destination attributes at Kumarakom backwaters.

The Statement of the Problem

Backwaters are always a point of attraction for pleasure and holiday enjoyments and the most sought after theme of tourism in Kerala for relaxation and enjoyments by domestic tourists. The contribution of this segment of tourism to the state exchequer is remarkable. It has the potential to give tourists an enchanting experience. As per the reviews of tourists in "Trip Advisor" the world's largest travel site, Kumarakom backwater provides a fantastic experience through cruising on a houseboat. They had an awesome visit. Travellers consider days at backwaters are just as a dream and something unique in all Kerala. They feel that this is the heaven on earth refreshing their mind and body. However, there are some allegations against backwaters in Kerala. One of the major issues is the cost of availing the facilities because of greedy promoters and agents. Security issues, disturbance from insects and mosquitoes, rush in houseboats, lack of public toilet facilities are some serious problems they face during their days at these backwater destinations ("Trip Advisor"). In this situation, this chapter makes an attempt to unearth fact whether the domestic tourists' experience exceeds expectation on the facilities, tourism products and services.

Objectives of the Study

In lieu of the problem, the chapter intends to achieve the following objectives:

1. To assess the level of domestic tourist satisfaction on various destination attributes at Kumarakom backwaters.
2. To identify the major factors motivating the tourist to select Kumarakom backwater destination.

Description of the Study Area

The coverage of the study is limited to the assessment of the level of domestic tourists' satisfaction on various attributes of Kumarakom backwater destination. It concentrates on the five dimensions of the HOLSAT model developed by Tribe and Snaith (1998) for measuring the gap score of expectation and experience of holiday-makers at Kumarakom Backwaters region. This chapter is an attempt to trace out the factors influencing the tourists to select Kumarakom backwater destination and identify constraints to be overcome by the destination.

Methodology

The study is a descriptive research as it is a fact-finding study and based on the assessment of the degree of satisfaction on the various destination-based attributes by applying the dimensions of HOLSAT model. The accessible population for the study is the domestic tourists who visit Kumarakom backwater destination; Kottayam that includes a sample of 80 respondents who visited and stayed at various resorts and hotels there. The sample was drawn from the accessible population through convenience sampling method as the exact size of the population is unknown. The required data were collected from both primary as well as secondary sources. The primary data were collected from first time domestic tourists by administering a detailed questionnaire. The secondary data were collected from Journal Articles, Existing literature, websites etc. The analysis of the data and interpretation of the result was made with the help of SPSS 16.0 software.

Variables and Model Used

Tourist satisfaction is the dependent variable of this study. Meanwhile, the independent variables are the dimensions of HOLSAT Model developed by Tribe and Snaith (1998) like Attractions, Activities, Accessibility, Accommodation and Amenity. The HOLSAT Model (Tribe & Snaith, 1998) was used for assessing tourist satisfaction on various destination attributes. The HOLSAT is a new model that attempts to address the complexity of measuring tourist satisfaction with a destination. Tribe and Snaith (1998) developed this model and used it to evaluate holiday satisfaction in the popular resort area of Varadero Cuba. This model defines tourist satisfaction as the degree to which a tourist assessment of the attributes of that destination exceeds his or her expectations for those attributes. The peculiarity of the model is its ability to measure a tourist satisfaction with their holiday experience at a destination rather than a specific service provider. The HOLSAT model administered a questionnaire where in respondents are asked to rate the expectation of each holiday attribute and to rate the experience or performance on the same set of attributes following the holiday experience. A Likert scale was used to score each attribute for both states. Mean scores for each attribute determines for both expectation and for experience. The difference between the mean expectation and experience scores for each attribute gives a quantitative measure of the level of satisfaction shown by the tourists.

Results of the Study

The demographic descriptions of the sample collected (n=80) show that

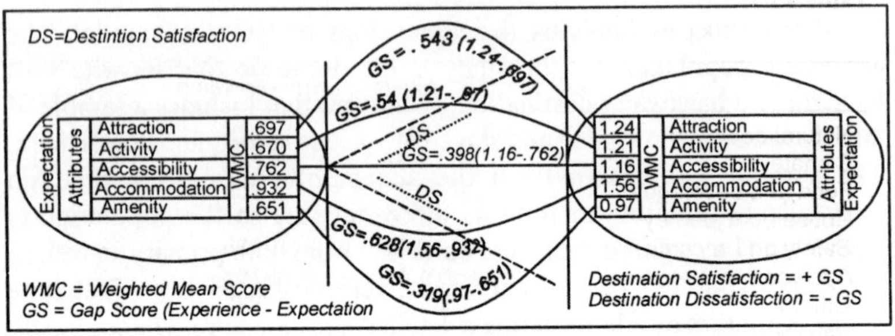

Fig. 15.1: Proposed theoretical model of the application of HOLSAT in Kumarakom Backwaters.

Source: Primary Data.

65 per cent of the respondents are male. Most of the tourists (70%) are below the age of 45. A considerable per cent of tourists (38%) are students, (23%) are professionals and others are from business and allied activities. The main purpose of visit is for pleasure and relaxation. Most of them (78%) are spending up to 3 days at these destinations.

Application of the HOLSAT Attributes

For applying the HOLSAT model, the respondents were asked to describe their expectation and experience of 'attraction', 'activities', 'accessibility', 'accommodation' and 'amenity' (Tribe and Snaith, 1998) before and after visiting in Kumarakom backwater destinations using a five point scale. The questionnaire was administered only once among first time visitors after their travel had been completed, because of the difficulty of getting the responses and maintaining contact with them before and after visiting the destination. The gap scores of the expectation and experience of domestic tourists on various holidays-attributes and dependency of responses were ascertained with the help of descriptive statistics and Wilcoxon test respectively.

Major Findings and Discussion

The natural beauty of Kerala and climatic condition are the main factors behind the selection of Kumarakom Backwaters as a destination for pleasure and holiday enjoyments. They were being ranked as the main factors for selecting a destination (mean score 6.35 and 5.07 respectively). Kumarakom backwater is gifted with fascinating natural beauty and is

Table 15.1: Descriptive Statistics-Factors Influencing the Selection of Kumarakom Backwaters

	Mean	*Std. Deviation*	*Rank*
Natural beauty	6.35	1.075	1
Climate	5.07	1.228	2
Food and beverages	4.23	1.209	4
House boat journey	4.20	1.381	5
Safety and security	2.68	1.185	6
Ayurvedic treatment	4.47	1.754	3
Others	1.00	.000	7
Valid N (list-wise)			

Source: Primary data.

bestowed with a pleasant and tranquil climate throughout the year which attracts a number of domestic tourists every year. It gives real joyful days under the cloudy sky, refreshing scent of the wet soil for revitalizing the body, mind and soul. Kerala's own Ayurvedic treatments have high demand in the tourism industry as the tourist want to treat their body through harmless means, i.e. harmonising with the nature. The success of backwater tourism depends on the level of facilities available in the houseboat (Kuriakose, 2012). Spicy foods and enchanting house boat journey gives an unforgettable experience to the visitors at Kumarakom backwater region. Feeling safe or having a perception of safety is very important and a key competitive advantage over rival destinations (Akin Aksu, 2010). It is not an issue at Kumarakom as it is a calm and quiet place suitable for spending holidays in an ecstatic manner.

Kumarakom is a popular backwater destination with many attractive features. Tourists come to see and enjoy the eye catching natural beauty, experience the tranquil climatic conditions, visit the bird sanctuary, relish the delicious dishes of Kerala and to rejuvenate themselves through Kerala's own Ayurvedic treatments. The HOLSAT result depicts that domestic tourists' experience on various elements of attraction exceeds their expectation level, i.e., they are satisfied with the attractions of Kumarakom backwater destinations. The Wilcoxon test result also substantiates the significant difference between their impressions before and after travel for holiday enjoyments. The clean and hygienic destinations, occasions to experience culture and traditions, tasty and spicy foods, safety and security mechanism at Kumarakom are always highlighted to capture attention of tourists. The backwater offers a peaceful atmosphere free from disturbances of beggars and street vendors and is capable of giving an enchanting experience to those who want to enjoy their holidays.

Table 15.2: Attractions-Expectation V/s Experience

	Descriptive Statistics				*Gap*	*Wilcoxon Test*	
	Expectation		*Experience*			Z	Asymp. Sig. (2-tailed)
	Mean	*SD*	*Mean*	*SD*			
Natural beauty of Kumarakom is attractive	.97	.423	1.65	.483	.68	–4.508a	.000
Climate condition would be enjoyable	.97	.480	1.57	.501	.60	–4.179a	.000
I would be able to see bird sanctuary at Kumarakom	.62	.540	1.30	.516	.68	–4.354a	.000
There would not be rush at this destination	.15	.864	.48	1.26	.33	–2.427a	.015
The destination would be clean and hygienic	.62	.628	1.28	.506	.66	–4.245a	.000
There would be no disturbance from beggars and street vendors.	.05	.316	.45	.639	.40	–3.578a	.000
There would be adequate security and safety at Kumarakom backwaters	.82	.636	1.40	.496	.58	–4.413a	.000
I would get ample opportunities to experience the culture and traditions at this destination	.77	.530	1.30	.464	.53	–4.001a	.000
There would be many opportunities for Ayurvedic treatment	.98	.577	1.42	.549	.44	–3.819a	.000
I would be able to enjoy tasty and spicy food and beverages of Kerala at this destination.	1.02	.530	1.55	.504	.53	–4.185a	.000

Source: Primary data.

It is always a delightful experience to tourists to take part in the activities at tourist destinations that they visit. This is considered as an effort to learn and mingle with the specialities to fetch maximum pleasure from backwater experiences. Such an experience of involving is capable of carving long lasting memories in the minds of tourists. No one can forget the amazing experience of the house-boat journey on the ripples of the lakes to explore the beauty of the backwaters and its surroundings.

Table 15.3: Activities—Expectation *V/s* Experience

	Descriptive Statistics				Gap	Wilcoxon Test	
	Expectation		*Experience*			*Z*	*Asymp. Sig. (2-tailed)*
	Mean	*SD*	*Mean*	*SD*			
I would be able to get pleasure from indoor and outdoor games at Kumarakom backwater Destination	.45	.552	1.10	.496	.65	–4.564a	.000
I would be able to get pleasure from the backwaters of Kumarakom	.90	.441	1.63	.490	.73	–4.874a	.000
I would be able to get memorable house boat journey through lakes/rivers	1.00	.506	1.70	.464	.70	–4.613a	.000
Sunset viewing and sea bath at beaches would be comfortable	.15	.362	.41	.637	.26	–2.500a	.012
I would be able to get an unforgettable sightseeing at different destinations in Kumarakom.	.85	.427	1.20	.516	.35	–2.952a	.003

Source: Primary data.

The descriptive statistics disclosed that the domestic tourists had a fabulous experience on sightseeing, sea bath and other recreations at this heaven on earth. Destination marketing organisations are keen to arrange indoor and outdoor games at Kumarakom backwater destinations as they are the best means for relaxing tourists' body and mind through physical as well as intellectual exercises.

All endeavours to market tourist attractions, products and services will be vain unless it is accessible to tourist at reasonable fares and comfortable means. The availability of proper national and local transportation faciiities with greater safety at affordable charges is inevitable for enabling the accessibility of a tourist destination. The gap scores state that Kumarakom backwaters provide better transport facilities at reasonable rates and ensure availability of sufficient number of air, train and bus tickets according to tourists' preference as and when they want

Table 15.4: Accessibility—Expectation *V/s.* Experience

	Descriptive Statistics				*Gap*	*Wilcoxon Test*	
	Expectation		*Experience*			*Z*	*Asymp. Sig. (2-tailed)*
	Mean	*SD*	*Mean*	*SD*			
Checking and clearance would be fast and efficient	.27	.452	.88	.335	.61	–4.899a	.000
I would be able to get national air, train and bus tickets when I want to visit Kumarakom	.90	.441	1.25	.494	.35	–3.500a	.000
I would be able to get the products and service at affordable prices	.40	.496	.83	.446	.43	–3.900a	.000
There would be proper transportation facilities in Kumarakom	.92	.350	1.25	.439	.33	–3.153a	.002
I would be able to use local transportation facilities at reasonable rates	.48	.506	.92	.417	.44	–4.025a	.000
I would be easy to reach the destinations Kumarakom region	1.05	.320	1.50	.506	.45	–4.025a	.000
I would be safe while travelling	1.03	.362	1.28	.456	.25	–2.887a	.004
I would be able to get necessary information about Kerala Tourist Destinations and various facilities available there	1.05	.450	1.35	.483	.30	–3.207a	.001

Source: Primary data.

to visit this destination. The contribution of information centres at the backwater destination in disseminating detailed information about the peculiarity of the destination, various facilities, products and services is remarkable to direct the tourists to have an outstanding tour of this romantic place. In addition, waiting in long queues for clearance and checking at aerodromes and other check-posts is generally a dreary matter while travelling to somewhere else. But, the tourists at Kumarakom had a different experience than the usual.

Table 15.5 : Accommodation—Expectation *V/s* Experience

	Descriptive Statistics				*Gap*	*Wilcoxon Test*	
	Expectation		*Experience*			*Z*	*Asymp. Sig. (2-tailed)*
	Mean	*SD*	*Mean*	*SD*			
I would be able to get a hotel/resort reservations when I want to visit Kumarakom	1.10	.304	2.18	3.08	1.08	–4.811a	.000
I would be able to get superior/deluxe/Standard rooms etc. according to my preference	1.10	.379	1.57	.501	.47	–4.359a	.000
Rooms would be well furnished, equipped and clean	1.03	.480	1.60	.496	.57	–4.104a	.000
I would be able to get an accommodation facility in calm and quiet atmosphere	.92	.572	1.70	.464	.78	–4.803a	.000
I would get most privacy and safety in my accommodation facility	.87	.516	1.67	.474	.80	–5.166a	.000
I would be able to get adequate room services as and when I need it	.85	.533	1.47	.506	.62	–4.291a	.000
I would be able to get an outstanding dining experience from Kerala dishes	.97	.480	1.47	.506	.50	–3.879a	.000
Cost of accommodation, food and beverages would be cheap	.62	.490	.85	.427	.23	–2.496a	.013

Source: Primary data.

The accommodation facilities at Kumarakom assure the tourists a separate destination and a unique holiday experience itself. It clubs modern and traditional architectural sonata to extend the pleasure of the traditional hospitality of Kerala. The properties at this destination offer reservations ranging from well furnished, equipped and clean deluxe rooms to budget rooms in calm and quiet atmosphere with utmost privacy and security according to their preference. The Resorts and Hotels provide a homely experience away from home by giving an outstanding dining experience

Table 15.6 : Amenity–Expectation *V/s* Experience

	Descriptive Statistics				*Gap*	*Wilcoxon Test*	
	Expectation		*Experience*			*Z*	*Asymp. Sig. (2-tailed)*
	Mean	*SD*	*Mean*	*SD*			
I would be able to get a detailed itinerary from my Destination Manager	.75	.439	1.00	.000	.25	–3.162a	.002
I would get proper insurance, medical care and medicines	.44	.502	.87	.404	.43	4.123a	.000
I would be able to get the local history, geographical, historical and other significances of the places which I intended to visit	.68	.474	1.02	.357	.34	–3.742a	.000
There would not be the problem of the availability of Multilanguage guide service	.70	.564	1.03	.357	.33	–3.606a	.000
I would be able to obtain the banking services at the destinations	.93	.417	1.22	.423	.29	–3.464a	.001
There would be bona fide information Centres at Tourist Destinations to provide me genuine Information and instructions to have a safe and comfortable tour	.75	.543	1.07	.350	.32	–3.606a	.000
I would be able to get my complaints and grievances redressed	.57	.594	1.15	.362	.58	–4.600a	.000
I would get whole-hearted support from Police and other law and order bodies and arrangements	.13	.335	.62	.490	.49	–4.264a	.000
There would be a full-fledged front office to help me to get information relating to accommodation, F&B, billing, clearance etc.	.90	.591	1.53	.506	.63	–4.630a	.000
I would be able to get proper facility to keep my valuables under safe custody	1.12	.516	1.55	.552	.43	–3.900a	.000
I would get proper entertainment facilities	.70	.608	1.30	.516	.60	–4.707a	.000

(Contd.)

	Descriptive Statistics				*Gap*	*Wilcoxon Test*	
	Expectation		*Experience*			*Z*	*Asymp. Sig. (2-tailed)*
	Mean	*SD*	*Mean*	*SD*			
I would be able to shop in the local market/business centres	.40	.545	.95	.504	.55	–4.491a	.000
I would be able to use my Credit cards at purchasing centres	.82	.385	1.10	.496	.28	–3.051a	.002
The local public would have a very supportive attitude	.32	.474	.78	.423	.46	–3.838a	.000
There would be ease of using phoning, internet and Wi-Fi facilities	1.10	.441	1.47	.506	.37	–3.638a	.000
There would be adequate public toilet facilities	**.10**	**1.17**	**–1.10**	**.928**	**–1.2**	**3.697b**	**.000**

Source: Primary data.

of Kerala cuisines at their own rooms at a cheaper cost with greater quality. The outcome of the Wilcoxon test proves the substantial difference between the level of expectation and experience of domestic tourists on various attributes related to accommodation at Kumarakom.

Infrastructural development plays a crucial role in the promotion and marketing of a tourist destination. The success of backwater tourism depends on the level of facilities available in the houseboat (Kuriakose, 2012) and destinations. The absence of these facilities may discourage them from travelling to enjoy the attractions of backwaters. In order to complete a tour successfully within the stipulated time and resources, the tourists will demand for a detailed itinerary from the destination marketers prior to the fixation of the mutual terms and conditions of their deal. The result depicts that tourists in Kumarakom backwater regions were able to get detailed plan to travel from their travel agents and tour operators. The collective responsibility of both the organized and unorganized destination management organizations in the Kumarakom region to arrange proper medical and insurance provisions for tourists' life protection was met satisfactorily. Availability of Multilanguage local guide service is always a concern of tourists when they want to visit a place away from their home country. Descriptions and narrations of local culture, traditions, geography and historical significances of the destinations in their own mother tongue are significant to cover up the scope of the trip with an exact sense of experience. Well trained tourist guides are available at Kumarakom backwater destinations to assist the tourists in completing their trip most successfully. Domestic tourists are of the opinion that banking and credit facilities for safe money handling and exchange transactions, grievance handling mechanism for solving tourists' problems, cloakroom facilities for keeping valuable under safe custody while travelling, internet, phoning and information facilities to keep them away from loneliness, and shopping facilities to make available Kerala's own spices, handicrafts and other traditional products are above their level of expectation. But, it is important to note that the tourists are dissatisfied with the public toilet facilities at different destinations in Kumarakom region. This is the only one factor where the tourists have a negative impression.

Conclusion

In summary, the extracts of HOLSAT model applied in Kumarakom backwaters portray that the destination experience exceeded the level of expectation. Backwater tourism can be considered as a productive strategy for social as well as economic development of Kumarakom region. It is blessed with a number of backwater destination with high potentials to carve remarkable contributions to the state exchequer. The abstract of findings states that natural beauty, climate conditions, house boat journey and Ayurveda are the main factors influencing domestic tourists to have a trip to Kumarakom Backwaters.

REFERENCES

1. Aksu, A.; İçigen, E.T.; and Ehtiyar, R. (2010). A comparison of tourist expectations and satisfaction: A case study from Antalya region of Turkey. *TURIZAM International Scientific Journal*, 14(2): 66-77.
2. Homsud, N., & Samransart, T. (2012). Expectation and Satisfaction of Tourists Travelling to Historic Town of Ayutthaya. *European Journal of Social Sciences*, 401.
3. Kuriakose, I.G. (2012). A Study to analyse the Satisfaction Level of Tourists relating to facility available in the Backwater Tourism in Alleppey. *IJEMR*, 2 (3).
4. Mingfang, Z. (2011). Assessing Inbound Tourists' Overall Satisfaction Using the Tourist Satisfaction Index : A case study of Shenzhen, P.R. China.

Inter-national Conference on Economics and Finance Research. IPEDR 4. Singapore: IACSIT Press.

5. Siby Zacharias, D.J. (2008). Back Water Tourism in Kerala: Challenges and Opportunities. *Conference on Tourism in India–Challenges Ahead* (pp. 524-529). Kozhikode: IIMK.
6. S. Sivesan (2012). Heritage Attributes and Its Role in the Satisfaction of Tourist in Sri Lanka. *KKIMRC IJRSSM*, 1 (1).
7. Truong, T.H., & Foster, D. (2006). Using HOLSAT to evaluate tourist satisfaction at destinations: The case of Australian holidaymakers in Vietnam. *Tourism Management*, *27*(5): 842-855.
8. V. J. Patil, R.V. (2009). A Study of Hill Station Tourist Satisfaction : A Case Study of Mahabaleshwar. *Shodh, Samiksha aur Mulyankan International Research Journal*, II (5).

WEB REFERENCES

http://www.keralatourism.org/rt-keralaupdate.php, retrieved on July 14, 2013.

http://osakaair.com/kerala-new-trends/retrieved on July 14, 2013.

http://www.rtkerala.com/events.php, retrieved on July 14, 2013.

http://www.keralaholidays247.com/saparya-kerala-tourism-initiative-to-boost-community-tourism/retrieved on July 14, 2013.

http://www.hindu.com/2007/10/16/stories/2007101653900500.htm, retrieved on July 14, 2013.

http://gitpac.com/new/?p=573, retrieved on July 14, 2013.

http://www.hindu.com/2011/02/03/stories/2011020361810300.htm, retrieved on July 14, 2013.

16

An Empirical Analysis of Tea Tourism in the Tea Estates of Darjeeling

A Tea-Tourist's Perspective

Gaurav Deep Rai

Introduction

It is well accepted, that Tea is one of the most popular and cheapest beverages with prominent production economies *viz.* China, India, Kenya, Sri Lanka, Turkey and Vietnam. The tea industry has been one of the oldest organized industries in India bearing a well-established network of tea producers, retailers, distributors, auctioneers, exporters and packers. (Onicra Report, 2014). India is the second largest producer and consumer of tea, after China. It contributes around 30 per cent of the global tea production and exports around 12 per cent of world tea exports. Tea exports have remained flat over the years due to increasing competition in the global market and declining quality of tea produced in India. Thus, the prices are expected to be stable with domestic consumption expected to be rising steadily.

The history of tea plantation can be dated back to the year 1834, when Major Robert Bruce, an army officer of the British Battalion, discovered tea bushes growing wild in the fields of Assam. Lord William Bentinck, Governor, General of India, formed a committee to ascertain the possibility of tea cultivation in India. Dr. Campbell, planted the first tea seeds at his backyard in Beechwood in 1840 (O'Malley, 1907). Darjeeling presently has 87 major tea gardens employing almost 52,000 permanent workers (including both garden and factory workers) (Tea Board Statistics).

Tea Tourism is gradually emerging worldwide as a niche market, promoting sustainable cultural and ethnic eco-tourism bearing tremendous potential. With the inherent teething troubles namely, erratic weather affecting the quality of tea, increased competition in the global tea market, alarming increase in domestic consumption, frequent conflicts between the management and employees, inadequate funds, high cost of production and social welfare cost, Tea Tourism can be an impeccable solution to revive the tea industry. Several countries like United States, China, and Sri Lanka have already resorted to Tea Tourism for sustained growth to combat competition. In India, the concept of Tea Tourism has not received much academic attention. It can serve as a means of alternative source of revenue, bringing employment opportunities and income for local communities and to the ailing tea industry, as a whole. The term 'Tea Tourism', includes a wide range of activities, and not just appreciating tea, an entirely new experience of tourism in the midst of a tea garden or estate. The visitors stay in a heritage bungalow inside the tea gardens having the essence of the colonial era, which once belonged to the British tea garden managers, exciting long treks experiencing the natural beauty of a tea garden and its locality. Tea estates provide the entire package of appreciating tea through undertaking tea-drinking and tea-tasting sessions, experiencing the whole process of tea production, from watching, participating in the plucking of tea leaves to the entire cycle of processing of tea in factories and simultaneously witnessing local culture, traditional dances performed and patronizing local artisans. Long leisure walks or treks, bird-watching, fishing and indulging in the natural beauty of the tea garden.

Overview of Literature

Tea has an intriguing history of being considered as an agricultural product, a beverage, a meal service, a pastime and as an integral part of food service (Jolliffe, 2007). In the United States, a tea garden was reopened in 2003 that provides tea factory tours and trolley rides through tea fields in South Carolina (Sanchez, 2008). Tea Tourism has received very little academic attention and there is very little literature on tea tourism published in English and Chinese besides the works by Hall *et al.* (2003) and Boniface (2003). Tea Tourism has been defined as "tourism that is motivated by an interest in the history, traditions and consumption of tea" (Jolliffe, 2007). It relates to experiencing many aspects of tea from its history, growth, production, processing, blending to its final consumption. This concept has led to the emergence of 'Tea Tourists' who are "tourists experiencing history, culture and traditions related to the consumption of tea". Jolliffe also commented on the wide range of experiences and opportunities which tea can provide for travellers, including tea shop trails, the partaking of the tea ceremony and visits to tea gardens or museums.

Tea tourism events in China have wide coverage including tourist attractions to the National Tea Museum in Hangzhou (Dewar & Li, 2007) and tea arts and ceremonies in the Fujian province (Xiao, 2007). Zhang (2004) indicates that tea tourism has developed to showcase tea planting areas with beautiful natural environment or special historical heritage. Tea culture (local tea customs) is conveyed through a variety of activities promoting sightseeing, learning, shopping and other forms of entertainment and tourism experiences. Ji (2006) demonstrated that tea tourism in China was developed in the forms of tea museums, tea gardens, tea related activities, tea shops, tea events, tea folk performance, and tea related products. Cheng (2001) pointed out that tea tourists of Xing yang, China are mainly tea lovers between the ages of 31 and 40, and tea drinking habits had significant influences on people's attitude towards tea tourism.

(Goowalla and Neog, 2011) Tea Tourism in Assam is positively impacted by natural beauty, heritage, and wildlife, but negative factors *viz.* poor road transport, weather and unorganized planning of activities have wedged its success. There persists lack of proper awareness of tourism services provided by the tea estates of Assam.

(Rai, 2015) Tea Tourism yields economic development through additional funds which largely caters to the needs of the management and workers. The cultures of the locality are transmitted worldwide, through the ethnic dances and songs performed for the entertainment of the tourists. Tea Tourism can also be considered as establishment of brand image, promoting niche marketing to ultimate consumers abating blatant imitation of Darjeeling Tea to certain extent through the direct purchase of genuine tea from the very factory itself, where it is produced.

Research Objective

There is a dearth of adequate literature on Tea Tourism, as it is still in its infancy. It is gradually emerging as a new type of sustainable cultural tourism with immense potential. This chapter endeavours to fill-up the lacuna of literature and understand the exigent need for a proper implementation of Tea Tourism policy to aid the sickness and pump additional revenue of the tea estates in the hills of Darjeeling (small town in northern part of India).

- To understand the importance of Tea Tourism.
- To analyse the present scenario of Tea Tourism in Darjeeling Tea Industry.
- To fathom the perspective of the domestic and foreign tourists regarding the tea tourism activities.
- To provide suggestions for proper implementation of Tea Tourism Policy.

Research Methodology

This study has been conducted incorporating both primary and secondary data. Primary data were collected through a structured questionnaire eliciting the qualitative factors through a four point Likert Scale (4-very interesting to 1-dull). Personal interviews with the tourists, interaction through cell phones, Facebook and emails were also administered in collecting primary data. Respondents were questioned regarding their experience with tea cultures, their expectations from tea tourism and the actual reality, regarding the various tea tourism activities (*e.g.*, tea garden tours, lodging near tea gardens, tea museums, tea factory tours, tea tasting, tea festivals, and buying genuine tea products from the factories). A sample size of 110 tourists was initially chosen, but it boiled down to 86 successful respondents, due to incomplete filling of questionnaires and communication bottlenecks. T-tests were conducted at .05 level of significance to elucidate statistical variation between the perceptions of domestic and foreign tourists. Secondary data were collected from tea board reports, statistics and website. The demographic profile of the respondents is exhibited in Table 16.1.

Findings and Discussions

Importance of Tea Tourism

The Indian Tea Industry faced sharp decline in the auction prices during 1999 to 2006, which adversely impacted the very survival of the tea estates and the millions of workers employed. Around 130 gardens were closed, abandoned or suspended their operations for some time due to this recession of which majority of tea gardens have reopened with the gradual improvement in tea prices from 2008 onwards. The decline in the prices has mainly been due to strong growth in supply in the face of sluggish demand on account of low productivity and lack of investment on

Table 16.1: The Demographic Profile of the Respondents

	Socio-Economic Indicators	*Frequency*
1.	**Nationality of Tourists:**	
	(a) Domestic (Indian)	60
	(b) Foreign	26
2.	**Gender:**	
	(a) Male	48
	(b) Female	38
3.	**Age Group:**	
	(a) Less than 20 years	12
	(b) 20-40 years	29
	(c) 40-60 years	25
	(d) Above 60 years	20

Source: Tea Board Statistics.

developmental activities. The urgent need to diversify such risks, led to the idea of Tourism with Tea. If the vineyards of Europe can be exotic tourist attractions, Tea Tourism can be India's answer to such wine tourism.

Graph 16.1 the aggregate annual production of Indian tea and the corresponding consumption within the financial years. It is perceived from Graph 16.1, that there is a sluggish increase in demand and the domestic consumption is also relatively on the high. It is estimated that 75 per cent of the total produce in 2013-14 has been consumed in India; this in turn led to the international demand unmet. There has been a sharp decline in the prices of Darjeeling Tea on account of low productivity and intense

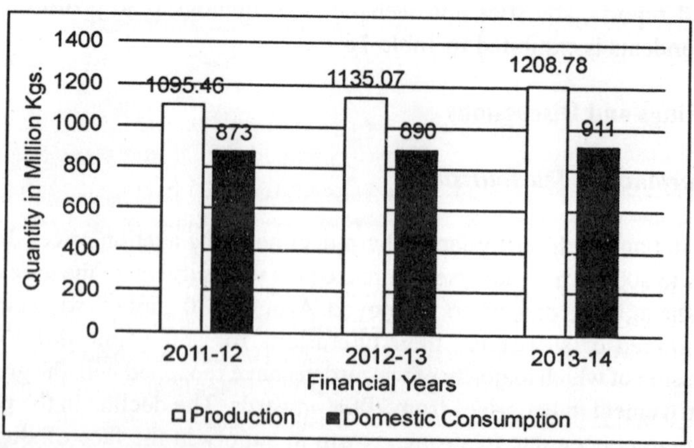

Graph 16.1: Total Production
Source: Tea Board Statistics.

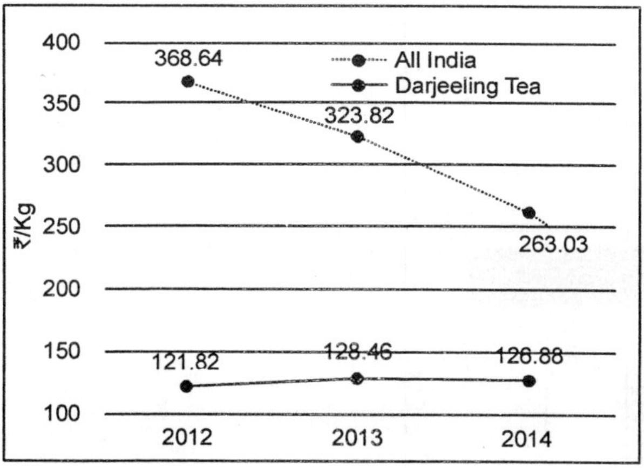

Graph 16.2: Auction Prices
Source: Tea Board Statistics.

competition faced in the global arena with China, Kenya, Sri Lanka and Vietnam in the forefront. Tea Tourism can aid to such problems, serving as an alternative strategy, pumping funds all-round the year through a well-established tourism network.

India is the fourth largest exporter of tea with China topping the chart (Graph 16.3). Kenya has also been a major competitor in the global market. India is slowly losing its grip in the market share, due to decline in quantity and quality and the competition is very high in the international level. The erratic climatic factors have resulted into variation in the quantum and frequency of rain and rise in the temperature have resulted into lower production, decline in quantity of tea due to a high incidence of pests and diseases. One of the major factors affecting quality and quantity of tea is slower pace of replantation of old bushes. Lack of bush replantation and rejuvenation of bush health are major deterrents for Indian tea production. (Onicra Report, 2014) Over 1,48,305 hectare or 37 per cent of entire Indian tea land hosts bushes over 50 years of age, which has crossed its optimum producing age. Comparatively, over 70 per cent of tea bushes of Kenya and 68 per cent in Sri Lanka are less than 40 years of age. The entire tea plantation of Vietnam is less than 20 years old and 35 per cent of Chinese plantation is less than 10 years old. Younger the tea bushes, higher is the quality and productivity of tea. Ageing and senile bushes is a major problem for the Indian Tea Industry.

Tea Tourism has emerged as a form of eco-tourism venture with a huge amount of potential. Creating a tourism industry around tea production would supplement tea growers with an alternative source of

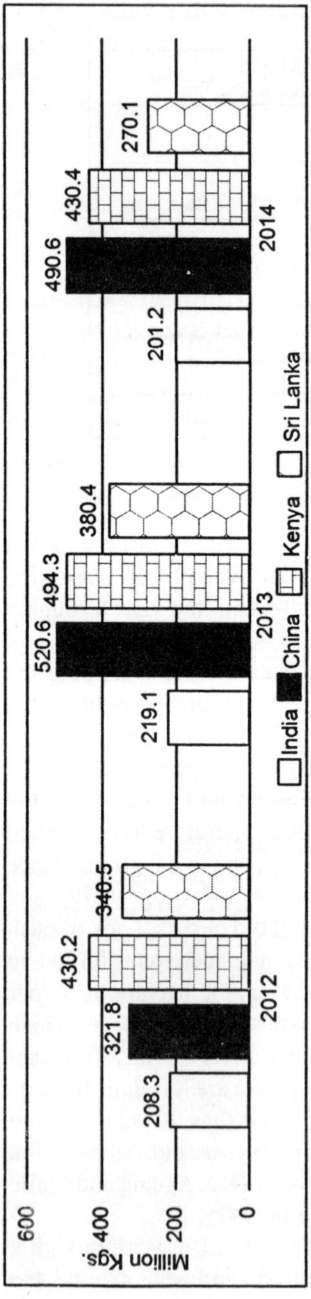

Graph 16.3: Exports.

Source: Tea Board Statistics.

revenue, bringing employment opportunities and income for local communities, which are typically very poor. The concept of Tea Tourism has been initiated by some tea estates of Darjeeling, mainly due to the falling fortunes in tea production business. Tea Tourism ventures has the following advantages:

- Creates additional revenue stream, which is indispensable for some tea estates.
- Reduces maintenance cost of these properties.
- Wages of the workers in the tea gardens is Rs. 90 and no wages for Sundays and holidays, hence even the survival becomes a challenge to a worker. Tea Tourism can generate employment as local folks can be hired as travel guides, waiters, entertainers, etc.
- Tea is seasonal in nature; workers are fully employed only during the peak season i.e., February to June. Tea Tourism, if properly implemented, can generate income almost throughout the year.

The local ethnicity and traditions are also exhibited through dances and songs performed for the entertainment of the tourists, which in a subtle manner provides global transmission of cultures and traditions of the local masses.

Present Scenario of Darjeeling Tea Industry

Tea tourism has been implemented only in a few of the tea estates of Darjeeling. It is not mandatory for all the tea estates to compulsorily indulge in Tea Tourism activities. The government has laid down strict guidelines for the tea estates adopting tourism, such that the production of tea and the tea growing areas are not hampered. The prominent tea estates which can be exotic tourist destinations in Darjeeling are:

1. Glenburn
2. Makaibari
3. Selim Hills
4. Goomtee
5. Ambootia
6. Runglee Rungliot
7. Sourenee
8. Happy Valley

Tea Tourism Packages include wonderful stay in some of the best resorts. These luxurious resorts are beautifully placed in the tea estates and are well facilitated making the stay of its guests comfortable. The following are a few of the services one can expect from the tea estates of Darjeeling.

(a) Visitors stay in the heritage bungalows experiencing the colonial ambience of the British era.
(b) Guided Garden Tour (witnessing and participating in tea tasting, tea processing, and plucking sessions).
(c) Nature walks and treks accompanied by travel guides.
(d) Birding & fishing.
(e) Toy train ride in the famous Darjeeling Himalayan Railway (DHR).
(f) Picnic lunch with barbeque by river side and river rafting.
(g) Gurkha cultural songs and dances.
(h) Herbal massages.
(i) Ethnic cultural shows and meals

Comparative Empirical Analysis of the Perception of Domestic and Foreign Tourists

Table 16.2 exhibits the opinions of the domestic and foreign tourists regarding the various services provided by the tea estates. The t-tests specify verification of whether or not a difference between two groups' (Domestic and Foreign Tourists) averages, reflecting a significant difference (in the level of perception) in the population from which the groups were sampled.

It is elucidated from Table 16.2 that there persists a significant variation in the sentiments of Indian tourists with regard to their international counterparts in four of the above statements, at .05 level of significance. Judging by the mean scores, domestic tourists have relatively enjoyed their stay at the heritage bungalows, savouring a glimpse of the colonial era (mean score 3.27), in regard to the international tourists (2.04). Contrariwise, foreign tourists have found, witnessing and participation in tea plucking sessions in the gardens (2.73), Cultural dances and songs (namely Nepali and Hindi) (3.42) and knowing the manufacturing, processing of tea and the drinking styles, fairly remarkable with regard to Indian tourists. From the above analysis, we can infer that there is no variation in the levels of perception to other activities performed by the

Table 16.2: Perception of Demestic and Foreign Tourists

Tourism Activities:	*Domestic*		*Foreign*		*t-value*	*p-value*
	Mean	*SD*	*Mean*	*SD*		
1. Stay at heritage bungalows	3.27	.841	2.04	0.720	6.483*	.000
2. Tea plucking	2.17	1.224	2.73	1.002	–2.067*	.042
3. Tea tasting sessions	3.43	.981	3.62	.637	–.869	3.87
4. Tea processing	3.58	.850	3.31	.928	1.344	1.83
5. Nature Treks	2.78	.993	2.92	.977	–.602	.549
6. Wild life	3.05	1.096	3.15	1.047	–.409	.684
7. Toy train rides	3.23	1.015	3.38	.983	–.641	.523
8. Picnics and river rafting	2.93	.972	3.27	.827	–1.536	.128
9. Cultural shows	2.78	.940	3.42	.809	–3.017*	.003
10. Learning about the processing, tea culture and drinking style	3.07	.880	3.50	.812	–.2144*	.035
11. Purchase of genuine tea from the factory	3.17	.847	3.27	.827	–.519	.605
12. Overall satisfaction of the tourism process	2.67	.951	2.85	.925	–.811	.420

* Values significant at 5 per cent level of significance
Source: Tea Board Statistics.

tea estates. Witnessing the tea processing in the factories (3.58), the various production levels and segregation of tea in order of their quality and aroma was given high regard by the domestic tourists, followed by sipping of different flavours in the tea tasting sessions (3.43), staying at the bungalows, which once was used by the British planters (3.27) and finally the rides in the famous Darjeeling Himalayan Railway or simply the toy train rides, through the picturesque hills. The foreigners were delighted with the tea tasting sessions (3.62), knowing the history of tea, its culture and the drinking styles (3.50), understanding the ethnicity through various cultural dances and songs (3.42) and toy train rides (3.38).

In general, the tourists are aesthetically satisfied with relatively low mean scores, 2.67 for domestic tourists and 2.85 for international tourists. Further, the analysis also revealed that the satisfaction of tourists were dampened by the poor connectivity of roads, lack of proper drinking water facilities and inferior quality of food, a sense of insecurity, inclement weather and language barrier. Adequate steps are to be taken by the authorities to understand the needs of the domestic and international tourists, in order to provide a better avenue for tourists' attraction.

Suggestions for Sustainable Development

Tea tourism in Darjeeling encompasses a large potential market, as a result of its green and sustainable tourism characteristics, as well as the global transmission of tea culture. The concept of "Tea Tourism" is gradually setting in the tea estates producing the "Champagne of Teas", attracting domestic and foreign tourists. A well chalked out plan for tourism could be an alternative strategy for tea estates as a source of constant inflow of funds.

It is explicitly clear that the tea estates lack proper infrastructural facilities, especially proper network of transport, and adequate drinking water and lighting facilities. A proper Tea Tourism policy fostering the coordination of the tea managers, Tea Board, government and the tourism department is the need of the hour. The most important role to be played is the government, through sanction of funds. Government has to come up with huge investment to break the geographical isolation and remove communication-bottlenecks from the Hills.

There is lack of awareness of such tourism facilities provided by the tea estates, hence international and national seminars are to be administered for attracting domestic and foreign investors as well as tourists. The government should open four information hubs each at Kolkata, Chennai, Mumbai and Delhi to inform and motivate both the domestic and foreign tourists and investors.

Innovative variants of Tea would increase the appeal, consumption and attraction to these tourist destinations. Promotion of more added flavours of fruits and herbal tea namely ginger, lemon, grape, *elaichee*, etc. could add a spark to the tea drinking styles and the arena of tea tourism as a whole. Meditation and yoga centres could also be established for tourists who want to experience the beauty and relax in the freshness of nature. Separate rooms for meditation classes intended for physical and mental benefits, removing tensions, insomnia, anxiety and emotional stability could add an extra definition to the concept of Tea Tourism.

Many of the tea gardens in Assam (north-eastern state, India) have polo fields and golf courses (Rai, 2015). There are as many as 30 air strips and helipads maintained by the tea garden management. These facilities can also form into an attractive packages for tourism in the tea estates of Darjeeling. Strategies should be developed by the concerned agencies to exploit the positive aspects meaningfully for tea tourism promotion. Hence, formulation of a need-based tea tourism policy is an urgent requirement for the promotion of Tea Tourism.

Tea Tourism can also be an effective tool to curb blatant imitation of Darjeeling Tea, as guests are also invited to tea tasting sessions where tea lovers can directly purchase genuine tea from the very factory itself, where it is produced. It also helps to sell value added tea at premium price with their own branding.

Tea tourism can also be considered as establishment of brand image, promoting niche marketing to ultimate consumers.

Conclusion

Tea tourism, though relatively new in concept has tremendous potentiality. This chapter attempts to fill a lacuna in the literature of Tea Tourism. This area of tourism has received very little academic attention, but given the proper resources, it will yield additional source of continuous funds. The authorities need to first understand the needs of the tourists (domestic and foreign) and accordingly devise marketing strategies. The participation in the tea tasting sessions, tea plucking, processing in the factories, toy train rides, learning of the history of tea culture and drinking styles have to be given due importance while designing the tourism activities. The purchase of genuine tea produced in the very factory can be an effective measure to curb the blatant imitation of Darjeeling Tea. The enrichment of the lives of the local masses through employment as chauffeurs, waiters, travel guides and entertainers is also a positive contribution towards the local masses and furthermore, there is global transmission of cultures and traditions.

Being the second largest producer of tea in the global market, contributing almost 30 per cent of global tea production, still it has not been able to perform effectively in the international arena. With the inherent glitches namely unpredictable weather, high cost of production leading to a high market price, stiff competition faced imitation of tea and high consumption rate of 75 per cent of its own production. The Indian tea is gradually losing its market share in the global arena, which has been reflected through its decline in its exports. Tea Tourism, if properly implemented can be a solution to the glitches and a perfect diversification of its risks. With Tea Tourism, the tea industry, which was in the doldrums, can finally live up to its full potential and can be a major strategy for sustainable economic and regional development.

REFERENCES

Bhatterchaije, P. (2004). *Tourism in Assam: Trend and Potentiality*, Utpal Hazarika Publications, Guwahati.

Bhowmik, S.K., *et al.* (1996). *Tea Plantation Labour in India*, Friedrich Ebert Publications, New Delhi.

Bi, J. and Yin, Z. (2006). Study on the tea cultural tourism development and the Xinyang Tea events of Hennan China. *Journal of Zhengzhou Economics & Management Institute*, pp. 44-47.

Bora, S. and Mahesh, C. (2005). *The Story of Tourism*, UBS Publishing Distributors Pvt. Ltd., New Delhi.

Cheng, S., *et al.* (2010). Tourists' attitudes toward tea tourism: a case study in Xinyang, China. *Journal of Travel & Tourism Marketing*, pp. 211-20.

Chen, Z. (1992). *Chinese Tea Classics*. Shanghai Culture Publishing House, Shanghai.

Das, D. (2013). Prospects and Problems of Tourism Industry in Assam, *Global Research Methodology Journal,* Vol. II.

Darvishi, G.A. (2013). An analysis of changing pattern in area, production and productivity of coffee and tea in India. *International Journal of Marketing, Financial Services & Management Research*. Vol. 2, No. 9.

Dutta, B. Tourism in North East—prospects and problems. *The Assam Tribune* (dated: 30th May, 2005).

Goowalla, H. & Neog, D. (2011). Problem and Prospect of Tea Tourism in Assam—A SWOT Analysis. Vol. 20. Retrieved from: http://www.ipcsit.com/vol20/45-ICAIT2011-G2023.pdf

Jolliffe, L. (2006). *Tea and Tourism: Tourists, Traditions and Transformations,* Clevedon: Channel View Publications, pp. 180-205.

Jolliffe, L. (2007). *Tea and Tourism: Tourists, Traditions and Transformations*, Clevedon: Channel view Publications, pp. 3-20.

Jolliffe, L. & Aslam, M.S.M. (2009). Tea heritage tourism: evidence from Sri Lanka. *Journal of Heritage Tourism*, Vol. 4.

Kalisch, A. (2001). *Tourism as Fair Trade—NGO Perspectives*, Tourism *concern.*

Khan, M.A. (2005). *Introduction to Tourism*, Anmol Publications Pvt. Ltd., pp. 248-60.

Kreishan, F.M. (2008): "Tourism and Economic Development": The Case of India, *European Journal of Social Sciences,* Vol. 34, No. 8: 255-259.

Luo, Y. (2006). Study on the significance, advantages and strategies of tea tourism development in Xinyang. *Journal of Higher Correspondence Education in Natural Sciences*, Vol. 19(6): 6-21.

O'Malley, L.S. (1907). *Bengal District Gazetteers Darjeeling*, Logos Press, New Delhi.

Onicra Credit Rating Agency of India (2014): Report, The Indian Tea Industry FY 14-15: Healthy Domestic Demand to Keep Tea Prices Firm.

Rai, G.D., 2015. Tea Tourism: An Unconventional Strategy for Sustainable Rural

Development in the Tea Gardens of Darjeeling, *Rural Development in India: Issues and Challenges,* Abhijeet Publications, New Delhi, India, pp. 113-31.

Sanchez, P. (2008). Tea and coffee trips: the new trend in tourism. *Tea & Coffee Trade Journal*, Retrieved from: http://www.teaandcoffee.net/0508/speciality.html

Sharma, K. (1999). *Tea Industries in India: An Introduction,* L. Publishers, Dibrugarh, Assam.

Sinclier, D. & T. Huybers (2005). Tourism and Economics Development: A Survey, *Journal of Development Studies,* pp. 22-28.

The Statesman (06 July, 2013). "Tea estates' land to be used for tourism", Kolkata, India.

The Telegraph (28 November, 2010). "Plea to promote tea tourism", Kolkata, India.

The Telegraph (15 February, 2012). "Nod to tea tourism without land lease", Kolkata, India.

Wang (2001). *Chinese Tea Culture: The Origin of Tea Drinking*. Subang Java, Malaysia: Pelanduk Publications.

www.maamatimanush.tv/articles.php?aid=321

Xiao, H. (2007). Tea culture and tourism in Fujian province, China: Towards a partnership for sustainable development. *Tea and Tourism: Tourists, Traditions and Transformations,* Clevedon: Channel View Publications, (pp. 115-132).

Zhou, M., *et al.* (2011). *Tea Tourism: Examining University Faculty Members' Expectations*. Tourism Travel and Research Association: Advancing Tourism Research Globally, University of Massachusetts, International Conference. 2012.

Part 3: Dynamics of Health Tourism

17

Predictors of Behavioural Intention of Health Tourists

Padmasani and *Remya, V.*

Introduction

With the advent of the globalisation and open economy, tourism emerged as one of the world's fastest growing industries and a leading contributor to GDP in many countries. According to a survey by World Tourism Organisation, tourists movement throughout the world can touch 1600 million mark by 2020. This has engrossed considerable attention from the government, practitioners and researchers in many developing nations.

In India, over the decade, a rapid growth in the tourism industry is witnessed with the tourists arrival of 8.03 million in 2015 compared to 3.92 million in 2005. Tourism, being the biggest foreign exchange earner of India, helps in generating maximum employment opportunity through its interconnection with number of subsidiary industries, brings advancement in the infrastructural development, which in turn, helps in regional and economic development. Thus, acknowledging the great potential of tourism, the Government of India declared tourism as an industry in the year 1980. Though tourism is recognised as an important economic contributor to the nation, it is faced with several challenges. The major challenge faced by the Indian tourism sector is negligible market share in the world tourism market. Thus, it has become crucial for the country to identify its competitive advantage and induce the tourists for greater usage of these services so as to acquire large market share in the world tourism industry.

Against this background, developing and fostering behavioural intention as a major source of competitive advantage is an important business strategy in the market economy system and consequently directs the efforts of service managers, academicians and researchers in comprehending the dynamics involved in behavioural intentions. Thus, establishing relationship with customers that shapes behavioural intention has been considered a key factor in obtaining market share and creating a sustainable competitive advantage (Deng *et al.*, 2010). According to Chen & Tsai (2007) by understanding the relationships between future behaviour and its determinants, tourism destination managers would know how to build up an attractive picture and improve their marketing efforts to maximise resource utilisation. Therefore, it is imperative to know the ways to attract the tourists to revisit and to recommend the destination to others for the success of destination tourism development.

This chapter is organized by presenting the theoretical background and hypotheses of the proposed model, methodology, followed by empirical results and discussions with a conclusion.

Theoretical Background and Hypotheses

Health Tourism

Health tourism refers to cross-border healthcare motivated by lower cost, avoidance of long waiting times or services not available in one's own country. Bookman and Bookman (2007) defines medical tourism as travel overseas with the aim of improving one's health. Health tourism is distinguished from tourism as the combination of travel to an overseas vacation destination for a potential leisure experience and a specific medical intervention.

Several studies have been conducted in health tourism context which contributed to the body of knowledge. Smith and Forgione (2007) created a two-stage model to determine the impacting factors on patient when selecting overseas medical services. In the first stage, the locations for medical tourism are selected, the main factors are economic environment, political climate and regulation. In the second stage, when an institution is selected, factors such as cost, medical quality and professional certification are considered. Caballero-Danell and Mugomba (2007) showed that factors determining customer decisions about medical tourism include: customer benefits, brand, law, facility, target market, product, communication channel, operator and social conditions. Ye *et al.* (2008) researched the medical tourism customer motivation and impedances in Hong Kong by developing a one-tier structural model with a push-pull viewpoint, which showed that medical tourism customers are more concerned about health related factors rather than location. Heung *et al.* (2010) proposed a conceptual model for medical tourism to create a correlation between customers and companies based on supply and demand whereas Shieh *et al.* (2010), Quintela *et al.* (2011) and Yang and Huang (2013) analysed service quality indicators in medical tourism context and revealed that individual concerns, immediate services provided to customers, symptom diagnosis, professional explanation and discussion with doctors, detailed medication process and results from doctors are critical success factors for medical service quality.

Thus, most of the past studies are about medical tourists motivation, service quality, medical tourism market based models and determinants of medical tourism destination selection. As a result, the identification of behavioural intention indicators for health tourism and their interrelationship reveal significant research value and contributions.

Destination Image

Destination Image is one of the important constructs in tourism marketing as it influences tourists' choice or decision making and their behaviour at a particular destination. Gartner (1989) stated that destination image influences destination choice process and a positive image promises the travellers a rewarding life experience. Thus, relative images, tourists hold towards destinations, will form one of the bases for identifying destination's strength and weakness, competitive advantages and distinctive competencies for each destination relative to other destinations.

A number of researchers have carried out research in this concept, some attempted to conceptualise the components of destination image (Gunn, 1985; Baloglu and Brinberg, 1997) whereas others discussed the management and formation of destination image (Echtner and Ritchie, 1991; Fakeye & Crompton, 1991) while some studied the destination image construct and its influence on tourists' behaviour, the travel selection process and travel satisfaction (Hunt, 1975; Chon, 1990). Kotler, Bowen and Makens (1996) tried to establish a sequential relationship between image-quality-satisfaction-post purchase behaviour and found tourism image exercises a positive influence on perceived quality and satisfaction. Bigne, Sanchez and Sanchez (2001) pointed out the influence of tourism image on behavioural intentions and the post-purchase evaluations of the stay and they also examined the relationship between quality, satisfaction and tourists' behaviour variables using SEM. The results showed that tourism image is a direct antecedent of perceived quality, satisfaction, intention to return and willingness to recommend the destination. Thus, it is confirmed that the role of image is a key factor in destination marketing. Thus, the following hypothesis is framed:

H1: Destination Image Positively Influences Behavioural Intention

Service Quality

Service quality is a measure of how well the services delivered match customer expectations (Joewono and Kubota, 2007). Therefore, the extent to which service performance matches customer expectations would influence the degree to which customers feel satisfied. The SERVQUAL scale proposed by Parasuraman *et al.* (1985, 1988) based on the disconfirmation of expectations model (Oliver, 1980) is widely used to measure service quality. This scale contains 22 items under five dimensions including tangibility, reliability, responsiveness, assurance, and empathy. However, these five dimensions and 22 associated items have been challenged as being inappropriate for some service businesses (Cronin and Taylor, 1992).

The service quality is studied by several researchers (Hanzaee *et al.*, 2012; Kandampully and Susartanto, 2000; Landhari, 2009; Choi *et al.*, 2004; Lee *et al.*, 2005; Alexandris *et al.*, 2002; Baker *et al.*, 2000; Zabkar *et al.*, 2010; Bei & Chiao, 2001). Its influence is not limited to the selection phase of the destination, but also affects the behaviour of tourists in general, their loyalty to the destination, their intention to revisit and recommend to others (Bigne *et al.*, 2001; Chen and Tsai, 2007; Lee *et al.*, 2005). This construct is a crucial determinant of patient satisfaction as well as patient loyalty (Hanzaee *et al.*, 2012). Researchers in the medical tourism sector, investigated the crucial role of service quality and its relationship with behavioural intention and established a significant positive relationship (Ho *et al.*, 2015; Jyothis and Janardhan, 2009). Thus, the following hypothesis is framed:

H2: Service Quality Positively Influences Behavioural Intention

Satisfaction

Satisfaction is an overall affective response to a perceived discrepancy between prior expectations and perceived performance after consumption

(Oliver, 1980). There are two general conceptualizations of satisfaction in the literature: transaction-specific satisfaction (individual level) and cumulative satisfaction (customers' total consumption experience) (Johnson *et al.*, 1995). In practice, service quality and satisfaction are often used interchangeably, but differences between service quality and customer satisfaction are also clarified in the literature. Oliver (1997) suggests that service quality judgements are more specific while customer satisfaction judgements are more holistic. Service quality is also related to cognitive judgements while customer satisfaction is associated with affective judgements.

Service quality refers to transaction-specific while satisfaction, concerns the (dis)confirmation in the expectance gap of individual attributes, while cumulative satisfaction is conceptualized as overall satisfaction. In other words, overall satisfaction pertains to a holistic evaluation after a service delivery experience, and acts as a consequence of satisfaction with individual attributes (i.e. service quality) (Chen, 2008; Fornell, 1992). Past studies have shown evidence that customer satisfaction significantly affects customer loyalty and behaviour intentions in various industries (Anderson and Sullivan, 1993; Cronin and Taylor, 1992; Fornell, 1992; Oliver, 1980; Petrick and Backman, 2002). Thus, the following hypothesis is framed:

H3: Satisfaction Positively Influences Behavioural Intention

Behavioural Intention

Behavioural intention is an affirmed likelihood to engage in a certain behaviour. It can be viewed as signals that show whether a customer will continue to utilize a company's services or switch to a different provider (Zeithaml *et al.*, 1996). This can be assessed by both attitudinal and behavioural measures. The attitudinal measure refers to a specific desire to continue a relationship with a service provider while the behavioural perspective refers to the concept of repeat patronage (Chen and Chen, 2010). The degree of behavioural intention is frequently reflected in tourists' intentions to revisit the destination and their willingness to recommend it (Chen and Tsai, 2007). Favourable behavioural intentions encompass three dimensions: word-of-mouth, purchase intentions and price insensitivity. Two behaviours, i.e. repeatedly patronizing the service provider and recommending a service provider to others, are viewed as key manifestations of behavioural intention (Fornell, 1992). Most researchers tend to employ the behavioural-intention measure to represent customer loyalty, since action loyalty is difficult to observe and is often equally difficult to measure (Yang and Peterson, 2004). The current study thus employs the behavioural-intention measure of customer loyalty, which includes repurchase and recommendation intentions.

It is acknowledged that factors such as service quality, consumer satisfaction, and value are frequently viewed as key building blocks of customer loyalty (Chen, 2008). A higher quality of service and levels of satisfaction can result in positive behavioural intentions. Hence, the study adopted destination image, service quality and satisfaction as important indicators and examined their influences on behavioural intention.

Methodology

Kerala a Health Tourism Hub of India

The quality of service coupled with comparatively low charges has made India a preferred destination for health tourism. The competitiveness of India in health tourism is enhanced by the attractiveness of the alternative systems of medicine, Ayurveda in particular, for the foreign tourists. A large number of tourists, both domestic and foreign, undergo Ayurvedic treatment not only for improving their fitness and well-being but also for curing many types of chronic diseases. Kerala is the most popular destination for tourists for treatment under Ayurveda. The unique position that the state enjoys with respect to Ayurveda is due to the fact that the treatment has proved effective in dealing with certain diseases, which are incurable by other systems. The state is also well endowed with herbs and medicinal plants, which are used for treatment. With *yoga*, meditation, ayurveda, allopathy and natural herbal treatments, Kerala offers a unique basket of services to foreign patient-tourists that are difficult to match by other countries. The preference for health tourism in Kerala is so strong that Ayurveda Centre has been established at multiple locations in various major cities. For ensuring the quality of service in accordance with traditional methods, the Ministry of Health, Government of India, has accredited the Ayurveda Health Centres. Kerala is having the potential and the capacity to attract more than one million tourists per annum even then the tourists flow to the state is very low compared to the global tourists arrival. Therefore, understanding tourists' behavioural intentions after experiencing the services of a destination is an essential task for attracting and retaining the tourists. In this context, the present research aims to develop a conceptual model that incorporates the main determinants of tourists' behavioural intention and explores their effects on behavioural intention.

Measures

The study is purely based on primary data which was collected from the international health tourists visiting Kerala for Ayurvedic treatment. The instrument used to collect empirical data was a self-administered questionnaire developed based on the review of related literature. To have adequate content validity, the survey instrument was revised and finalised according to feedback given by physicians and healthcare centres' managers. The questionnaire is used to gather information with respect to destination image of Kerala, service quality of health tourism providers and finally, overall satisfaction and behavioural loyalty of the health tourists.

Data Collection

An on-site survey was conducted at select Ayurvedic Health Centres accredited by Kerala Tourism Department where tourists availed their treatment. The convenience sampling technique was employed due to the fact that the population of tourists availing the treatment was not available. Tourists who were ready to participate in the survey were asked to fill in the questionnaire. Thus, a total of 194 questionnaires were returned with usable responses. The data so collected was analysed using SPSS software. This study is pertinent to foreign tourists and cannot be generalised into domestic tourists population. If the responses were also collected from domestic tourists, it would provide a more comprehensive picture of tourism industry in Kerala.

Empirical Results

Predictors of Tourists Behavioural Intention to Ayurvedic Health Tourism

To identify the predictors of tourists behavioural intention in health tourism context, a hierarchical multiple regression analysis was performed. As a first step, to check the assumptions of linearity and homoscedasticity met by the data, the normal probability plot and residuals scatter plot test were undertaken. In a normal probability plot, the straight line represents the normal distribution and the points represent the observed residuals. Therefore, in a perfectly normally distributed data set, all points will lie on the line. A visual inspection of Fig. 17.1, depicted the normal probability plot revealing that the residual plots were almost close to the normal straight diagonal line, suggesting that the residuals were approximately normally distributed. Additionally, Fig. 17.2, shows the scatter plot (a plot of the standardised residuals versus the standardised predicted values) revealed that most of the plots are randomly and evenly dispersed throughout the graphs (without any curvilinear trend or plots very closer at one end and widely dispersed at other end indicating heteroscedasticity or increasing variance across the residuals) specifying linearity and homoscedasticity.

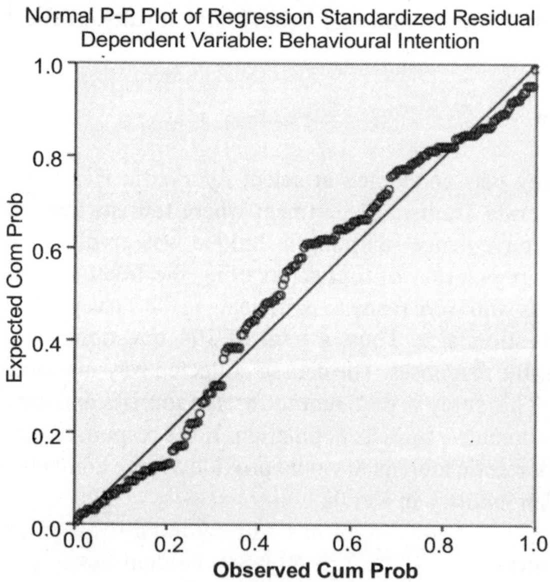

Fig. 17.1: Normal Probability Plot.
Source: Primary Data.

To test the presence of multi-collinearity, the tolerance and VIF values of the independent variables were assessed while the regression analysis was run. For a model to be safe from multi-collinearity problem, all the independent variables VIF value should be below 10 and the tolerance statistics should be above 0.2 (Hair *et al.* 2010). The analysis, in Table 17.1 showed that all independent variables in the regression equation had high

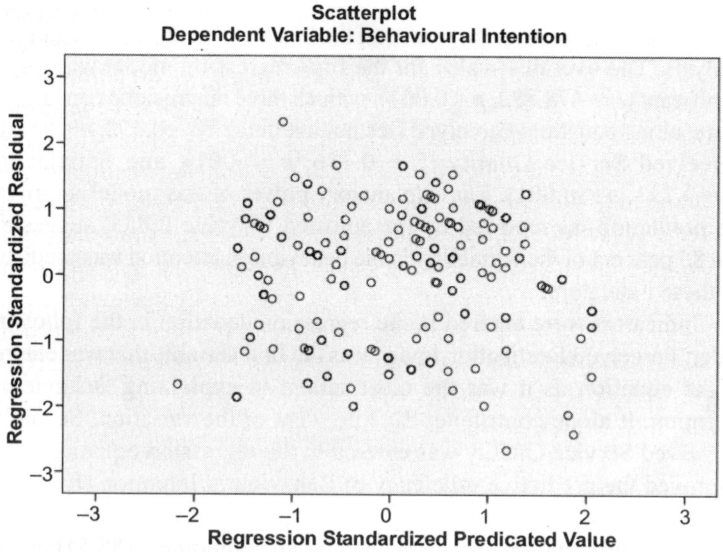

Fig. 17.2: Scatterplot.

Source: Primary Data.

Table 17.1: Collinearity Statistics

Independent Variables	*Tolerance Value*	*VIF Value*
Perceived Destination Image	0.64	1.81
Perceived Service Quality	0.77	1.94
Satisfaction	0.92	4.48

Source: Primary Data.

tolerance values ranging from 0.64 to 0.92 and the VIF values were all below 10, indicating an absence of multi-collinearity. Thus, the data satisfied the regression assumptions of multi-collinerarity, normality of residuals and homoscedasticity as no outliers were identified.

Relationship between Perceived Destination Image, Perceived Service Quality, Satisfaction and Behavioural Intention

To identify the factors influencing health tourists' behavioural intention, a hierarchical multiple regression analysis were performed using three dimensions (perceived destination image, perceived service quality and satisfaction) as independent variables. The dependent variable was behavioural intention. This regression helps in knowing the amount that each successive variable adds to the overall prediction.

Table 17.2 presents the results of the hierarchical multiple regression analysis. The overall *F*-value for the final regression model was highly significant ($F = 478.882, p < 0.001$), with all three dimensions constituting the resulting equation: Perceived Destination Image ($\beta = 0.498, p < 0.001$), Perceived Service Quality ($\beta = 0.186$, $p < .001$), and Satisfaction ($\beta = 0.293, p < 0.001$). The explanatory power of this model improved the prediction, as reported by the adjusted R^2 value 0.855, suggesting that 85 per cent of the variability in the behavioural intention was predicted by these indicators.

Indicators were entered in the regression equation in the following order: Perceived Destination Image was the first variable that was entered in the equation as it was the most salient in explaining Behavioural Intention. It alone contributes 80.7 per cent of the variation. Secondly, Perceived Service Quality was entered in the regression equation and it improved the predictive efficiency of Behavioural Intention (R-square) from 80.7 to 82.8 per cent. Satisfaction was the next variable which was entered in the equation, this accounted for an additional 3 (85.5) per cent of the variation. The relative importance of the dimensions was indicated by their Standardized Beta Coefficients. As it is evident from Table 17.2, the strongest impact on Behavioural Intention was by Perceived Destination Image ($\beta = 0.498$). The next most important was Satisfaction ($\beta = 0.293$), followed by Perceived Service Quality ($\beta = 0.186$).

Table 17.2: Factor influencing Health Tourists Behavioural Intention

Model	*Predictor*	*B*	*Beta (β)*	*t-value*	*p-value*	*F-value*	*Adjst R^2*
1	(Constant)	.200		2.295	.023	1017.369	0.807
	Perceived Destination Image	1.107	.899	31.896	.000	(.000)	
2	(Constant)	.306		3.625	.000	587.444	0.828
	Perceived Destination Image	.722	.586	9.451	.000	(.000)	
	Perceived Service Quality	.418	.346	5.575	.000		
3	(Constant)	.337		4.336	.000	478.882	0.855
	Perceived Destination Image	.613	.498	8.508	.000*	(.000)	
	Perceived Service Quality	.225	.186	3.018	.003*		
	Satisfaction	.333	.293	6.737	.000*		

Source: Computed data.

Discussion and Conclusion

This study investigated health tourists behaviour by constructing a comprehensive model considering perceived destination image, perceived service quality, satisfaction and behavioural intention. The conceptual model was tested using data obtained from tourists' questionnaire survey at Ayurvedic healthcare centres. The results of the relationship between the constructs suggest important implications for destination marketers. According to the results, the foreign tourists were more influenced by destination image, followed by satisfaction and service quality. Thus, the findings revealed that if the foreign tourists perception towards destination image is favourable, then they may be willing to revisit and recommend the destination in future. Therefore, the destination managers are suggested to capitalise on these dimensions while promoting Kerala as health tourism destination at the international level.

Increasing the inflow of foreign tourists is extremely important for Kerala Tourism Industry, which is a matured market with very low resource utilisation capacity. Therefore, in addition to retaining existing tourists, more importance should be given to attracting new tourists. A more marketing-oriented approach rather than the traditional supply-oriented approach is thus believed to be more appropriate for Kerala Tourism Industry. From a practical standpoint, the findings offer important implications for the development of destination marketing strategies. In today's competitive climate, creating and managing the right destination image has become vital for effective positioning and differentiation to ensure continuous inflow of foreign tourists into the state.

REFERENCES

Ajzen, I. (1991). The Theory of Planned Behaviour. *Organisational Behaviour.* 50:179-211.

Alexandris, K., Dimitriadis, N. & Markata, D. (2002). Can Perceptions of Service Quality Predict Behavioural Intentions? An Exploratory Study in Hotel Sector in Greece. *Managing Service Quality.* 12 (4): 224-232.

Anderson, W. & Sullivan, M. (1993). The Antecedents and Consequences of Customer Satisfaction for Firms. *Market Science.* 12: 125 143.

Baker, D.A. & Crompton, J.L. (2000). Quality, Satisfaction and Behavioural Intentions. *Annals of Tourism Research.* 27(3): 785-804.

Baloglu, S. & Brinberg, D. (1997). Affective Images of Tourism Destinations. *Journal of Travel Research.* 35(4): 11-15.

Bei, L.T. & Chiao, Y.C. (2001). An Integrated Model for the Effects of Perceived Product, Perceived Service Quality and Perceived Price Fairness on Customer Satisfaction and Loyalty. *Journal of Customer Satisfaction Dissatisfaction and Complaining Behaviour*. 14: 125-140.

Bigne, J.E.; Sanchez, M.I.; Sanchez, J. (2001). Tourism Image, Evaluation Variables and After Purchase Behaviour: Interrelationship. *Tourism Management*. 22: 607-616.

Bookman, M.Z.; Bookman, K.R. (2007). *Medical Tourism in Developing Countries*, Palgrave MacMillan, New York.

Caballero-Danell, S. & Mugomba, C. (2007). *Medical Tourism and its Entrepreneurial Opportunities: A Conceptual Framework for Entry into the Industry*. Master's Thesis, Unpublished. Sweden: University of Gothenburg.

Chen, C.F. & Chen, F.S. (2010). Experience Quality, Perceived Value, Satisfaction and Behavioural Intentions for Heritage Tourists. *Tourism Management*. 31: 29-35.

Chen, C.F. & Tsai, D. (2007). How Destination Image and Evaluative Factors affect Behavioural Intentions? *Tourism Management*. 28(4): 1115-1122.

Chen, C.F. (2008). Investigating Structural Relationships between Service Quality, Perceived Value, Satisfaction, and Behavioural Intentions for Air Passengers: Evidence from Taiwan. *Transportation Research*. 42 (4): 709-717.

Choi, K.S.; Cho, W.H.; Lee, S.; Lee, H. & Kim, C. (2004). The Relationship among Quality, Value, Satisfaction and Behavioural Intention in Health care Providers Choice: A Korean Study. *Journal of Business Research*. 57: 913-921.

Chon, K.S. (1990). The Role of Destination Image in Tourism: A Review and Discussion. *The Tourist Review*. 45 (2): 2-9.

Cronin, J.J. & Taylor, S.A. (1992). Measuring Service Quality: A Re-examination and Extension. *Journal of Marketing*. 56(3): 55-68.

Deng, Z.; Lu, Y.; Wei, K.K. & Zhang, J. (2010). Understanding Customer Satisfaction and Loyalty: An Empirical Study of Mobile Instant Messages in China. *International Journal of Information Management*. 30 (4): 289-300.

Echtner, C.M. & Ritchie, J.B. (1991). The Meaning and Measurement of Destination Image. *Journal of Tourism Studies*. 2: 2-12.

Fakeye, P.C. & Crompton, J.L. (1991). Image Differences between Prospective, First-time, and Repeat visitors to the Lower Rio Grande Valley. *Journal of Travel Research*. 30: 10-16.

Fornell, C. (1992). National Satisfaction Barometer: The Swedish experience. *Journal of Marketing*. 56: 6-21.

Gartner, W.C. (1989). Temporal Influences on Image Change. *Annals of Tourism Research*. 13: 635-644.

Gunn, C.A. (1985). *Vacation Scape: Designing Tourist Regions*. 2nd sub ed. Van Nostrand Reinhold, USA, pp. 152-178.

Hair, J.F.; Black, W.C.; Babin, B.J. & Anderson, R.E. (2010). *Multivariate Data Analysis: A Global Perspective*. Pearson Prentice Hall. New York.

Hanzaee, K.H.; Bigdeli, F.; Khanzadeh, M. & Javanbakht, A. (2012). Assessing

Patients Behavioural Intentions through Service Quality and Perceived Value. *Journal of Basic and Applied Scientific Research*. 2(10): 10686-10692.

Heung, V.C.S.; Kucukusta, D.; Song, H. (2010). A Conceptual Model of Medical Tourism: Implications for Future Research. *Journal of Travel and Tourism Marketing*. 27: 236-251.

Hunt, J.D. (1975). Image as a Factor in Tourism Development. *Journal of Travel Research*. 13(3): 1-7.

Joewono, T.B.; Kubota, H. (2007). User Satisfaction with Paratransit in Competition with Motorization in Indonesia: Anticipation of Future Implications. *Transportation*. 34: 337-354.

Johnson, M.D.; Anderson, E.W.; Fornell, C. (1995). Rational and Adaptive Performance Expectation in a Customer Framework. *Journal of Customer Research*. 21: 595-707.

Joythis, T. & Janardhanan (2009). Service Quality in Health Tourism: An Evaluation of the Health Tourism Providers of Kerala (India). *South Asian Journal of Tourism and Heritage*. 2(1): 77-82.

Kandampully, J. & Suhartanto, D. (2000). Customer Loyalty in the Hotel Industry: the Role of Customer Satisfaction and Image. *International Journal of Contemporary Hospitality Management*. 12(6): 346-351.

Kotler, P., Bowen, J. & Makens, J.C. (1996). *Marketing for Hospitality and Tourism*, Pearson Prentice Hall, Upper Saddle River, New Jersey.

Landhari. (2009). Service Quality, Emotional Satisfaction and Behavioural Intentions. *Managing Service Quality*. 6: 1085-1108.

Lee, C.K.; Lee, Y.K. & Lee, B.K. (2005). Korea's Destination Image formed by the 2002 World Cup. *Annals of Tourism Research*, 32(4): 839-858.

Li-HsingHo & Tai Yi. (2014). Constructing Quality of Service Indicators and Improvement Strategies for Medical Tourism in Taiwan. *Ethno Med*., 8(1): 23-31.

Li-HsingHo, Shu-Yun Feng, Tieh-Min Yen. (2015). Using Fuzzy gap Analysis to Measure Service Quality of Medical Tourism in Taiwan. *International Journal of Health Care Quality Assurance*. 28(7): 648-659.

MarcioFavilla Lucca de Paula (2011). *Tourism Towards 2030*. World Tourism Organisation. Geneva.

Oliver, R. (1980). A Cognitive Model of the Antecedents and Consequences of Satisfaction Decisions. *Journal of Marketing Research*. 17: 460-469.

Oliver, R. (1997). *Satisfaction: A Behavioural Perspective on the Consumer*. McGraw-Hill, New York.

Oliver, R.L. & Swan, J.E. (1989). Consumer Perceptions of Interpersonal Equity and Satisfaction in Transactions: A Field Survey Approach. *Journal of Marketing*. 53(2): 21 35.

Oliver, R.L. (1999). Whence Consumer Loyalty? *Journal of Marketing*. 63: 33-44.

Parasuraman, A.; Zeithaml, V.A.; Berry, L.L. (1988). SERVQUAL: A multi-item Scale of Measuring Consumer Perceptions of Service Quality. *Journal of Retailing*. 64: 12-41.

Parasuraman, A.; Zethaml, V.A.; Berry, L.L. (1985). A Conceptual Model of Service Quality and its Implications for Future Research. *Journal of Marketing*. 49(4): 41-50.

Petrick, J.F. & Backman, S.J. (2002). An Examination of the Construct of Perceived Value for the Prediction of Golf Travellers' Intentions to Revisit. *Journal of Travel Research*. 41 (1): 38-45.

Petrick, J.F. (2004). The Roles of Quality, Value, and Satisfaction in Predicting Cruise Passengers' Behavioural Intentions. *Journal of Travel Research*. 42(4): 397-407.

Quintela, J., Correia, A., Antunes, J. (2011). Service Quality in Health and Wellness Tourism—Trends in Portugal. *International Journal of Business, Management and Social Sciences*. 2(3): 1-8.

Shieh, J.I.; Wu, H.H.; Hung, K.K. (2010). *A DEMATEL Method in Identifying Key Success Factors of Hospital Service Quality*. Knowledge-Based System. 23(3): 277-282.

Smith, P.C. & Forgione, D. (2007). Global Outsourcing of Healthcare: A Medical Tourism Model. *Journal of Information Technology Case and Application Research*. 9(3): 19-30.

Um, S.; Chon, K. & Ro, Y. (2006). Antecedents of Revisit Intention. *Annals of Tourism Research*. 33(3): 1141-1158.

Yang, C.L. & Huang, R.H. (2013). Systematic Approach for Improving Medical Service Quality. *International Journal of Economics, Finance and Management Sciences*. 1(2): 108-114.

Yang, Z. & Peterson, R.T. (2004). Customer Perceived Value, Satisfaction, and Loyalty: The Role of Switching Costs. *Psychological Market*. 21 (10): 799-822.

Ye, B.H., Yuen, P.P., Qiu, H.Z., Zhang, V.H. (2008). Motivation Medical Tourism in Taiwan of Medical Tourists: An Exploratory Case Study of Hong Kong Medical Tourists. Proceeding of the 2008 Asia Pacific Tourism Association (APTA) Annual Conference, July 25-31, Bangkok, Thailand.

Zabkar, V.; Brenc, M.M. & Dmitrovic. (2010). Modelling Perceived Quality, Visitor Satisfaction and Behavioural Intentions at the Destination Level. *Tourism Management*. 31(4): 537-546.

Zeithaml, V.A.; Bitner, L.L. & Parasuraman, A. (1996). The Behavioural Consequences of Service Quality. *Journal of Marketing*, 60: 31-46.

18

Dental Tourism

Evolution, Relevance and Scope

Aishwarya Biju

Dental tourism is a subset of the sector known as medical tourism. It involves individuals seeking dental care outside of their local healthcare systems. Normally, it may be accompanied by a vacation. Dental tourism is growing worldwide. As the world becomes ever more interdependent and competitive, technique, material, dental tourism enables dental care at significant cost savings when compared with their peers in the developed world. Against this backdrop, this chapter illustrates and investigates into the facets of dental tourism from hospitality perceptive. The introductory part traces the origin, evolutionary process and significance of hospitality industry in a global perceptive. The second part unfolds, on the rise of dental tourism as a potential element of medical tourism. Part three focuses on the components of dental tourism with special focus on its strategy and concluding part presents the major findings of the study.

PART I: INTRODUCTION

Tourism

Tourism is the travel for recreational, leisure, family or business purposes, usually of a limited duration. Tourism is commonly associated with trans-national travel, but may also refer to travel to another location within the same country. The World Tourism Organization defines tourists as people "travelling to and staying in places outside their usual environment for not more than one consecutive year for leisure, business and other purposes".

Tourism has become a popular global leisure activity. Tourism can be domestic or international, and international tourism has both incoming and outgoing implications on a country's balance of payments. Today, tourism is a major source of income for many countries, and affects the economy of both the source and host countries, in some cases it is of vital importance.

Origin of the Concepts

The word 'tourist' was used in 1772 and 'tourism' in 1811. William F. Theobald (1994) suggested that "etymologically, the word 'tour' is derived from the Latin, 'tornare' and the Greek, 'tornos', meaning "a lathe or circle; the movement around a central point or axis". This meaning changed in modern English to represent 'one's turn'. The suffix–*ism* is defined as "an action or process; typical behaviour or quality", while the suffix,–*ist* denotes "one that performs a given action". When the word 'tour' and the suffixes–*ism* and–*ist* are combined, they suggest the action of movement around a circle. One can argue that a circle represents a starting point, which ultimately returns back to its beginning. Therefore, like a circle, a tour represents a journey in that it is a round-trip, i.e. the act of leaving and then returning to the original starting point, and therefore, one who takes such a journey can be called a tourist."

Today, three schools discuss on the roots of tourism. The French School, led by A. Houlot argued that the term tourism comes from the old Aramaic Tur, which was used for the trip, exploration and movement of people in the Bible. This word had been used, for the first time, when Moses begins his expedition to the lands of Canaán. Nevertheless, another school of thought—the Onomastic School—considers the origin of the concept not from a linguistic perspective but rather links it to the last name of the French aristocracy Della Tour. According to this school, after Carlos-V signs a treaty with England in 1516, in celebration of this event, the future king gives the Della Tour family exclusive rights to conduct commercial transport and related businesses. Finally, a third school focuses on the Anglo-Saxon world, situating the Theobald´s development under the lens of scrutiny. Surmising that the roots of the word tourism comes from the Ancient Anglo-Saxon term Torn, these scholars found evidence to think the term was coined in the 12th century which by farmers to denote those travels with intentions to return. Over centuries, the meaning of the word has been shifted to be politically adopted. By the middle of the 18th century, the English noblemen used the term "turn" to refer to the trips undertaken for education, search and culture exploration. In reality, the purpose of the noblemen's trip to the different parts of Kingdom was to acquire knowledge that was later useful for governing.

Definitions

In 1936, the League of Nations defined a *foreign tourist* as "someone travelling abroad for at least twenty-four hours". Its successor, the United Nations, amended this definition in 1945, by including a maximum stay of six months. In 1941, Hunziker and Krapf defined tourism as people who travel "the sum of the phenomena and relationships arising from the travel and stay of non-residents, insofar as they do not lead to permanent residence and are not connected with any earning activity." In 1976, the Tourism Society of England's definition was: "Tourism is the temporary, short-term movement of people to destination outside the places where they normally live and work and their activities during the stay at each destination. It includes movements for all purposes." In 1981, the International Association of Scientific Experts in Tourism defined tourism in terms of particular activities selected by choice and undertaken outside the home.

In 1994, the United Nations identified three forms of tourism in its Recommendations on Tourism Statistics:

- Domestic tourism, involving residents of the given country travelling only within this country.
- Inbound tourism, involving non-residents travelling in the given country.
- Outbound tourism, involving residents travelling in another country.

The terms *tourism* and *travel* are sometimes used interchangeably. In this context, travel has a similar definition to tourism, but implies a more purposeful journey. The terms *tourism* and *tourist* are sometimes used pejoratively, to imply a shallow interest in the cultures or locations visited by tourists.

Significance of Tourism

Strandkorb chairs on Usedom Island, Germany. Not only the service sector grows thanks to tourism, but also local manufacturers (like those producing the strandkorb), retailers, the real estate sector and the general image of a location can benefit a lot. Tourism is an important, even vital, source of income for many countries. Its importance was recognized in the *Manila Declaration on World Tourism of 1980* as "an activity essential to the life of nations because of its direct effects on the social, cultural, educational, and economic sectors of national societies and on their international relations."

Tourism brings in large amounts of income into a local economy in the form of payment for goods and services needed by tourists, accounting for 30 per cent of the world's trade of services, and 6 per cent of overall exports of goods and services. It also creates opportunities for employment in the service sector of the economy associated with tourism.

The service industries which benefit from tourism include transportation services, such as airlines, cruise ships, and taxicabs; hospitality services, such as accommodations, including hotels and resorts; and entertainment venues, such as amusement parks, casinos, shopping malls, music venues, and theatres. This is in addition to goods bought by tourists, including souvenirs, clothing and other supplies.

PART II: DENTAL TOURISM

Dental tourism is an important segment of the growing health tourism industry. Patients generate relevant tourism revenues for the destination country beyond the direct income of the dental clinics.

Reasons for Travel

While dental tourists may travel for a variety of reasons, their choices are usually driven by price considerations. Wide variations in the economics of countries with shared borders have been the historical mainstay of the sector. Examples include travel from Austria to Hungary, Slovakia and Slovenia, from the US and Canada to Mexico, Costa Rica and Peru, from the Republic of Ireland to Northern Ireland, Hungary, Poland, Turkey and Ukraine, and from Australia to Thailand and other countries of South-East Asia. While medical tourism is often generalized to travel from high-income countries to low-cost developing economies, other factors can influence a decision to travel, including differences between the funding of public healthcare or general access to healthcare.

Mobility of Labour

For countries within the European Union, dental qualifications are required to reach a minimum approved by each country's government. Thus, a dentist qualified in one country can apply to any other EU country to practice in that country, allowing for greater mobility of labour for dentists (Directives typically apply not only to the EU but to the wider designation of the European Economic Area-EEA). The Association for Dental Education in Europe (ADEE) has standardization efforts to harmonize European standards. Proposals from the ADEE's Quality Assurance and Benchmarking taskforce cover the introduction of accreditation procedures for EU dentistry universities as well as programmes to facilitate dental students completing part of their education in foreign dentistry schools. Standardization of qualification in a region reciprocally removes one of the perceptual barriers for the development of patient mobility within that region.

Pricing and Quality

Dental tourists travel chiefly to take advantage of lower prices. Reasons for lower prices are many: dentists outside the "developed world" are able to take advantage of much lower fixed costs, lower labour costs, less government intervention, lower education fees and expenses, and lower insurance costs. Much of the bureaucratic red-tape that engulfs businesses in the developed world is eliminated abroad, and dentists are free to focus on their trade, dentistry. The flip-side of this is less legal recourse for patients when something goes wrong, but the result is that procedures, such as dental implants and porcelain veneers, which are simply financially out of reach for many people in the developed world, are made affordable overseas.

Much of the debate about dental tourism and medical tourism in general centres on the question of whether or not price differentials imply quality differentials. Another concern is whether or not large scale dental procedures can be safely completed abroad in a relatively short, "holiday-sized" time period. Another issue affecting this debate is the lack of an independent inspections committee for dental similar to the Joint Commission International for medical.

An instructive case study an analysis of patient outflows from the United Kingdom and Ireland, two large sources of dental tourists. Both countries were the subject of a report from the Irish Competition Authority to determine whether consumers were receiving value for money from their dentists. Both countries' professions were criticised for a lack of pricing transparency. A response to this is that dentistry is unsuitable for transparent pricing: each treatment will vary, an accurate quote is impossible until an examination has occurred. Thus price lists are no guarantee of final costs. Though they may encourage a level of competition between dentists, this will only happen in a competitive environment where supply and demand are closely matched.

The 2007 Competition Authority report in the Irish Republic criticised the profession on its approach to increasing numbers of dentists and the training of dental specialities–orthodontics was a particular area for concern with training being irregular and limited in number of places. Supply is further limited as new dental specialities develop and dentists react to consumer demand for new dental products, further diluting the pool of dentists available for any given procedure.

Aside from the above issues, it is possible to compare the prices of treatment in different countries. With the international nature of some products and brands it is possible to make a valid comparison. For instance, the same porcelain veneer made in a lab in Sweden can be as much as 2500 AUD in Australia, but only 1200 AUD in India. The price difference here is not explainable by reference to the material cost.

Clearly, undergoing extensive dental procedures abroad, even when allowing for travel expenses, can be significantly cheaper than the same procedures at home. Pricing and qualifications of the dentists may be researched through websites or by contacting the dentists. Another important consideration is location: if one travels all the way to India or Peru for a dental procedure and something goes wrong, it is a long way to return to fix it.

Many Americans choose to go somewhere relatively accessible from the US, such as San Salvador, Tijuana, Los Algodones, Tecate, Agua Prieta orLima. Due to the ongoing narco-violence in towns such as Tijuana and Ciudad Juarez, clinics in safer towns 1,000 miles south of the border—Cabo San Lucas, San Jose del Cabo, Puerto Vallarta, Cancun, Playa del Carmen and Cozumel Mazatlan etc. have recently started offering large and small dental treatments. (See info below.) More than 70 per cent of Mexico's US patients travel from the border states of California, Texas, or Arizona.

Since procedures often require multiple steps, or subsequent check-ups, the patient may have to return to the same doctor for those reasons. Typically, a patient takes two trips to have implants. The first trip is to set the base and the provisional crown. The second trip is typically 4-6 months later after the implant has stabilized in the bone. One Day Implants are not recommended for dental tourists due to the higher failure rate of the system. When combined with a holiday, as the name implies, dental tourism can be an opportunity to receive low-cost, quality dental care. Dental tourism is expected to continue growing, as consumers continue to seek out lower-cost options.

PART III: KEY COMPONENTS IN DENTAL TOURISM

The dental tourist's decision starts with a health problem which creates a more or less urgent need for an intervention by a dentist. If the price differences among services "at home" and "abroad" at some perceived quality level are important enough to incite the patient to travel abroad for the intervention, the dental patient becomes a potential dental tourist who is choosing a dentist, and—seemingly—in a simultaneous way a destination. However, if the destination has no touristic value as such for the patient other than being the location of the more convenient offer for a dental service, we cannot usefully consider this as being dental tourism. Medical services are dominant in the experience, while tourism spending is not significant.

Travellers who buy health care abroad usually get a package deal including the treatment, air transport, transfers and accommodation. Tourism is thus rather a by-product of packaging, but creates substantial benefits to the travel industry. Although as will be argued below, the tourism part is not necessarily sustainable as it depends completely on the price differences of medical treatment. We will, therefore, discuss the potential for increasing the tourism value of dental tourism to the patient and to the destination.

Among the economic factors determining the demand for medical tourism, several components can be identified; the most important being differences in treatment price, in national health systems and in conditions of private health insurance. The reduced prices can compensate for the absence of insurance overall or for some treatments (e.g. cosmetic surgery). These push factors are well-known from UK and USA who are important source countries of medical tourism in general. Concerning dental treatments, the British national health system, scarcely funded by tax revenue, results in long, up to half year stays on the waiting lists, while some treatments are hardly available in some regions. At the same time, UK's private clinics are offering their treatments at unaffordable prices for many. As far as the US is concerned, an estimated 50 million of citizens are without health insurance and 120 million without dental coverage which creates an important potential for medical and dental tourism. To what extent this translates into effective demand depends on the type of treatment. Bookman and Bookman (2007) claim, that the price elasticity of demand depends on the importance of the operation less complicated and more available treatments being more price sensitive. The implication for destinations is that they have to closely observe the development of relative, all inclusive prices to the patient between the source country and their own for different kinds of treatments before they ponder about additional tourism services. Apart from price differences, the necessary elements for the development of medical tourism (Bookman and Bookman, 2007) are: skilled local human capital, domestic research and development, developed infrastructure, stable political and regulated legal institutions, liberalized market economy, available tourist attractions.

Finally, as in general in tourism, good and cheap accessibility (i.e. mostly air transport services) will enhance the competitiveness of a dental tourism destination. Improved mobility gives better access to health services for the patients, and allows for a more efficient use of existing medical capacities (Österle, 2007).

Strategy for Dental Tourism

Prof. Judit Zoltan and Rico Maggi, Faculty of Economics, University of Lugano, Switzerland, have developed an innovative strategy for Dental Tourism. According to them, in order to describe a strategy for dental tourism that would take dental tourism closer to tourism, we apply the "Get there—stay there—live there" model (Croce, Maggi, 2005), which distinguish these three phases of the tourism experience. The GET THERE phase covers holiday start-up activities as information gathering ("Virtual Get There") and mobility ("Real Get There"). STAY THERE regards the satisfaction of basic holiday needs, i.e. accommodation and food, and LIVE THERE is about the satisfaction of secondary holiday needs and including all the activities of tourists at destination. The overall experience of a tourist is integrated among the three phases, but the degree of integration can vary in the different organizational models.

Dental treatments are the primary motivation of the dental trips. As cited above, for obvious reasons the treatment is placed in three varied phase—Get, Stay and Live (Details are furnished in Table 18.1). Visiting dental clinics constitutes a basic need of the patients, dental tourism would not be possible without them. The clinic is the anchor point of the dental tourism experience, much like the business meeting of the conference is for business tourism.

Table 18.1: Dental Tourism Activities Model as Developed by Judit Zoltan and Rico Maggi

	Get There	*Stay There*	*Live There*
Activities	Information gathering	Dental treatment	Entertainment
	Contact with operators	Accommodation	Wellness
	Transportation	Food	Sightseeing
Stakeholders	Marketing and Information platform	Dental Clinic	DMO
	Dental Travel agent	Partner Hotel	Excursion organizer
	Dental Travel Agency	Controlling authority at the destination	Entertainment provider
	Controlling authority in the source country		
	Insurance Company		
	Airline company		

Source: www.https://ssl.lu.usi.ch>pdf–pub 5354

The challenge for the development of dental tourism lies in the currently dominating focus of the tour organization on the stay there phase, hence the dental treatment complemented by the accommodation. Table 18.1 shows the three actual dominating organizational models of dental tourism. While in the first of the three cases illustrated, the organizational anchor point (i.e. the TO) is the clinic, in the other two cases the organization of the experience is in the hand of a specialized tour operator. When the first model applies, the tourism experience at destination represents just an accessory, organized eventually by the hotel or the clinic upon request from the patient. As there is no integration with the destination, the scope of a DMO to target the market via the TO is very limited and the business will never become more touristic. The intermediation between the clinic and the patient by a TO, as in the second case shown in Table 18.1, makes the organization of the experience more efficient and consequently will enlarge the market. However, neither this model includes the tourism experience at the destination in the dental tourism market. Only the third model where the anchor is again the TO but with direct access to the destination, i.e. packaging, arranging, offering the whole experience will give scope for a development of a real dental tourism market. Dental Travel Agencies have the potential to link effectively DMOs with the dental industry.

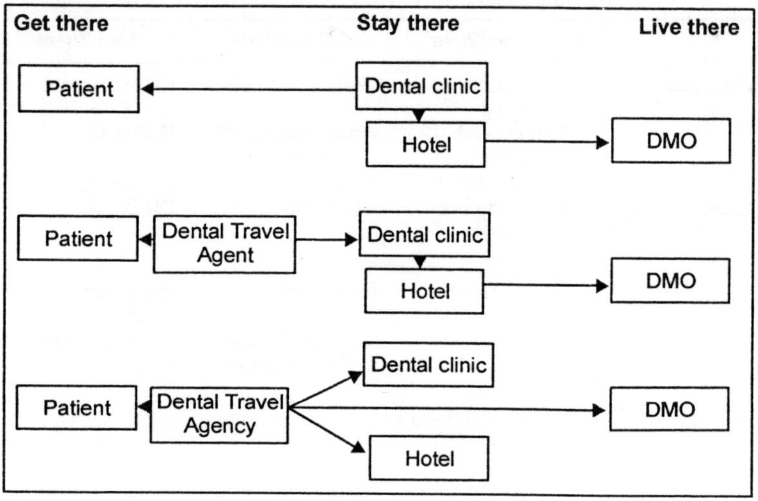

Fig. 18.1: Dental tourism organizational models in the Get there-Stay there-Live there frame as Developed by Judit Zoltan and Rico Maggi.
Source: Ibid.

PART IV: CONCLUDING OBSERVATIONS

Global Scenario : The World Tourism Organization (UNWTO) forecasts that international tourism will continue growing at the average annual rate of 4 per cent. With the advent of e-commerce, tourism products have become one of the most traded items on the internet. Tourism products and services have been made available through intermediaries, although tourism providers (hotels, airlines, etc.), including small-scale operators, can sell their services directly. This has put pressure on intermediaries from both on-line and traditional shops.

It has been suggested there is a strong correlation between tourism expenditure per capita and the degree to which countries play in the global context. Not only as a result of the important economic contribution of the tourism industry, but also as an indicator of the degree of confidence with which global citizens leverage the resources of the globe for the benefit of their local economies. This is why any projections of growth in tourism may serve as an indication of the relative influence that each country will exercise in the future.

Latest Trends

As a result of the late-2000s recession, international arrivals suffered a strong slowdown beginning in June 2008. Growth from 2007 to 2008 was only 3.7 per cent during the first eight months of 2008. This slowdown on international tourism demand was also reflected in the air transport industry, with a negative growth in September 2008 and a 3.3 per cent growth in passenger traffic through September. The hotel industry also reported a slowdown, with room occupancy declining. In 2009 worldwide tourism arrivals decreased by 3.8 per cent. By the first quarter of 2009, real travel demand in the United States had fallen 6 per cent over six quarters. While this is considerably milder than what occurred after the 9/11 attacks, the decline was at twice the rate as real GDP has fallen.

However, evidence suggests that tourism as a global phenomena shows no signs of substantially abating in the long term. It has been suggested that travel is necessary in order to maintain relationships, as social life is increasingly networked and conducted at a distance. For many people vacations and travel are increasingly being viewed as a necessity rather than a luxury, and this is reflected in tourist numbers recovering some 6.6 per cent globally over 2009, with growth up to 8 per cent in emerging economies.

People all-over the world have been visiting India to explore its scenic beauty. Now-a-days, these tourists are not only here for sightseeing, but, for availing reasonable dental treatments while they travel. Dental treatment is truly expensive abroad, and, getting treated without a dental insurance can be a complex task for them. So, tourists abroad are now looking at the option of getting dental treatments done while abiding their journey. Dental Tourism has come out as a respite for those seeking low cost dental treatment, and, India emerged as a major tourism destination for dental treatments within the means.

Dental treatment and its cost is a major drawback for people searching for reasonable dental care procedures. Visitors coming from US, UK and other nations expect much better savings on dental costs. They can set aside substantial amount of money on most dental treatment courses, even after the totalling on travel, lodging etc. Dental Tourism in India has turn out to be the widely accepted sector of medical tourism. Dental clinics in India blow visitors with its state of the art facilities.

Highly proficient and skilled dentists are there in India to carry out effective dental implants. Indian dental clinics always offer highly standardized clinical care for the patients. Dental procedures in India are on a par with the dental services in UK, US and other nations. Indian dental clinics never conciliate on quality, even though the dental procedures are offered at low cost. Tourists from other nations found that, India is the best destination for dental tourism, as it offers affordable dental treatments. Visitors can also take pleasure in their trips without affecting the treatment schedule.

Dental Tourism in Kerala: Kerala has also been established as a destination for dental tourism for decades. Kerala dental treatments are less susceptible and the patients never ever feel distressed before and after the course. The reasons for the abundance of dental tourists in Kerala are as a result of the excellent dental procedure, quick and easy treatment options and also the specialist's appointments without the need of much waiting. Above all, visitors flock to Kerala owing to its position as the topmost tourism destination round the globe. Dentists are getting appreciated for their degree of professionalism and for their concerned care. Moreover, Dentists in Kerala are highly treasured for their expert dental care. Kerala dental procedures are highly standardized and are done under strict etiquettes of sterilization and disinfection to keep away from adverse effects of dental treatments.

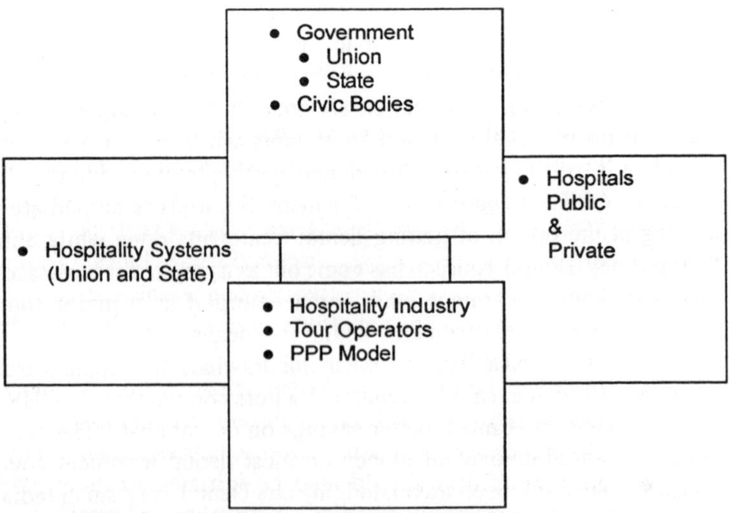

Fig. 18.2: The Partners of Dental Tourism—Proposed.

Source: Developed by the author.

Promote Dental Tourism

With over 3000 dentists and 1200 dental clinics, Kerala has a distinct advantage in dental tourism. The fact that the treatment requires multiple sittings with liberal gaps in between sittings and hence requiring around 30-40 days stay makes the dental patient an ideal candidate for medical tourism. Hence, more efforts should be made to market the dental tourism product.

Suggestions to Revamp

- The government should take more active role for the growth of medical and dental tourism. It should function as a facilitator and catalyst.
- It would be advisable to follow a Private-Pubic-Partnership Model (PPP) in promoting Dental Tourism.
- The Central Government could also help popularise Medical and Dental Tourism through Embassies and through Health Ministries in various foreign countries.
- More financial and fiscal concessions need also be offered to this sector which has tremendous employment and foreign exchange earning potential. Only then they can be encouraged to make the necessary investments needed for upgradation, standardisation and accreditation of the medical facilities/ institutions.
- Other areas which will require government/statutory support is in the field of insurance facilities, visa on arrival with special facilities for medical visas, quality control and certification/ accreditation.
- Moreover, Government of Kerala should also take initiative to organise Dental Tourism Fairs and Road-shows for promoting Dental tourism besides participation in international medical tourism events. Special efforts targeted at SARC countries may also be considered.
- In this, there must be active participation from all category of Dental and Medical Tourism players, industry associations like CII and Central and State Governments as shown in Fig. 18.2.
- Sincere efforts should also be initiated to incorporate the involvement of civic bodies—both urban and rural.

- Steps should also be initiated to explore the possibilities to introduce Ayurveda in Dental Treatment.

REFERENCES

Bookman, M.Z. and Bookman, K.R. (2007). *Medical Tourism in Developing Countries*, Palgrave MacMillan, New York.

Connell, J. (2006). "Medical Tourism", *Tourism Management,* Vol. 27, Issue 6, December, 2006.

Croce, V., and Maggi, R. (2005). "*Lugano Tourism Indicator—A Competitiveness Indicator for City Tourism Destination in Europe*," UNWTO Coimbra.

en.wikipedia.org

Government of Kerala, Department of Tourism (2000). Tourism Policy : Mission 2020.

Government of Kerala, State Planning Board, *Economic Review*, Various years.

Horowitz, M.D. and Rosenweig, J.A. (2007). "Medical Tourism : Globalization of the Healthcare Marketplace," *Medscape General Medicine Journal*, Vol. 9(4).

Joseph M. Cherukara and James Manalel, *Medical Tourism in Kerala—Challenges and Scope*, dspace.iimk.ac.in/.../1/369-379+Joseph+ Cherukara.pdf &embedded =true

Judit Zoltan and Rico Maggi, *What is Tourism in Dental Tourism*, https:// ssl.lu.usi.ch/entityws/Allegati/pdf_pub5354.pdf

Pruthi Raj (2006). *Medical Tourism in India*, Arise Publishers and Distributors, New Delhi.

www.academia.edu/4106727/dental_tourism_in_india

19

Outbound Business Travel—An Emerging Trend among Pharma Companies

Anitha, R.

I. Introduction

The Indian Pharmaceutical industry today is in the front rank of India's science based industries with wide ranging capacities in the complex field of drug manufacture and technology. A highly organized sector, the Indian pharma industry is estimated to be worth $ 4.5 billion, growing at about 8 to 9 per cent annually. It ranks very high in the Third World, in terms of technology, quality and range of medicines is manufactured. From simple headache pills to sophisticated antibiotics and complex cardiac compounds, almost every type of medicines is now made indigenously.

Playing a key role in promoting and sustaining development in the vital field of medicines, Indian Pharma Industry boasts of quality producers and many units approved by regulatory authorities in USA and UK. International companies associated with the sector have stimulated, assisted spearheaded this dynamic development in the last 53 years and helped to put India on the pharmaceutical map of the world.

The Indian pharmaceutical sector is highly fragmented with more than 20,000 resisted units. It has expanded drastically in the last two decades. The leading 250 pharmaceutical companies control 70 per cent of the market with market leader holding nearly 7 per cent of the market share. It is an extremely fragment market with severe price competition and government price control.

The pharmaceutical industry in India meets around 70 per cent of the country's demand for bulk drugs, drug intermediates, Pharmaceutical formulations, chemicals, tablets, capsules, orals and injectibles. There are about 250 large units and about 8000 small scale units, which form the core of the pharmaceutical industry in India (including 5 central public sector units). These units produce the complete range of pharmaceutical formulation, i.e. medicines ready for consumption by patients and about 350 bulk drugs, i.e., chemicals having therapeutic value and used for production of pharmaceutical formulations.

To motivate the field force now most of the companies organize meetings, conferences and incentive travel to their employees to top to bottom. The field force is the backborn of promoting brands and products.

II. Objectives

Outbound business travel as an emerging trend among pharma companies.
To analyse the impact of outbound tourism among pharma companies.
To evaluate the role of pharma companies towards incentive travel.

Methodology

A detailed questionnaire was designed and developed with a view to obtain the trend among various pharma companies regarding outbound business travel, tourist experience, choice of destination, selection of accommodation, duration of visit, travel agency assistance, marketing strategy etc. During the survey altogether 20 effective face to face interviews were made from different categories between age group of 22 to 26 years of aged medical representatives all-over Kerala. They belongs to the top ten pharma companies at that time and other 6 major companies who joined outbound business travel. The study is being made to know the scope, impact of outbound tourism in the country and to evaluate the future of out bound incentive travel, whether it is an emerging trend, Pharma companies' role in promoting incentive travel etc. Most basic and outstanding samples are identified and analysed in detail.

III. Outbound Business Travel—An Emerging Trend among Pharma Companies

India's corporate travel market is today estimated at not less than US$3 billion (around Rs.150 billion). In the past there has been better growth in outbound business as compared to inbound. Travel costs have emerged as the third largest expense of corporate, salaries and raw-meterials. The companies offer incentive travel to the employees for motivating their field force and to withstand strong competition of Pharma products and marketing of branding position.

(A) Why pharma companies offer outbound business travel?

1. For attending international conferences.
2. For updating scientific and academic knowledge.
3. Sharing of experiences.
4. Familiarization of the application of modern technology.
5. Mutual support for business.

(B) Why the employees prefer International destination?

Other than the above reason some sort of entertainment mixed with leisure is common.

1. Cultural performances at the venue.
2. Discount for shopping in malls.
3. Duty free outlets.
4. Shopping and entertainment.
5. To feel the urban prosperity.
6. Excellent guide service.

IV. Top 10 Companies on the Basis of Net Sales

I. The Top 10 companies on the basis of net sales (2007 March sales)

I. Dr. Reddy's Laboratories
II. Ranbaxy
III. Cipla
IV. Lupin
V. SunPharma
VI. Nicholas Piramal India
VII. Glaxo SmithKline
VIII. Cadila Health Care
IX. Wockhardt
X. IPCA Lab

Source: *Business India,* September 23, 2007.

Top 10 Companies on the Basis of Volume of Sales of Medicine Supplied to Hospitals (According to Hospital Secondary Audit Survey. *Source*: *Business India*, December 30, 2007):

1. Glaxo SmithKline
2. Cipla
3. SanofiAventis
4. Alkem
5. SunPharma
6. Zydns Cadila
7. Pfizer
8. Ranbaxy
9. Nicholas Piramal India
10. Lupin Labs

V. Trends that Support Business Travel

(1) Corporate Travel Agents

Today the information is instant and available to everyone and agencies are automated and equipped to meet increasingly complex travel needs of the corporate traveller. Through such incentive business they got bulk business.

(2) Budget Airlines

The primary objective of low cost carriers where faster connectivity at a cheaper price—To transport passenger from origin to destination in the shortest possible time at the most affordable price. Now-a-days, even big firms are looking to reduce the cost of expenses to their employees. In such a background, the availability of cheaper airlines are highly admitable to reduce the cost of travel expenses from their company's side.

(3) *Budget Hotels*

Budget hotels offer an alternative for the big budget hotels. It provides same amenities at an affordable cost.

(4) Service Apartments

The concept of service apartments though a recent phenomenon in India, is an established global concept. Villas in Spain than flats in U.K. apartments, complexes in the US have all created a vibrant and viable market for those wanting more than just a room in a hotel. Service apartments are the latest trend in accommodation offering the comfort and convenience of a home without the hassles of having to maintain or look after it. [Four seasons is developing a destination resort in Puthenkayal Kumarkam which will have 75 villas and also 20 branded private residences. The resort will be operational by 2012]. Internet technology has helped expand the utility of global distribution system allowing end-consumers to directly interact with the GDS system. This means that the traveller can now book his itinerary with his travel agents, from anywhere in the world or any time of the day or night. Communication is another area where the travel distribution industry is witnessing a revolution.

(5) GPRS (General Pocket Radio Services)

GPRS offers instant connections and provides more bandwidth that will enable a host of interactive services and new products, making both planning travel and travelling a whole lot easier.

(6) Business Centre Facilities

The advent of broadband and wireless internet has brought about a drastic change in the role of a hotel business centre. The latest in this area is "small meeting rooms" with state-of-the-art technology *viz.*, video conferencing, phone conference web casting etc.

(7) Mobile Connectivity

The impact of mobile is becoming hard to overstate, especially for the corporate traveller, who is persistently on the go. So when the boundaries of mobile telephony, both in terms of hardware design and technological integration are being pushed, it means good news for the corporate road warrior.

VI. Sales Report

Number of Employees and Destinations
Selected for Out bound Business Travel

Table 19.1: Top 10 Companies and Six Other Companies

	Name of Pharma Company	*Trend*	*Number of Employees*			*Destination*		
			2006	*2007*	*2008*	*2006*	*2007*	*2008*
1.	Dr. Reddy's Lab	No trend				Dubai	Dubai	
2.	Ranbaxy		20	No trend	No trend	Amsterdam		
3.	Cipla		–	–	–	–	–	–
4.	Lupin		830	800		Thailand	Srilanka (optional)	
5.	Sun Pharma		No trend	800	900	–	Singapore, Malaysia	Thailand
6.	Nicholas Primal India			1200	200		Malaysia	
7.	Glaxo SmithKline		500	No trend	No trend	USA		
8.	Cadila Health Care		500	600		Malaysia	Singapore	
9.	Workhardt	No trend	–	–	–	–	–	–
10.	IPCA Lab	No trend	–	–	–	–	–	–
	OTHERS							
1.	Torent		375	500	No trend	Bangkok	Bali	No trend
2.	Intas		200	500	–	Singapore	Dubai, Singapore	—
3.	Pfizer		No trend	50	50	–	Bankgkok, Pattaya	Dubai
4.	Novartis		200	250	350	Thailand	Malaysia, Srilanka	Singapore
5.	Merc		50	60	95	Keiro	Singapore	Malaysia
6.	Aventis		No trend	120	120	–	Bankgkok, Pattaya	Malaysia

Source: Direct survey.

VII. Important Mice Destination—For Pharma Companies

I. Thailand
II. Indonesia
III. Singapore
IV. Dubai
V. Hong Kong
VI. Australia
VII. Mauritius
VIII. Canada
IX. USA

(MICE—Meetigs, Incentives, Conferences, Exhibitions.)

Table 19.2: Views and opinions of the respondents

Option	*No: of Participants*	*Total*
Government Agencies	Nil	Nil
Corporate Travel Agents	20	100%
Total	**20**	**100%**

Source: Direct survey.

(1) Public/Private Role

Pharma companies seek the Assistance of corporate travel agents. Among the 20 Respondents all companies seek the assistance of corporate T&A.

(2) Guide Service

Opinion	*Net Responds*	*Percentage*
Excellent	4	20
Good	8	40
Okay	4	20
Not Satisfactory	4	20
Total	20	100

(3) Travel Agents Assisted in Completing Travel formalities

Opinion	*No. of Respondents*	*Percentage*
Yes	17	85
No	3	15
Total	**20**	**100**

(4) Travel Agents Assisted in Foreign Currency Conversions

Opinion	*No. of Respondents*	*%*
Yes	15	85
No	5	15
Total	**20**	**100**

(5) Quality of Food

Opinion	No.	%
Excellent	2	10
Good	10	50
Average	6	30
Satisfactory	2	10
Total	**20**	**100**

(6) Shopping Assistance

Opinion	No.	%
Excellent	3	15
Good	13	65
Average	4	20
Total	**20**	**100**

(7) Duration of Stay in the Outbound Partition

Opinion	No.	%
Three days	8	40
Four days	10	50
>4 days	2	10
Total	**20**	**100**

(8) Is it the First Visit to a Foreign Destination and for the First Time Travel by Flight

Opinion	No.	%
First Time	15	75
No	5	25
Total	**20**	**100**

(9) Sightseeing

Opinion	No.	%
Excellent	4	20
Good	9	45
Average	3	15
Satisfactory	4	20
Total	**20**	**100**

(10) Outbound tourism—An emerging trend among pharma companies

Opinion	No.	%
Yes	20	100
No	NIL	0
Total	**20**	**100**

(11) Outbound tourism strongly promote marketing of brands and status and prestige leval of field force

Opinion	No.	%
Yes	*20*	*100*
No	*NIL*	*0*
Total	**20**	**100**

(12) Satisfaction Level of Respondents

Opinion	No. of Respondents	%
100%	4	20
75%	12	60
50 %	4	20
25%	Nil	100

(13) Incentive Travel Proceeds Strong Internal and External Competition between Pharma Companies

Opinion	*No. of Respondents*	*%*
Yes	17	85
No	3	15
Total	**20**	**100**

Source: Direct Survey.

VIII. Findings

Medical representatives are the major tools of product promotion. The companies offer them outbound incentive travel for motivating their field force and achieving their target. The outbound tourism trend among pharma companies is significant in many ways. It is an emerging trend. It builds strong internal and external competitions among and between companies. Bulk business is captured by corporate travel agents. Airlines, hotels, guide services, have significant role in promoting outbound tourism. It allows the citizen to make a comparison between India and the outbound destination in all streams of education technology, infrastructure etc. For many representatives attending a conference or meeting or achieving an outstanding performance award or an incentive trip could be his or her first visit in a foreign destination. So, the accommodation units usually keeps high service standards and it provide a good experience for the executives and will generate more spin off business opportunities in future. The findings are explained below:

1. Most of the field executives are the age group of 20-26 and they are graduates only and they belong to middle class families.
2. A field executive who achieve 110-120 per cent target get the advantage of incentive travel.
3. Out of the top 10 companies listed above 50 per cent companies only send field executive in a foreign land.
4. Medium and small sector companies are offering much better incentive structure to their company executives.
5. Most of the pharma companies offer outbound incentive travel to doctors and their family members. To marketing executives it is a new trend.
6. Each and every year the number of marketing executives going abroad is increasing.

7. The growth of outbound travel is remarkable when compared to inbound growth.
8. Corporate travel agents assisted in completing travel formalities for 85 per cent of the travel executives.
9. Duration of stay in a foreign land is minimum of three days for 40 per cent and four days for 50 per cent respondents.
10. The quality of food provided is excellent for 10 per cent and good for 50 per cent respondents and the rest average.
11. Sightseeing options are good for 45 per cent and excellent for 20 per cent and the rest average.
12. Outbound tourism strongly promote marketing of brand status and prestige level of field force.
13. Incentive travel provides strong internal and external competition among and between pharma companies.
14. Outbound business travel is a strong motivating factor for achieving sales target and making profit for the Companies.

The study reveals that the most preferred outbound destinations are Malaysia, Thailand and Singapore. Obtaining visa to these destinations are simple compared to other destinations. The conference meetings and award presentations in a foreign land is a prestigious experience. Shoppings, entertainments, food and beverages strongly attract executives towards an incentive travel.

Problemes Faced by Field Executives

1. Those who qualify this year may not be qualifying next year because of increase in target.
2. Executives may not be able to continue the per man per month growth productivity.
3. Due to one year achievement next year subject to market conditions they are not able to perform.
4. Due to sales pressure and other alternative jobs are available like insurance and IT sector, currently attrition rates are quite high.

IX. Conclusion

In conclusion the researcher could say that outbound business travel is a new trend among pharma companies. Even though companies are following the cost cutting norm the trend still exists. Those who archieve the sales target are only eligible for incentive travel. So, every person is striving for achieving sales target and they get monitory benefit as well as outbound incentive travel. It is also considered as a prestigious one for marketing executives. A recent study by the National business association (NBTA) has shown that Companies are recognizing the value of face to face meeting with customers, prospects, partners and colleagues, to build relationships and set the stage for topline growth. For this outbound business travel for conference, conventions, meetings, award presentations etc. will always be one of the best ways to reward and retain top talent. Even in the background of global economic recession the trend is still existing.

REFERENCES

http://www.ibef.org
http://www.businesstravellerindia.com
Pharmaceutical Industry, Indian Pharma Industry.
Business India Magazine 2007, September 23 & December 30.

20

Management of Archaeological Sites and Promotion of Heritage Tourism
Study of Nalanda

Sujata, Yashwant Singh and *Shyju, P.J.*

1. Introduction

Heritage is conceived of as identifying set of natural and cultural assets of a society (Repiso).

The concept of heritage tourism is associated with sites related to historical importance, old monuments, and artefacts. In the perspective of historical importance, archaeological sites in India, reflect the rich heritage of thousands of years. The excavated sites of civilizations, take us back to an era of prosperous life, flourished in the subcontinent. The territory under the jurisdiction of Indian state contains by far the most socio-cultural situation in the world (Oommen, 2004). A nation's identity primarily relies on the background of its claim on ancient heritage and the value assigned to it on the basis of life and prosperity by comparing with other countries. The archaeological sites in India have a predominant role in the making of the concept of Heritage Tourism. Excavated sites in Gujarat, Tamil Nadu, Karnataka, Madhya Pradesh, Bihar, Uttar Pradesh etc. proved the fact that the rich heritage of India has immense potential to attract tourists.

Heritage Tourism play a very important role in the development of the regions and the economic activities emerged out of tourism gained attention from different corners such as government, private and public sectors. Heritage tourism is representative of many contemporary visitors to directly experience and consume diverse past and present cultural forms. Nalanda, located in the state of Bihar in India, is well known for centuries. The ruins of ancient Buddhist establishments of Nalanda lie close to the place of Bargaon about 55 miles south-east of Patna and seven miles North of Rajgir (Rajagriha). As a destination of learning, its historical importance is beyond any levels of comparison. India's first multi-media museum located close to the ruins of Nalanda University gives an animated visualisation of the rise and decline of this historical place. Today, the remains of this great university attract tourists and it is a debatable issue whether the educational and historical importance of Nalanda has gone down.

The maintenance of this monument is taken care by the Archaeological Survey of India since the identification of this site. A.S.I. has declared the excavated sites as protected monuments, to conserve the buildings and remains from further degradation or collapse. The initial enthusiasm of a visitor may soon go down if he/she has not aware of the historical importance of this place. Rather departments like Archaeology or tourism have not given any interest to ensure a better tourist experience in these sites In addition to the problems of law and order in the state, lack of efforts from the side of government, to uplift this place as an international destination resulted in a low turn out of foreign tourists. This chapter attempts to discuss the interrelationship between archaeological sites and heritage tourism.

2. Literature Review

Several researches have been done in the field of Archaeology. Many archaeological sites have been reused as visitor attractions to tap the rapidly burgeoning demand for tourism (Dutta, Banerjee and Hussain, 2007). The literature survey shows that studies have been conducted on heritage tourism in different countries, and the most debatable part is the authenticity of information provided in a heritage site. A dynamic swift has taken place in period in evolving standards and philosophy in public archaeology and heritage interpretation in the last few decades (Jameson, 2008). Commoditisation of culture is one of the main drawbacks of tourism development, which is a major debatable issue (Medina, 2003). Quests for authenticity are one of the main part of motivating factor for tourists (MacCannel, 1976). MacCannel (1979) further suggests that staged authenticity is not at all advisable to attract tourists. Heritage tourism has got lot of attention in the recent years (Balcar and Pearce, 1996; Herbert,

2001). Heritage tourism offers opportunity to portray the past in the present (Patnaik, 2004). Zeppal and Hall (1991) view heritage tourism as based on the nostalgia for the past and desire to experience diverse cultural landscapes and forms. An important attribute of heritage tourism is authenticity (Boniface and Fowler, 1993, Taylor, 2001). Quality of heritage tourism is enhanced by authenticity (Cohen, 1988). Marketing of historic events can reinforce the locus identity (Ashworth & Larkham, 1994).

It is clear that the relationship between heritage tourism and national identity is an important area for research and debate. A better appreciation of the way in which these two areas interact can only lead to a more in-depth awareness of how national identity is formed and how it can change over time. A nation's history, or heritage is only one of the elements that combine to form a national identity (Palmer, C., 1999).

Heritage is not a monolithic representation, and it gives different dimensions of thoughts to different visitors (Cheung, 1999). Tourists to heritage sites expect interpretation of information on site visited (Poria, Butler, & Airey, 2003). Points of view, perceptions beliefs or powers can make things appear as authentic but it may not be inherently authentic (Wang, 1999). Tourists seek deep integration with existential intangible heritage while they link authenticity with the original spirit (Gonzalez, 2007). Importance in visitor experience in cognitive and emotional aspects is the base for satisfaction (Rojas and Camarero, 2008), which leads to the managerial part of visitor management in a destination. The inter-relationship between heritage tourism and archaeological sites have been discussed very less.

Brief History

Nalanda is a Sanskrit word, which means *giver of knowledge*. Lord Buddha is believed to be visited this place several times and stayed in the mangrove of Pavarika's mangrove. *Kevatta Sutta*, mentioned that during the period of Lord Buddha, Nalanda was a thickly populated town and very prosperous. Sariputta, the right hand disciple of Buddha, was born and died in Nalanda. The Chinese monk Xuanzang (Hiuen-Tsang) referred Nalanda in his works. According to Xuanzang, Nalanda Mahavihar (University) was established by Sakraditya. Historians identify Sakraditya as the Gupta Ruler Kumargupta-I. During the peak time, Nalanda University could accommodate approximately 10,000 students and 2,000 teachers. It was one of the master pieces of architecture and it had a great library, which had a most renowned repository of Buddhist knowledge.

Nine storey building, eight separate compounds, ten temples, and several meditation halls adorned this centre of learning.

The curriculum of this university had various subjects such as Astronomy, Medicine, Philosophy, *Yoga Shastra*, the *Vedas*, Scriptures of Buddhism, Grammar, Linguistics and Theology. Nalanda was destroyed thrice. But the complete destruction of the monument had taken place in 12th century A.D., when Bakhtiyar Khilji attacked the University. In addition to the above said monuments A.S.I. has listed the following monuments in its list—Tomb of Malik Ibrahim Bayu, Garh, Ancient Mount, Baragaon, Statue of Buddha, Jagdishpur etc.

3. Methodology

The study is conducted through various primary and secondary data sources. Secondary sources include books, publications by government, journals and other published reports. Information available from internet also helped to complete the study. Apart from the published sources, personal visit to these places helped a great extent to undertake this study. Observations made during the visits, interaction with the visitors, local people and the officials benefited in a way to understand the realities of visitor experience in these places.

4. Significance of the Study

As mentioned in the introduction, heritage tourism is one of the major segments of tourism products of India. The historical remains and archaeological sites constitute a chunk portion of heritage tourism. Many of such archaeological sites are located in Bihar and as a place fostered Buddhism in its course of development as a religion, throughout the world, and as the seat of learning of ancient India, the archaeological site at Nalanda has immense potential to promote heritage tourism. This study focuses on various issues associated with the archaeological sites and heritage tourism in the background of Nalanda. The study can initiate further discussions on various topics associated with issues like visitor management in historical sites, site interpretation, preservation etc. Understanding the tourists profile will lead to the better management of visitor facilities and preservation of historically important monuments.

5. Objectives

The study has been conducted to understand the problem areas of the archaeological sites and how heritage tourism is promoted in Nalanda. Main objectives of the study are the following:

- To understand the importance of Nalanda as a historical place.
- To explore the interfering areas of archaeological sites and tourism activities.
- To make a comparative study, whether tourism is overriding the protection of archaeological sites.
- To present the problematic areas of tourist presence in ancient sites.

6. Analysis

Nalanda has got back its pride and status after excavations done by ASI, and it stands as one of the identities of India in the world. This archaeological site proves the importance given to education in ancient India, (not corporate/commercial), teacher-student relationship (*gurushishya parampara)* and the advancements in experiments, meditation and knowledge. It took several years to demark the locations of the remains of this great University. But even today it is difficult to say exactly how much still remains unexcavated. Picture 20.1 shows the lay out of the main site of Nalanda University.

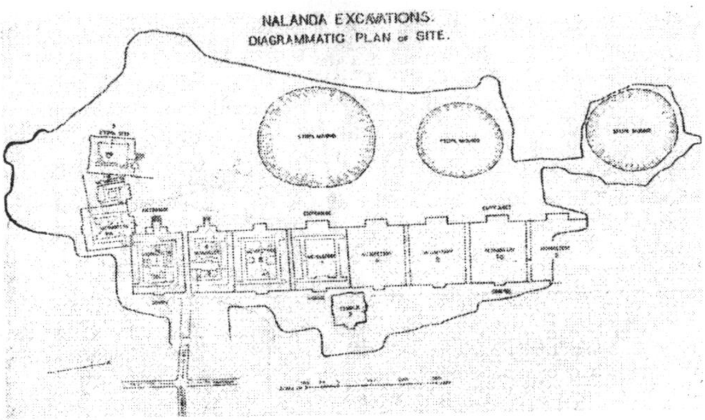

Picture 20.1: Nalanda Excavations.
Source: Kuraishi, M.H., 1931.

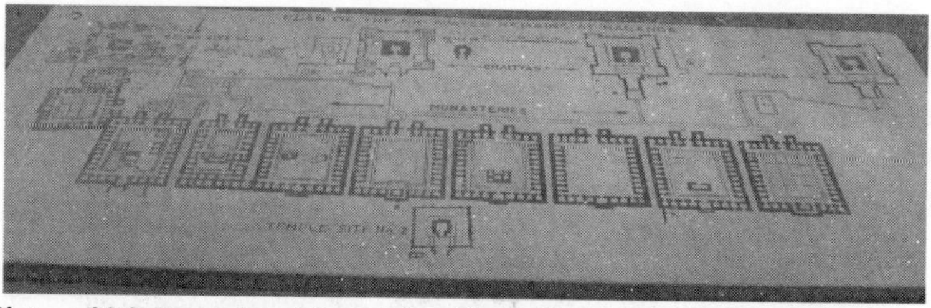

Picture 20.2: Reproduced from A.S.I. illustration at the site, Main entrance.
Source: A.S.I.

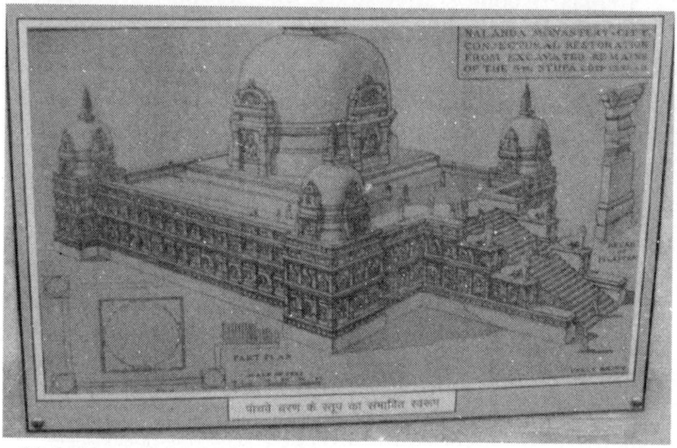

Picture 20.3: Plan of the Main temple.
Source: A.S.I.

Picture 20.4: Excavation works in pogress.
Source: A.S.I.

Picture 20.4: Excavations in progress.
Source: A.S.I.

Picture 20.5: After Excavations, Photo: author.
Source: A.S.I.

Pictures shown in the previous pages imply the beginning and progress of excavation works by A.S.I. Preservation works are still going on and it may take a couple of years to complete. The site is open to the visitors and large number of domestic tourists and a number of international tourists visit this monument. After entering the site, tourists will be curious to see a new world open to their eyes as one's thoughts of the holistic education of the past and a divine place in terms of learning come close to their eyes. But this astonishment and enthusiasm will go after covering few yards, as there is no one to help the visitors or provide authentic information about the lay-out of the buildings, main structures, and its importance. It is also seen that fabrication of stories by local guides who can change the characters and history time to time.

This phenomenon is found in all important places in India. In order to earn a day's livelihood, local guides who take the tourists inside a historical site, interpret the history in their own way, which raises serious questions on the national identity itself. When the authenticity of the information becomes a fabricated story consciously or unconsciously, the tourists have no other option left other than believing what the local guide says. The basic problem here is a dearth of trained guides in the destination. Further domestic tourism is high in India; the interest of domestic tourists to look for a guide is also another reason of inadequate information distribution. Even though the volume of domestic tourists is high, the team members who constitute a group are less in number, results in avoiding the additional burden to hire a guide. Fig. 20.1 displays flow of information management system in an archaeological site.

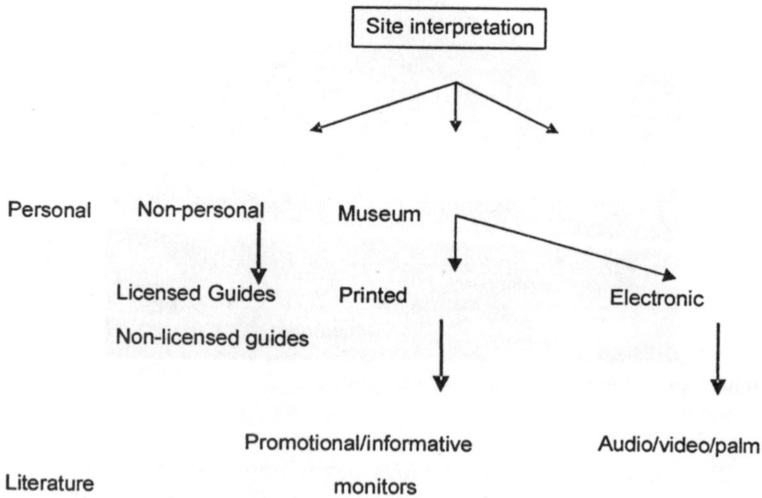

Fig. 20.1: Distribution of Information

Fig. 20.1 explains the distribution of information, which is channelled through personal and non-personal forms. Authenticity of information depends on the source. As mentioned earlier, A.S.I. has a vital role in providing accurate and reliable information but it could not take serious steps for controlling the false interpretation of sites. The role of A.S.I. change from preservation to *information management* and *visitor management* too.

Heritage tourism and archaeology are interrelated subjects. Curiosity is one of the main motivational factors in tourism. An ancient site cannot only generate common interest of visitors, but also fuel appreciating national identity, pride and patriotism. Visit to Nalanda definitely, will give a visualisation of the ancient learning system and understand the value given by the people of India in terms of learning. Interface of archaeological sites and the development of heritage tourism here means educating the visitor towards a historical site, and make one appreciate the value and importance of such sites, underline the need of preservation, and the role of each individual in a society to become part of the preservation activities. Thus the archaeological sites will be protected in one way and at the same time the visitors will be part of the preservation activities.

Apart from this, generation of income from the visitors on various ways like entry fee, user charges, souvenir sales etc. can be a fund source for that site. At present the entry fee in any A.S.I. site in India not even constitute 1 per cent of the total investment required for survey, excavation and preservation works. The recurring expenditure of preservation of a site is so huge that a government, which has many other priorities cannot simply help. So, the interaction between tourism and archaeological sites will help to solve these problems up to certain extent. The summary of the above discussion can be explained as follows:

Archaeological Sites	*Heritage Tourism*
Main purpose Protection and preservation	Opening the heritage (archaeological) sites for tourists
Problem areas Overcrowding Disfiguring Theft of artefacts Manipulation of facts in Reproduction (Loss of images/materials) mismanagement	Advantages Income generation Awareness/educating visitors Creating a sense of pride/patriotism Maintenance of standards

Source: Primary Data.

With the help of various agencies and State Governments, A.S.I. is in the forefront of every activity of preservation of heritage and ancient sites in India. Yet, several problems exist in the management of archaeological sites. A question arises here is whether tourism activity hijacks the preservation efforts of A.S.I. or state agencies who are responsible for the preservation activities. The basis for the doubt is in Rajasthan, monuments of historical importance have been well preserved, than in any other states in India. A lion share of foreign tourists arrivals are recorded in Rajasthan which also indicates the sites covers historical monuments and palaces which are well maintained. Forts, palaces, and ancient sites which are dilapidated, collapsed have less number of tourist turn out. This fact indicates that revenue from tourism attract the investors who are eager to protect a monument if there will be an anticipated return from that monument. At the same time, a monument of historical importance, is neglected which can generate less income from tourism. Another fact is that for the convenience of tourists, refreshment centres, comfort stations etc. will slowly change the structures permanently and thereby loose the authenticity. Sometimes, it will result in the permanent destruction of the site. Government is having a dominant role in the preservation of the heritage of the nation, but it seems to be silent in the case of financing such monuments are concerned.

Researches and excavations conducted in Nalanda, could unearth copper plates, stone inscriptions, brick inscriptions, ceiling and plaques, coins and potteries, carved bricks and stone images. Bargaon, located north of the main site of excavations, is an important site in terms of archaeology, having a Surya Temple, from where the collection of Brahmanical and Buddihst images can be seen. Another site, Begampur, located between the village of Bargaon and Begumpur, has extensive mounds representing ancient buildings. This place probably marks the northern extremity of the ancient establishments of Nalanda and give an idea of how extensive Nalanda was in the days of its glory. Nalakgram, is the birthplace of Sariputta, one of the main disciples of Lord Buddha. Kundalpur which is hardly one km away from Nalanda, is a site associated to Jainism. These sites are least cared by tourism department and no proper sign boards of these places are erected in and around Nalanda. Other than research scholars, or students of Archaeology, the number of tourists visiting these places, are very less. In simple words, tourism hijacks the archaeological importance of sites.

Another point of discussion here is the presences of tourists create impacts on the monument. Once upon a time, admission to this great place was based on the intelligence of an individual. Today there is no restriction as such. But from the observations and personal experience, the employees deputed in the site are giving attention to the main area, i.e. the first temple. The structure seems to be weak, but the staff must give much care to protect this monument from visitors. But this is not the case of other temples, *viharas*, or the meditation halls. Drawings and writings disfigured some walls in the site. Permission to walk on the roofs of some structures can create problems in future. Other than the main board directs the visitors at the entry no other visible sign boards are placed inside the site. Marking places with diagrams which indicate beds, wells etc. cannot be difficult for a layman is concerned, especially a visitor from low education background.

7. Conclusion and Implications of Future Research

The debate of impacts of heritage tourism in preserving our cultural heritage opens new areas of research. The process of convergence between heritage management and tourism activity certainly helped to protect the site, and at the same time make the project sustainable. In order to maintain the site as a destination, a detailed study of individual preference pattern, motivating forces etc., should be carried out at a site. The result of this study will help the administrators to change the approach towards an archaeological site and how efficiently they can incorporate with heritage tourism. Tourism acts as a tool for sustainability here. However, promotion of tourism activity should not disturb the existing conditions of a site. Tourism highlights the importance of a site, at the same time modifications are required from the side of the archaeological department authorities regarding the management of information, site interpretation, behaviour of the staff, amenities for visitors etc.

REFERENCES

Ashworth, G. & Larkham, P. (Eds.) 1994. *Building a New Europe: Tourism, Culture and Identity in the Europe*, London: Routledge Kegan Paul.

Balcar, M. and D. Pearce (1996). Heritage Tourism on the west coast of New Zealand, *Tourism Management*, 17: 214-220.

Boniface, P. and P. Fowler (1993). *Heritage and Tourism in the Global Village*, Sage Publications, London.

Cheung, S.C. (1999). The Meaning of a Heritage Trail in Hong Kong, *Annals of Tourism Research*, Vol. 26.3: 570-588.

Dutta, M., Banerjee, S. and Hussain, Z., 2007, Untapped Demand for Heritage: A Contingent Valuation Study of Prinsep Ghat, Calcutta, *Tourism Management*, 28.1: 83-95.

Ghosh, A. (1939), *A Guide to Nalanda*, A.S.I., Delhi.

Gonzalez (2007), Intangible Heritage Tourism and Identity, *Tourism Management*, 29.4: 807-810.

Herbert, D. (2001), Literary Places, Tourism and Heritage Experience, *Annals of Tourism Research*, 28:312-333.

Jameson, H.J. (2008), Interpretation of Archaeology for the Public, *Encyclopaedia of Archaeology*, Elsevier, pp. 1529-1543.

Kuraishi, M.M.H. (1931), *A Short Guide to Buddhist Remains Excavated at Nalanda*, A.S.I., Central Circle, Patna.

MacCannell, D. (1976), *The Tourist, A New Theory of Leisure Class*, New York.

Shocken (1979), Staged Authenticity, Arrangements of Social Space in Visitor Settings. *American Journal of Sociology*, 79(3): 589-603.

Medina, L.K. (2003), Commoditizing Culture, Tourism and Maya Identity, *Annals of Tourism Research*, 30.2: 353-368.

Oommen, T.K. (2004), Futures India, Society-Nation, State, Civilization, *Futures*, 36:6-7.

Palmer, C. (1999), Tourism and symbols of identity, *Tourism Management*, 20: 313-321.

Patnaik, S.K. (2004), Heritage Tourism, Places of Tourist interest in the district of Puri, *Orissa Review*.

Poria, Y., Butle, R., & Airey, D., (2003), The Core of Heritage Tourism, *Annals of Tourism Research*, Vol. 30.1: 238-254.

Repiso, L.I., Heritage, Tourism, and Sustainability: An Archaeological Park as a tool for local sustainable development, www.holcimfoundation.org/portals.

Rojas, C. and Camarero, C. (2007). Visitors' experience, mood and satisfaction in a heritage context: Evidence from an interpretation centre, *Tourism Management*, 2008. Vol. 29.3: 525-537.

Sashi, T., (2006), Reconstructing Nalanda, *The Hindu*, December 24, 2006.

Taylor, J., (2001), Authenticity and Sincerity in Tourism, *Annals of Tourism Research*, 28: 7-26.

Wang, N. (1999), Rethinking authenticity in tourism experience, *Annals of Tourism Research*, Vol. 26.2: 349-370.

www.ai.nic.in, monuments list, accessed on 18.08.2008

Zeppal, H. and C. Hall, (1991), Selling art and history, cultural heritage and tourism, *Tourism Studies*, 2, 47-55.

Index